FIVE
STARS

FIVE STARS

★★★★★

THE COMMUNICATION SECRETS TO GET FROM
GOOD TO GREAT

CARMINE GALLO

ST. MARTIN'S PRESS
NEW YORK

www.stmartins.com

Designed by Meryl Sussman Levavi

Library of Congress Cataloging-in-Publication Data

Names: Gallo, Carmine, author.
Title: Five stars : the communication secrets to get from good to great /
Carmine Gallo.
Description: New York : St. Martin's Press, [2018] | Includes bibliographical
references and index.
Identifiers: LCCN 2017059648| ISBN 9781250155139 (hardcover) | ISBN
9781250183477 (ebook)
Subjects: LCSH: Business communication. | Communication in management. |
Persuasion (Psychology)
Classification: LCC HF5718 .G35324 2018 | DDC 658.4/5—dc23
LC record available at https://lccn.loc.gov/2017059648

ISBN 978-1-250-19384-1 (international, sold outside the U.S.,
subject to rights availability)

Our books may be purchased in bulk for promotional, educational,
or business use. Please contact your local bookseller or the Macmillan
Corporate and Premium Sales Department at 1-800-221-7945,
extension 5442, or by email at MacmillanSpecialMarkets@macmillan.com.

First U.S. Edition: June 2018

First International Edition: June 2018

1 3 5 7 9 10 8 6 4 2

To Josephine and Lela,
the shining stars who brighten my world

CONTENTS

FIVE
STARS

INTRODUCTION

Rise Up!

I am not throwing away my shot.

LIN-MANUEL MIRANDA, *Hamilton*

Alexa, who was Alexander Hamilton?

"Alexander Hamilton was an American statesman and one of the Founding Fathers of the United States."[1]

Lin-Manuel Miranda, who was Alexander Hamilton?

"A bastard, orphan, son of a whore and a Scotsman, dropped in the middle of a forgotten spot in the Caribbean by providence, impoverished, in squalor . . ."

Siri, who was Alexander Hamilton?

"Alexander Hamilton was an American statesman and one of the Founding Fathers of the United States."

Lin-Manuel Miranda, who was Alexander Hamilton?

"The ten-dollar Founding Father without a father. Got a lot farther by working a lot harder. By being a lot smarter. By being a self-starter . . . young, scrappy and hungry."

Siri and Alexa are digital personal assistants that live in the cloud; Lin-Manuel Miranda is a human composer who lives in our hearts.

Powered by artificial intelligence, Siri and Alexa do their jobs remarkably well. They retrieved the same answer to the question in the blink of an eye. By turning breath into bytes, encoding speech into digital packets, identifying key words, and matching those words against a vast amount of retrievable data, these digital assistants came up with an answer that had the highest probability of being accurate. And they both agreed on it.

Alexa, Siri, and their more "cognitive" cousin, IBM's Watson, respond to queries much faster than any human ever will. But Miranda's job is different; his job is to make you *feel*.

Miranda combines words and ideas in a way no human has ever done and no computer can ever match. For example:

- On vacation in Mexico, Miranda visited a bookstore and randomly chose Ron Chernow's biography of the American Revolutionary War hero Alexander Hamilton. Miranda was "thunderstruck." He imagined a direct line between Hamilton writing his way off the island of St. Croix and the pioneers of rap music writing their way out of poverty.
- Miranda chose to write his famous musical *Hamilton* as hip-hop because it's the language of ambition, defiance, and rebellion. It has the most words per measure of any musical genre, which makes it uniquely suited to reflect the density of Hamilton's writing.
- America's Founding Fathers were white men, but Miranda deliberately cast black and Latino actors to play them. *Hamilton* is the story of America *then* told by people who live in America *now*.
- Each character raps or sings in a distinct vocal style that reflects their personality. George Washington's style is deliberate and controlled, a combination of the hip-hop artist Common and the singer-songwriter John Legend. Hamilton is modeled after Miranda's favorite polysyllabic rhyming heroes, Rakim and Eminem. The character of Lafayette (who left the French aristocracy at the age of 19 to join the American Revolution) is unsure of himself early in the musical. When we first meet Lafayette, he raps in a simple, early 1980s rap cadence. As he grows in confidence, the character of Lafayette becomes a "Rap God," singing rhymes in double and triple time. The character of King George III does not rap. Why would

he? He's not rebelling. King George walks on stage as though he's wandered in from another musical. He sings his ballad "You'll Be Back" in a throwback British pop sound.

- Alexander Hamilton wrote in long paragraphs. Miranda wrote the first verse of *Hamilton* as a "crazy, run-on sentence" of 37 words.
- Miranda spent more than one year writing Hamilton's signature song, "My Shot." Miranda says it's the "Rosetta Stone" of Hamilton's brain, and, to prove that Hamilton was the most fearsome intellect in the room, Miranda felt that every couplet, every verse, had to live up to Hamilton's verbal dexterity.

Hamilton is a leap of imagination, a somersault into the world of creativity. Miranda has a gift. He makes us feel differently about ourselves and the world we live in. In this book, I'll build the case that we all have that gift: the potential to move people, excite them, and ignite their imagination. You will also learn why the world's most successful people say that accessing the gift is the key to thriving in an ultra-competitive global economy in which rapid technological advances are disrupting every industry, business, and career. The scholars, neuroscientists, economists, historians, entrepreneurs, investors, and leaders who you will meet all agree: *Mastering the ancient art of persuasion—combining words and ideas to move people to action—is no longer a "soft" skill. It is the fundamental skill to get from good to great in the age of ideas.*

Master the Ancient Art of Persuasion to Thrive in the Modern World

This book evolved from conversations with people who are stars in their fields, and who credit superior communication skills for much of their success. They lead companies like Google, Airbnb, and McKinsey. They are investors who have funded the world's most admired startups. They are astronauts who look down at the Earth from 250 miles in space, and they are scientists on Earth who look up at the stars to explore worlds outside of our solar system. They are recent college graduates thriving in their first jobs, mid-level career professionals getting promoted above their peers, and people leaving their jobs to start successful businesses or nonprofit adventures. They are Navy SEALs and CEOs, scholars, writers, adventurers, explorers, and trailblazers. They stand out. They are exceptional.

While writing this book, I was invited to join a team of elite U.S. military officers attending a secretive class in a remote air force base in the desert. Carefully selected from the top 1 percent of the air force, army, and navy, the students were being trained to help the country avoid massive conflicts. Two of my previous books were among the assigned course material: *Talk Like TED* and *The Storyteller's Secret*. "These men and women will be asked to analyze, write, and present their findings to political leaders, generals, admirals, and the president," an instructor told me. "In many cases, they'll get ten minutes or less. They're often the smartest people in the room, but if they can't make a persuasive argument quickly and concisely, it could have catastrophic consequences." It's worth repeating: The ancient art of persuasion is not a soft skill. It's fundamental.

Why "ancient"? In the last 20 years, the advent of functional magnetic resonance imaging (fMRI) has given researchers the ability to see brain activity in real time. Scientists studying blood flow in the brain have now discovered the secrets to effective communication—the exact reasons why certain words, speakers, and styles make an emotional connection with the rest of us. According to scientists, while the tools we use to communicate have evolved, the way our brains are wired to consume information has not. Become a great communicator by mastering the art and science of persuasion and you'll thrive in the modern world.

At no time in history have interpersonal communication skills been as important as they are today. In the Agrarian Age, a farmer who ploughed the field a little better than their neighbor could not acquire significantly more wealth. In the Industrial Age, a factory worker who assembled widgets a little faster than the person next to them could not acquire significantly more wealth. Today, anyone, anywhere in the world, who is *a little better* at expressing their ideas can see a sudden, massive increase in wealth that is unprecedented in human history.

In the twenty-first century knowledge economy, you are only as valuable as your ideas. The ability to convince others that your ideas matter is the single greatest skill that will give you a competitive edge at a time when the combined forces of globalization, automation, and artificial intelligence trigger a wave of anxiety across every profession in every country. In the next decade, your ideas—and the ability to articulate those ideas successfully—will count more than ever. Persuaders are irreplaceable.

Persuaders Are Irreplaceable

For business professionals today, average performance only guarantees below-average results. "In the past, workers with average skills, doing an average job, could earn an average lifestyle. But, today, average is officially over," writes *New York Times* columnist and bestselling globalization expert Thomas Friedman.[2] "Everyone needs to find their extra—their unique value contribution that makes them stand out in whatever is their field of employment."

The phrase *average is over* is more than a catchphrase, says economist Tyler Cowen. He argues that the irreversible forces of intelligent machines and economic globalization should lead you to ask the following key questions: "Are you good at working with intelligent machines or not? Are your skills a complement to the skills of the computer, or is the computer doing better without you? Worst of all, are you competing against the computer?"[3] According to Cowen, "If you and your skills are a complement to the computer, your wage and labor market prospects are likely to be cheery. If your skills do not complement the computer, you may want to address that mismatch." Consider this book the solution to the mismatch.

The very nature of work is changing, and so are the skills required to stand out, get ahead, and achieve greatness in one of the most transformative moments in history. If you can persuade, inspire, and ignite the imagination of others, you will be unstoppable, irresistible, and irreplaceable.

Anthony Goldbloom is a world-renowned expert in using big data to tackle big tasks. His company, Kaggle, uses predictive modeling to solve complex problems for NASA, automakers, insurance companies, and drug and medical device manufacturers, among others. No problem is too big for Kaggle's team of scientists to resist tackling. Goldbloom, named by MIT as one of the top 35 innovators in the world, believes that "machine learning" is the most powerful branch of AI and will be responsible for much of the disruption we can expect to see in the workplace. Machine learning is the technology that allows machines to learn from data and, in some cases, mimic things humans can do. Kaggle operates on the cutting edge of machine learning, which gives Goldbloom a unique perspective on what machines can do and what they can't.

"By construction, machines are very good at learning things that have been done before and repeating them again and again and again," Goldbloom told me.[4] "But in order to touch somebody emotionally, you have to surprise people. Machines have made very little progress in tackling novel situations. They can't handle things they haven't seen many times before."

One project undertaken by the Kaggle community of data scientists demonstrated the promise—and limitations—of machine learning. In a competition co-sponsored by the Hewlett Foundation, scientists were invited to create software that could grade a student-written essay as well as or better than a human evaluator. It's an important area of software development. The Hewlett Foundation is a philanthropy dedicated to providing America's public school students with the skills they need to excel in the twenty-first century. Chief among those skills are critical thinking and effective communication. One way to improve the quality of instruction in those areas is to move from multiple-choice tests to essays, which require higher-level thinking and writing skills. However, grading essays by hand is expensive and time consuming. That's why Hewlett challenged the Kaggle community to take their best shot at automating the task of scoring essays.

The results of the Kaggle/Hewlett challenge were promising.[5] The winning software evaluated 22,000 hand-scored essays. By analyzing sentence structure, spelling, and punctuation, the software did a reasonably good job of replicating scores given by human graders, especially for the average essay. But according to Goldbloom, the algorithm came up short in one crucial area. It failed to recognize essays that were above average—unusual, novel, and groundbreaking. In fact, creative essays received lower grades than they actually deserved! Machines learn from crunching large amounts of existing data while we humans use our imaginations to propose and communicate novel ideas that, by definition, have never been seen before. "We can connect seemingly disparate threads to solve problems," says Goldbloom.[6] "This puts a fundamental limit on the human tasks that machines will automate." If a computer can recognize average, it can replicate average. Average simply isn't good enough to stand out in the digital age.

In another essay experiment, this time in Japan, mathematician Noriko Arai sparked a wave of anxiety when she built an AI system that outperformed 80 percent of high school students in a competitive college entrance exam. The "Todai Robot" scored in the top 1 percent in the math and science section of the exam and could write a 600-word essay better than most students. Despite these results, Arai is convinced that humans can thrive in an AI-saturated world *if* they reconsider the types of skills they must master. In Arai's experiment, she discovered that AI did better than 80 percent of students because it could retrieve facts more quickly and accurately, which is what most students are taught to do—memorize facts and repeat them. But Todai failed to beat the 20 percent of students who stood out because they could think creatively and extrapolate meaning "beyond the bounds of a question."[7] In other words, AI doesn't read or think as humans do. The Todai Robot recognizes keywords and combines text and facts retrieved from existing information to provide an answer to a question. According to Arai, if "knowledge" means memorizing and retrieving facts, then AI can do what humans do, only better. She says the skills that give humans an edge are those that no robot or machine can currently replace: critical thinking, creativity, and communication.

Machines are fast; humans are creative. Machines glean insights from data; humans shed light on what the data means. Machines teach us about the past; humans build the future. Machines make us more productive; humans improve the world in imaginative, unexpected ways. Lin-Manuel Miranda didn't win a MacArthur Foundation Genius Award for writing a song faster than a computer. He won for igniting and inspiring the human spirit.

A Tectonic Shift Is Here

Emotional connection is, indeed, the winning ticket in a world where technologies such as automation, big data, artificial intelligence, and machine learning are eliminating millions of jobs and disrupting entire industries, businesses, and careers. People around the world are understandably anxious about the pace of change and what it could mean for the future of work. The good news is that fears of a "robot apocalypse" might be overblown, at least according to the evidence we have from the last 500 years.

Every technological shift has destroyed jobs, but also created more new jobs than were previously available. Economists studying the history of innovation as far back as the 1500s in Europe have found that, in those cases where new products and services sparked the highest anxiety, new job growth was also higher than expected. In the 1970s, Automated Teller Machines (ATMs) were widely expected to reduce the number of bank branches and human tellers. Today, banks employ more tellers than they did in 1980, but their roles have changed. Relationship management has replaced simple transactions. The disruption that technology triggers is very real and very scary for many. But in every economic shift—and especially in the digital revolution—communication skills become more valuable, and not less.

The exponential growth in technology has made our lives immeasurably better. By almost any metric today is the greatest time to be alive . . . ever. But unprecedented progress has also triggered what consulting firm Towers Watson calls a "tectonic shift" in global business; a shift that demands new skills from the twenty-first-century workforce.

In a detailed analysis of more than 700 occupations, Oxford researchers concluded that automation will eliminate *47 percent* of jobs that humans do today.[8] Let me say that again for emphasis: nearly half of all jobs performed by humans are on the road to elimination in the next decade. This is the extension of a process that started with blue-collar workers, men and women who used their hands, whose jobs are now done by machines. In the near future, automation may replace 140 million full-time knowledge workers around the world, whose work can be done more quickly and efficiently by "smarter" cognitive systems. The research suggests the risk will be the same across countries, regions, and nearly every field from transportation to technology, from healthcare to retail, and from law to finance.

"I think people are going to be surprised at how fast machine learning is going to displace routine jobs," says Neil Jacobstein, chair of the artificial intelligence and robotics department at the Silicon Valley think tank Singularity University.[9] "We're talking about a transition that's going to occur over the next 10 to 15 years that is really significant."

While it's difficult to predict exactly which jobs will be automated out of existence and over what time frame, we can predict which roles humans will want filled by other humans. People who know how to talk—and talk well—will be rewarded, and those with the ability to inspire people—to ignite another person's imagination—will be especially well positioned. "Machines can learn to read human emotion, but they don't *have* human emotions. It's a very important distinction," says Jacobstein.[10]

The hard data show that "soft skills" are in high demand. In one study of 400 human resource (HR) and recruiting professionals, 94 percent said an employee with stronger communication skills has a better chance at being promoted to a leadership position than an employee with more years of experience but weaker verbal skills.

Company leaders across the board say it's difficult to find applicants who can communicate clearly and precisely, inspiring and engaging co-workers and customers. "These traits can make the difference between a standout employee and one who just gets by," according to *The Wall Street Journal*.[11] "While such skills have always appealed to employers, decades-long shifts in the economy have made them especially crucial now. Companies have automated or outsourced many routine tasks, and the jobs that remain often require workers to take on broader responsi-bilities that demand critical thinking, empathy or other abilities that com-puters can't easily simulate . . . it's really the more fundamental skills like communication that seem to matter the most."[12]

A study by Burning Glass, a software company that matches people with jobs, revealed that employers face a real skills gap. The research combed through millions of job postings on social media. It found that in the most technical careers (IT, healthcare, engineering, finance), writ-ing and communication skills were highly valued, "far more than you'd expect based on standard job profiles." However, the same survey found that people with such skills—which they called the "human factor"—were "notoriously hard to find."[13]

Survey after survey, study after study, arrive at similar conclusions. And yet, according to a Hay Group study, "Poor communication skills hinder Millennials in the workplace. The Hay study of 450 Human Resources Directors in the U.S., India, and China concluded that 80 percent of HR professionals are having trouble finding graduate and entry-level employees who have technical proficiency *and* communication skills. "Social and emotional competencies are vital to future business success, but can be lacking in today's graduates."[14] In addition, 92 percent of HR directors believe emotional and social skills are increasingly important as global-ization accelerates and organizational structures change, which leads them to conclude that entry-level graduates with communication skills are "worth their weight in gold." The vast majority of those surveyed say graduates who do not develop emotional and social skills quickly will never be high performers, especially those in more complex roles. The communication skills gap is real, but so is your ability to bridge the gap.

"If you have the ability to communicate ideas that grab people's attention, then you won't be replaced anytime soon," says data expert An-thony Goldbloom.[15] "The unusual person will jump out," says billionaire Warren Buffett.[16] "And it's not because they have an IQ of 200 or any-thing like that. You will jump out, much more than you can anticipate, if you get really comfortable with public speaking. It's an asset that will last you 50 or 60 years and it's a liability if you don't like doing it."

Early in his career Buffett himself was so terrified of speaking in public, he signed up for a public-speaking course. He dropped out of the course on his first try because he was too afraid to speak up. Buffett worked up his courage a second time and completed the course. Today in Buffett's office he doesn't have a framed diploma of his college or business degrees, but he proudly displays his public-speaking certificate.

Speaking to a class of business students at Columbia University, Buf-fett said, "Right now I would pay $100,000 for ten percent of the future earnings of any of you, so if you're interested, see me after class. Now, you can improve your value by 50 percent just by learning communication skills—public speaking. If that's the case, see me after class and I'll pay you $150,000."[17] Buffett was reinforcing the point that mastering the art of public speaking is the single greatest skill a person can acquire today to boost their career in the future.

Entrepreneurs and small business owners, CEOs, and managers are only as valuable as their ideas. As automation replaces much of the work we used to do by hand, your ideas matter more than ever. If you cannot persuade others to back those ideas and if you cannot excite others, moti-vate, and inspire them, then you'll never fulfill your destiny. Bridge the skills gap and you'll shine in the marketplace of ideas.

The good news is that standing out through persuasion requires developing empathy with your listeners, a skill that "artificial" intelligence cannot replace. Machines don't have a heart; storytellers do.

Five Stars Is for Those Who Believe Their Ideas Matter

Throughout the book I use the term "five stars" to describe the unique leaders, entrepreneurs, business professionals, and brands who stand out, who occupy their own universe. In some cases, they are the leaders who run companies that achieve five-star reviews, literally. You will meet CEOs, leaders, and entrepreneurs behind five-star brands in hospitality, healthcare, and many other industries. I also use "five stars" as a metaphor. For example, you'll learn how business professionals who occupy the top jobs in their fields were average or good communicators and transformed themselves into great ones. Their ability to get buy-in for their ideas is a skill that sets them apart. You'll meet sales stars who were once in the middle of the pack and catapulted themselves to the top of their profession. You'll meet employees who get promoted above their peers, again and again. You'll meet managers who rise to the top 1 percent in ultra-competitive fields. You'll meet CEOs who have completely reimagined and reinvented entire business categories. You'll meet entrepreneurs whose companies are among the 0.5 percent of startups that received venture capital funding (and you'll hear directly from the investors behind the world's most admired companies). You'll also meet TED speakers, scientists, experts, and billionaires who credit their communication skills for catapulting their careers. Best of all, you'll learn the specific techniques they use to sell their ideas.

Five Stars is divided into three parts.

Part One: Why Great Communicators Are Irreplaceable

In the four chapters in Part One, we'll explore how ideas built the modern world. You will hear from top scientists, economists, historians, and business leaders who believe that—in the age of ideas—your ability to communicate persuasively is the single greatest skill that will set you apart in the next decade.

We'll also begin our discussion of the ancient brain. More than 2,300 years ago the Greek philosopher Aristotle argued that human beings are language animals and that "rhetoric"—persuasion—is an art and a science. Remarkably, most of the research conducted today in the science of persuasion and the brain reinforces Aristotle's original thesis. In Part One, you will learn why Aristotle's communication method remains as effective today as it was thousands of years ago.

Part Two: Who's Earned Five Stars

The five chapters in Part Two are divided into categories. Each category features individuals (and brands) who are five-star communicators. These standouts include: scientists, entrepreneurs, professionals, leaders, and TED stars, all of whom have inspired audiences through dynamic communication. They're all people and brands whose stories you'll want to hear. Along the way, you'll begin to recognize people from within your company or community who achieve five-star performance. They are the ones who command respect, inspire teamwork, and attract attention for their ideas and projects. They are the ones who create a virtuous cycle of successful results: (1) they persuade people to support their ideas, which helps them (2) launch creative innovations that further the goals of the organization, as well as (3) attract resources, funding, and support, which (4) elevates their status and reputation. And the cycle repeats itself again, and again, and again.

Part Three: How to Get from Good to Great

In Part Three you will learn specific, actionable methods to build the one skill that makes us uniquely human, the one skill that will propel you farther and faster in your career or chosen field. Most people who read this book likely have average or above-average communication skills. But today, average isn't good enough, and neither are skills that are a *little better* than average. Most people are perfectly happy living an average life. Average is comfortable and complacent. But Part Three is for the movers and doers, the explorers and adventurers. It's for those who want to propel their careers—and the world—forward. They're not content to watch.

They want to lead. If earning five stars is your goal, this section will help you to achieve it.

Remember, in the twenty-first-century knowledge economy, no machine, no software, no robot can replicate your ideas. But if you cannot sell your ideas persuasively, it doesn't matter.

As Wharton psychology professor Adam Grant argues, "originality" requires championing a set of novel ideas that go against the grain. Originals run up against a common hurdle: the human bias to remain in the status quo. "When you're pitching a novel idea or speaking up with a suggestion for change, your audience is likely to be skeptical."[18] If you cannot persuade people to buy into your vision, it will have damaging consequences for your career, your company, your industry, or the world, which may never stand to benefit from your idea. Developing original ideas and communicating those ideas effectively is the single greatest skill you can build today to own your future.

In a world of uncertainty, it's important to not lose sight of who we are. More than 3,000 years ago, Polynesian adventurers left their island home in outrigger canoes to cross thousands of miles of ocean. They populated modern-day Fiji, Hawaii, New Zealand, and hundreds of islands in the South Pacific. Remarkably, they did so with no maps, compasses, or GPS. They used the stars to chart their positions. The key to "wayfinding" is to remember where you started. To know where you're from is to know where you're going.

Why did these people risk their lives to venture thousands of miles from home? A five-hour plane trip today would have required 30 days at sea in a small canoe. Surely these travelers had to have a compelling reason. Famine? War? Overpopulation? Historians believe the strongest motivator may have been the spirit of adventure. We are natural explorers. The desire to discover something new is in our DNA. It will never leave us.

In a sense, we're all navigators—finding our way in a new world that is changing more rapidly than at any time in human history. Technological innovations are improving every aspect of our lives and disrupting entire fields, too. But if you can keep one eye on the stars and the other on where you're from—the qualities that make you uniquely human—it's likely that you'll embark on an epic adventure, and take the rest of us along for the ride.

Five Stars is for those who believe that their ideas matter. It's for men and women, students and entrepreneurs, teachers, managers, and leaders who want to gain a competitive edge in the age of ideas. No computer will replace you and no competitor will outsell you. Mastering the ancient art of persuasion will make you irreplaceable and irresistible. It will make you more likely to land the job of your dreams, build a career, start a company, evangelize an idea, rally a team, and pitch an innovative solution to a stubborn problem. You will stir people's souls. You will thrive, grow, and boldly lead others into the future. You will rise up into the fullness of your potential and achieve greatness.

PART ONE

WHY GREAT COMMUNICATORS ARE IRREPLACEABLE

1

POETRY, POWER, AND
MOONSHOTS

We have it in our power to begin the world over again.

—Thomas Paine

Alexander was a slightly built man with a grand plan.

He seemed younger than his 19 years as he climbed onto the platform and looked out at his audience of farmers and merchants, many of whom viewed him with a mix of skepticism and contempt. He would need to combine his passion and skills to build his case to a sharply divided audience. One-third of his listeners that day agreed with his opinion. The other two-thirds strongly disagreed or felt neutral about the subject. Alexander faltered at first. But as his confidence built, his rhetoric soared. He was an avid reader who loved poetry. He was known to have a "facility with words" that freed him from his humble birth and placed him among the giants of the time. On this day, his powers of persuasion allowed him to convert a largely hostile audience.

Alexander Hamilton's speech took place on July 6, 1774. He had taken a break from his college classes to argue for a boycott against British goods. "When his speech ended, the crowd stood transfixed in silence, staring at this spellbinding young orator before erupting in a sustained ovation."[1] Hamilton, whose spirit Lin-Manuel Miranda would resurrect 240 years later, "commanded attention with the force and fervor of his words." According to historian Ron Chernow, "no other articulated such a clear and prescient vision of America's future."[2] Hamilton's gift was to combine words and ideas to stir people's imagination.

Hamilton, along with Thomas Jefferson, Thomas Paine, Samuel Adams, and other gifted writers and speakers of the American Revolution, were influenced by the poets and philosophers who gave rise to the Enlightenment. The "trinity" of Francis Bacon, Isaac Newton, and John Locke taught America's founders to wrap their ideas in the radical rhetoric of rebellion. By doing so, they unleashed a wave of free ideas that built upon one another to usher in the greatest period of progress civilization has ever seen.

In 1835, the French sociologist Alexis de Tocqueville observed that "Every American is eaten up with longing to rise." One of these Americans was a young man born to a poor family in a log cabin. Abraham Lincoln studied the words of the founders, which he would later invoke in the Gettysburg Address, a speech that would remake the country. According to historian Doris Kearns Goodwin, Lincoln was a gifted storyteller who articulated his vision of a free society with contagious emotion. Lincoln's communication skills transformed a self-described "prairie-lawyer" into one of the greatest presidents of U.S. history. The ideas that shaped America didn't advocate for themselves.

Ideas built the modern world and it's the power of ideas that will build the world of tomorrow. But ideas in the absence of eloquence will fall on deaf ears.

One hundred and eighty-five years after poets and writers, orators and leaders ignited the flame of freedom, another son of Boston ignited the spirit of adventure. Robert Frost wrote that John F. Kennedy's election heralded "a golden age of poetry and power." Frost was right. In the speeches that Kennedy delivered to inspire the country to build a moon program, Kennedy translated his ideas into language that fueled one of the greatest achievements in human history. Recently scholars have identified some of his most effective rhetorical techniques.

I'm Not Mopping Floors; I'm Putting a Man on the Moon

Charlie Mars couldn't wait to get up and get back to work each morning. He'd graduated from Vanderbilt University with a bachelor's degree in electrical engineering. Five years later he joined NASA as a project engineer. Though he would never set foot on the moon, or travel in a rocket, or enjoy a ticker tape parade, years later, Mars spoke about the experience with the awe of someone who had done all three. "One of the things we had in common was a goal. We're going to the moon. We're putting a man on the moon! It so captured our imagination, and our emotion," Mars recalled.[3]

Wharton management professor Andrew Carton stumbled upon Mars's story as he pored over 18,000 pages of documents, transcripts, and internal NASA memos from the Apollo program, America's ambitious initiative, begun in 1961, to put a man on the moon. Carton noted a common thread among the writings of Mars and the other NASA employees across all functions—accountants and administrators, clerks and engineers. They'd all been profoundly inspired by the words of one man: John F. Kennedy.

When Neil Armstrong took one giant leap for mankind on June 20, 1969, it was the final step of a process that began when one leader with a bold idea lit the collective imagination of the 400,000 people who could turn it into reality. Carton identified the rhetorical formula behind Kennedy's successful communication and explained how his speaking skills triggered massive action.

First, "Kennedy reduced the number of NASA's aspirations to one."[4] When NASA was established in 1958, it had several objectives, among them to establish superior space technology, to achieve preeminence in space, and to advance science. Kennedy chose to focus on the single goal of sending humans to the moon and returning them safely to Earth. *It's easier to rally a team around one common goal than to divide their attention.*

Second, "Kennedy shifted attention from NASA's ultimate aspiration to a concrete objective." In other words, Kennedy took the abstract (advancing science by exploring the solar system) and made it tangible. On May 25, 1961, Kennedy told the U.S. Congress: "This nation should commit itself to achieving the goal, before this decade is out, of landing a man on the moon and returning him safely to earth." Kennedy articulated a concrete goal and attached a specific deadline to it.

Third, "Kennedy communicated milestones that connected employees' day-to-day work with concrete objectives." Kennedy outlined three programs and three objectives: The Mercury program would send an astronaut into orbit; Gemini would teach NASA what it didn't know about space walks and connecting two spacecrafts together; and Apollo would ultimately put a man on the moon. As you'll learn later, the "rule of three" is a powerful communication technique that superstar persuaders use to mobilize their listeners.

Fourth, "Kennedy emphasized the impressive scale of the objective with metaphors, analogies and unique figures of speech." Kennedy relied on a rarely used technique that linguists call "embodied concept." It binds a concrete event (landing on the moon) with an abstract aspiration (advancing science). The abstract and concrete become one and the same. For example, in a speech at Rice University in 1962, Kennedy said, "Space is there and we're going to climb it, and the moon and the planets are there, and new hopes for knowledge and peace are there." Kennedy gave abstract ideals like knowledge, peace, and exploration a real location.

The four steps proved to be irresistibly persuasive. Kennedy's "soft" skill led to one of the greatest achievements in the history of humanity. His words gave NASA employees a stronger connection between their work and the ultimate goal. They no longer saw their work as an isolated series of tasks like mopping the floors or building electrical circuits. Instead, they viewed their work as a critical component of putting a man on the moon, advancing science, and changing the world as we know it. "In this way, Kennedy positioned employees to experience greater meaningfulness from their work by changing the meaning of work," says Carton.

In the early 1960s, skeptics outnumbered those who believed a person could set foot on the moon by the end of the decade. Kennedy didn't persuade people with facts alone; he made them *feel*. He combined what Aristotle called Pathos and Logos: emotion and logic. Kennedy's words achieved emotional transcendence, making people believe that the impossible was possible. Skeptics became believers and believers became evangelists.

"It's important to remember what made the moonshot the moonshot," says Bill Gates.[5] "A moonshot challenge requires a clear, measurable objective that captures the imagination of the nation and fundamentally changes how we view what's possible . . . When we do that, we chart a course for a future that is safer, healthier, and stronger."

Kennedy Inspires a Tech Maverick

A 16-year-old Israeli boy read the text of Kennedy's Rice University "moon speech" in 1962. Seven years later, the boy, now in his earlier twenties, watched along with a billion other television viewers as Neil Armstrong stepped foot on the lunar surface. Kennedy's bold vision left a lasting impression on the boy, Eli Harari, inspiring him to pursue a lifelong passion in the physical sciences.

One month after Kennedy's vision was fulfilled, Harari arrived at Princeton University to begin his Ph.D. in aerospace and material sciences. It would lead to a career in tech; Harari would later start SanDisk, pioneering the technology that stores your digital photos. SanDisk's flash memory products are in your iPad, digital music player, smartphone, computer, laptop, and in the cloud where you send or retrieve files.

At the time that Harari started SanDisk in 1988, mobile phones were the size of bricks. Digital cameras were clunky and expensive. Laptop computers were in their infancy, "as luggable as a one-year-old child, and about as cooperative," as Harari put it. Digital music players, the world-wide web, phone apps, and cloud services were all in the future. So when Harari developed SanDisk, his potential investors told him he'd found the solution for a problem that didn't exist. Harari's hero was John F. Kennedy and he realized that, like Kennedy, he had to convince the skeptics. He had to bridge the chasm between his vision and what his audiences thought possible.

I first met Harari in 2008. The company was facing an existential crisis. The global financial meltdown had triggered the worst recession since the 1930s. As demand for flash-enabled consumer products plummeted, the industry faced a massive oversupply problem. Prices tanked, as did SanDisk's stock, which plunged 90 percent over the course of a year.

In August 2008, a competitor, Samsung, launched an unsolicited bid to purchase Sandisk for a 50 percent premium, or $10 billion. Mutual fund managers who owned a large percentage of stock pressed Harari to make the deal. But Harari believed the offer wasn't in the best interest of the company's shareholders, partners, and customers. When he turned down the offer of $26 a share, a popular television business personality put a picture of Harari on a "wall of shame" for rejecting the sale. "They don't understand our story,"[6] Harari told me at the time. Together we created a narrative that clearly explained Harari's vision and the long-term value of fighting for independence. Harari's story focused on the experience of the team, which had successfully weathered downturns in the past; its superb technology; SanDisk's exclusive patents; and its $2.5 billion cash position, which it had built up in the good times.

Although SanDisk's stock dropped precipitously to $6 a share, I never saw Harari panic. Optimism, he said, is a powerful weapon in times of crisis. Harari also understood the power of a story, simply told. In one notable meeting I attended, a group of executives and engineers were preparing for a major presentation to financial analysts. Although they had a lot of detail to cover, I suggested that they articulate one overarching and specific theme, just as John F. Kennedy had done. Many in the room pushed back. They argued that their story was too complicated to condense into a sentence. Harari, however, spoke up and said, "Nobody understands that Flash has reached an inflection point. Flash will be bigger than our critics can possibly imagine." I suggested that his statement become the rallying cry throughout the presentation. The first financial article to post after the analyst conference carried this headline: "Flash will be bigger than you think."

Flash forward seven years, to October 21, 2015, when Western Digital made an offer to buy SanDisk. This time, the company accepted. The price? More than $86.50 a share, or more than triple Samsung's original offer. SanDisk was sold for $19 billion. Eli Harari is a tech maverick, a leader who pursues ideas considered rebellious or disruptive. Mavericks often stand apart from the majority, which is why they must be persuasive *if* they hope to achieve tremendous things.

Let's return to the American Revolutionary period. The story of America is the story of persuasion. In January 1776, Thomas Paine published a pamphlet called *Common Sense* to persuade colonists to fight for America's independence. Paine had a gift, an ability to take sophisticated political arguments and make them accessible to the average reader at the time—farmers, merchants, and artisans.

Since many of the colonists could not read, they listened to the pamphlet being read out loud on street corners and in halls. George Washington even had the pamphlet read to his troops to lift their morale. Paine understood this and wrote for the ear, making the argument easy to follow and exciting to hear. *Common Sense* got its stirring rhythm from common techniques used by great persuaders. Among them:

> *Antithesis* (juxtaposing two contrasting ideas): "Society in every state is a blessing, but Government, even its best state, is a necessary evil."
>
> *Anaphora* (repetition of the same word or words in successive sentences or within clauses): "*Tis not* the affair of *a* city, *a* country, *a* province, or *a* kingdom, but of *a* continent. *Tis not* . . ."
>
> *Alliteration* (the repetition of similar letter sounds in two or more words in a group): "By referring the matter from *ar*gument to *ar*ms, a new *ar*ea for politics is struck; a new method of thinking hath *ar*isen."
>
> *Parallelism* (several parts of a sentence are expressed in a similar way to show the ideas are equally important, adding balance and rhythm to a speech): "I offer nothing more than simple facts, plain arguments, and common sense."

By framing the argument within a grand purpose—"The cause of America is in a great measure the cause of all mankind"—Paine elevated his writing from simple prose to a rallying cry for freedom. Paine's mastery of persuasive principles would help trigger the revolution and inspire independence movements around the world for years to come. When Paine wrote, "The sun never shined on a cause of greater worth," it changed what people thought was possible. For the first time in human history people who were not kings and monarchs began to think that they could govern themselves and secure their freedom against stronger, larger, wealthier armies. In much the same way, Kennedy's rhetoric persuaded people to do what they never imagined possible. And Harari, inspired by Kennedy's vision, created his own moonshot and stuck to his guns when his independence was threatened.

The world we live in today was not built brick by brick but idea on idea. In the next chapter you'll learn why these ideas have unleashed the greatest period of abundance the world has ever known and why the ability to communicate ideas persuasively is more valuable now than ever.

"A man may die, nations may rise and fall, but an idea lives on," John F. Kennedy once said. Your ideas deserve to live on. Let's make sure they do.

2

WINNING THE WAR OF IDEAS

We have never seen a time when more people could make
history, record history, publicize history, and amplify
history all at the same time.

—DOV SIEDMAN, American author

Libratus doesn't wear shades to cover its eyes. It doesn't watch an opponent's body language, looking for a "tell." But it can play a mean game of poker.

Libratus is a computer algorithm that beat four professional poker players in a 20-day competition in early 2017. The news triggered a cascade of dystopian headlines. One newspaper declared that the event represented "a crushing defeat for humanity, a major milestone for artificial intelligence." The headline was partly right and yet fundamentally exaggerated. The AI program did win at poker, marking the first time that a machine had done so. But its win didn't signal a crushing defeat for humanity. You see, the computer had an unfair edge—human help.

After 120,000 hands of Heads-up No-Limit Texas Hold 'em, one of the more complex poker variations, Libratus turned out to be a much more formidable opponent than the poker players had expected. Libratus relied on a form of AI called reinforcement learning, which uses extreme trial and error to make strategic decisions based on the probabilities of a particular outcome. To match wits with human poker players, Libratus had to train for months, playing trillions of hands of poker against itself and randomly experimenting with different strategies to figure out which worked and which didn't in certain situations. It still wasn't enough. The professional players detected patterns in the computer's play and exploited them. At the end of each evening, the computer scientists behind the program had to build another algorithm that identified those patterns and removed them. Advantage—human.

Noam Brown, one of the Carnegie Mellon researchers who helped to build Libratus, also pointed out that Libratus could not "read" the body language of the other players to tell if they were bluffing. A machine doesn't have intuition, feeling, or emotion. At certain tasks—scanning the cards, weighing the probabilities of a given outcome—it excelled. The Libratus AI connects to an enormous supercomputer that runs 30,000 times faster than a standard desktop computer at a cost of close to $10 million. Yes, Libratus is blazingly fast at weighing mathematical probabilities. But without empathy, Libratus has its limits. "I can't see a computer writing a prize-winning novel any time soon," Brown said.[1]

Libratus is a tough opponent, but it has a severe limitation. In the absence of empathy it cannot understand how people feel. It can beat a champion poker player, but it will never be a five-star leader or build a five-star brand. Libratus can never win in the war of ideas because it's incapable of *having* an original idea and advocating for it. But a human poker player who's mastered the art of persuasion has an ace in the hole, a skill that no algorithm can duplicate.

Let's meet Texas native Haseeb Qureshi, a former poker champion who began his card-playing career at the age of 16. In his first year he turned $50 into $100,000. He was a millionaire two years later. By 19, Qureshi was considered one of the best No-Limit Texas Hold 'em players in the world. But poker had lost its meaning for Qureshi. He felt isolated and unhappy. So he left the poker life behind and started anew—in San Francisco.

In 2015, Qureshi enrolled in an elite Silicon Valley software coding boot camp. He caught on quickly and, two months into the three-month program, began teaching one of the courses. Qureshi studied, coded, and taught for 80 hours a week. Yet his value on the job market was still uncertain. He had an unconventional background that didn't easily fit into a job description. He was also 26 years old, competing against 20-year-olds who had been coding since they were 10. On paper he had a losing hand: An English degree, a stint as a professional poker player, and less than one year of coding experience. Libratus would have given him a low probability of succeeding.

And sure enough, Qureshi's resume failed to stand out. He initially sent out 20 resumes and received 20 rejections. On paper, he was simply less impressive than his peers. He began to doubt himself. *Am I unsellable?* he wondered. Ultimately, through leveraging his referral network, Qureshi began to receive invitations for onsite, in-person interviews. The first company passed. Instead of considering the rejection a failure, Qureshi used it as an opportunity to refine his interview skills. If he could learn to code in a year, then he could learn to improve his communication skills. His practice paid off. Yelp was the first company to offer him a job at $105,000 a year. The dominos began to fall. Two other companies offered Qureshi $115,000. Then came an offer from his dream company— Google, where he'd nailed the interview. Their package was valued at $162,000 a year. Uber and Stripe made similar offers. In Silicon Valley, word gets around when there's buzz around a new hire. Airbnb got wind of the engineer who interviewed exceptionally well and came calling, ultimately offering $220,000. Google counter-offered. Qureshi decided to accept Airbnb's final package of $250,000, including salary, signing bonus, and pre-IPO stock.

So what made this person, so eminently resistable on paper, the subject of a Silicon Valley feeding frenzy? It came down to the interview.

"Interviewing is a skill, and not a particularly mysterious one," Haseeb told me.[2] "The first question is nearly always a version of 'What's your story?' Your answer will strongly influence their perception of you."

Qureshi says you can't charm your way into passing an interview for a software engineering position if you don't know the basics of the job. But communicators who craft compelling stories can differentiate themselves from their competition even when interviewing for highly technical jobs. "Consider yourself a character in a story and structure the story with a beginning, middle, and end. There should be inflection points, characters, and easy-to-understand motivations. Keep it as short as possible, while preserving the color that makes you interesting. When they ask, 'Tell us about a challenging bug you faced and how you solved it?,' tell a story." Qureshi practiced the stories he would tell, over and over again. He recorded himself telling the narrative and asked friends for feedback. He adapted the Hero's Journey, which we'll learn more about later, to frame his experience around a character (himself) who faced a technical problem and used the challenge to better himself. He strived to get so good at interviewing, "they couldn't ignore me."

Persuasion is a key skill for software engineers, because they do more than solve technical problems. The successful engineers act as "social orchestra conductors," according to Qureshi. Every software engineer works on a slightly different piece of the application, but they are highly dependent on their co-workers. A conductor keeps everyone in harmony and working as an ensemble. An engineer who can perform one task well might enjoy a fine career, but an engineer who can keep others on track will stand out as a leader. "In a job interview, if you only show you can solve technical problems and you have no communication skills, you are a much worse candidate than someone with good communication skills and pretty good technical skills. The key to communication is empathy. If you can create a connection in a job interview, you're much more likely to get what you want and to make a difference in your role," says Qureshi. "Even in the field of software engineering, the people with strong communication and presentation skills usually outperform the people with the best technical chops."

Qureshi concedes that he was up against coding specialists who had better qualifications and more experience. But the places that made Qureshi offers—many of the Valley's most successful and profitable companies—were looking for employees who could rise to leadership positions in the future. Great leaders combine great ideas *and* the ability to communicate those ideas effectively.

In addition to being highly successful, the companies that line up to pay top dollar for employees like Qureshi are at the leading edge of artificial intelligence, machine learning, cloud computing, and big data—the very trends that threaten to displace millions of workers. And yet they all came calling for Qureshi. They called because ideas move the world forward and they need people with good ideas. But ideas alone are not enough. The ability to sell those ideas persuasively is the single greatest skill that gives individuals a competitive advantage.

The Communications Skills Gap

Sam is a mid-career professional for a company that put the silicon in Silicon Valley. He works at Intel, legendary for powering many of the world's computers, servers, and devices. Sam's work advances Moore's Law, the famous 1965 prediction that computing power would double every 18 months. What Sam may not realize is that for every advance he makes in computing power, he's driving down his own value in the workplace.

During one of my visits to Intel's global headquarters in Santa Clara, California, a vice president stopped in a hallway, peered through a glass window, and pointed to Sam attending a meeting.

"You see that guy? He's the smartest guy in the room. He should be leading his division, but he's been stuck in the same position for years."

"Why?" I asked.

"He's a terrible communicator. He takes too long to get to the point. He can't deliver a clear and compelling presentation. He's not inspiring."

"You just said he's brilliant. Why wouldn't you want him in a leadership position?"

"These days, you can't lead without inspired followers."

For a decade, I had a front-row seat to the tech revolution, working directly with Intel's senior leaders as the company's primary media-training and communication skills advisor. People like Sam didn't always know that their failure to communicate effectively was holding them back. But many who were told didn't care—their job was to produce something, and it was other people's job to *sell* it. They thought polished communicators elevated style over substance. It's unfortunate because they had a chance to stand out, but their egos stood in the way.

It was during my work at Intel and other famous Silicon Valley companies that I began to notice a gap—a chasm, really—between the value professionals thought they were bringing to the organization and the skills senior leaders expected. CEOs, engineers, professionals, and managers who once considered their credentials and experience to be enough suddenly found themselves in a position where they were required to *talk* about the brand and its products. A surge of competitors began to vie for consumers and the company's top talent. Executives, managers, and engineers saw their roles shift. They were expected to clarify, excite, and inspire others. The quality of their presentation skills began to affect their value within the company and the industry.

For people running companies, these skills are especially important. One research study examined about 4,400 CEOs over a 10-year period.[3] Those who made regular media appearances on business programs or who were widely quoted in newspaper articles saw a large boost in compensation. Their appearances could increase their pay by as much as $210,000. The correlation was higher for CEOs of smaller firms, who benefited more from the increased visibility. The ability to articulate a company's strategy and to do so publicly is now a highly valued—and highly compensated—skill.

In *Only the Paranoid Survive*, legendary Intel CEO Andy Grove—mentor to Steve Jobs, Larry Ellison, and Mark Zuckerberg—coined the phrase "strategic inflection point." It's the point at which the fundamentals of a business or career are about to change. The change brings an opportunity to rise to new heights or "signals the beginning of the end." According to Grove, these inflection points "build up force so insidiously that you may have a hard time putting a finger on what has changed, yet you know that something *has*. It can be deadly when unattended to."[4]

Grove wrote those words in 1996, but he could have been describing today's workplace. Technology, he predicted, will increase the rate of change so quickly it will have an impact on everyone, in every field and in every country.

Grove said your career is your business. You are its CEO. Complacency, he said, breeds failure. As the CEO of your career, you must continually improve your skills, especially the art of communication.

Grove, born in Budapest, Hungry, survived the Nazi occupation. He didn't speak a word of English when he immigrated to the United States. Yet he realized that the gift of persuasion would help him navigate the inflection points in his own career. Grove built a reputation as a boss who demanded clear, concise, and compelling presentations from his subordinates. He viewed it as essential to his role as CEO to provide a clear vision for the company amid this period of great change. According to Grove, changes and new directions can leave employees confused, dispirited, demoralized, "or just plain tired." A leader's first task, he believed, is to form a mental image of what he or she wants the company or division to look like. The picture must be followed by a crisp communication of the vision.

A short 10-minute drive from Intel sits the sprawling Cisco campus. The giant networking company spans three cities and employs more than 70,000 people. Cisco isn't a household name like Amazon or Facebook, but without it, you wouldn't be able to order products from Amazon or post your favorite videos to Facebook. Cisco is one of the most important companies in the world, running much of the planet's IT infrastructure.

Cisco uses its own technology to raise productivity and to reduce labor costs. Employees save money on travel by sitting in "telepresence" videoconferencing rooms to have meetings with customers thousands of miles away. They enter one of 10 lobbies, all served by one receptionist on a digital screen. In Cisco's buildings, the company's own products are being used to automate tasks and replace jobs, but in many ways those very same products make human interaction a much more valuable skill, and one that—as we've learned—is in short supply among today's working professionals.

Cisco's chief executive, Chuck Robbins, wants everything done quickly, and for good reason. It took 50 years for television to reach 50 million people. It took Facebook 3.5 years. The addictive video game *Angry Birds* reached the same number of people in just 35 days. If a team of engineers tells Robbins they can have a product ready in 30 days, he gives them three weeks. At Cisco, top leaders believe communication skills are the "lubricant of execution" that gives the company its competitive edge.

As a technology company, Cisco relies on data to measure everything—including communication skills. Only above-average persuaders get promoted, literally.

Here's how it works. Employees, managers, and senior executives at Cisco frequently give presentations to internal teams and to customers and partners. Peers and customers rate the presentations for content and delivery. The score ranges from 1 to 5. A score of 4 or above is considered good. A score of 4.5 to 5 is considered high, but rare. Cisco's former CEO of 20 years—John Chambers—routinely scored 4.5 or above. When Chambers became CEO in 1996, the company had $70 million in annual revenue. Chambers was the company's evangelist, and he demanded five-star presentation skills from Cisco's senior leaders, as well. A little more than 10 years later Cisco was making $40 billion a year.

"Do the presentation scores really matter?" I asked one senior leader.

"Only if you want to keep your job or get a promotion," he said.

Even at firms deeply embedded in big data and artificial intelligence such as Cisco, Google, Microsoft, Salesforce, and IBM, some of the most influential leaders are those considered the best talkers. Across the board, the demand for communication skills is high while the supply of talent is low. This talent gap gives people who master the ancient art of persuasion a considerable advantage.

Before we learn more about who has this skill and how to sharpen it, we need to look back on how we got here and where we're going.

When Ideas Have Sex, We All Benefit

Thanks in large part to the freedom of ideas unleashed during the European Enlightenment and the American Revolution, much of the world has entered a golden age of innovation and prosperity. In the past 200 years, civilization has made its greatest advances ever in medicine, technology, and standards of living. It's all because ideas—as economist Matt Ridley once said—had sex. When the average person was free to express an opinion, ideas began to "combine and recombine, to meet and mate," according to Ridley in his book, *The Rational Optimist*.[5]

The mating period fueled an unprecedented period of innovation beginning around the year 1800. As a result, we're not just a little better off than those who lived before us; we're stunningly better off in nearly every way.

Deirdre McCloskey, the distinguished professor of history, economics, English, and communication at the University of Illinois at Chicago, calls the last 200 years "The Great Enrichment." It marks a period in which the number of goods and services available to the average person has expanded by an unprecedented 10,000 percent. McCloskey calls it the most important secular event since the invention of agriculture. It "restarted history."

Many leading economic historians share McCloskey's opinion. They've discovered that—beginning in the late eighteenth century—life in many places got better. Slowly at first, then quickly, and now unstoppable. "Material life got better not merely for Europeans or imperial powers or Mr. Moneybags, but for ordinary people from Brooklyn to Beijing," says McCloskey.[6]

Ian Goldin, professor of globalization and director of the Oxford Martin School at the University of Oxford, calls the modern world the "New Renaissance." "The world suddenly contains more brains, healthier and better educated, exchanging an exploding volume and variety of ever more vivid ideas—globally, instantly and at near-zero cost," he writes.[7] Goldin, a former vice president of the World Bank and an advisor to Nelson Mandela, says we are in a golden age in which the conditions are ripe for creative breakthroughs, unleashing progress that will far surpass any period in human history.

Swedish historian Johan Norberg agrees. "We are witnessing the greatest improvement in global living standards ever to take place . . . We've made more progress over the last 100 years than in the first 100,000," Norberg told me.[8] "Poverty, malnutrition, illiteracy, child labor, and infant mortality are falling faster than at any other time in human history . . . a child born today is more likely to reach retirement age than his forebears were to live to their fifth birthday."

These historians describe progress in different ways, but they all agree on its foundation. In a free society ideas have sex, and when they do, they multiply.

In the centuries following the invention of the printing press, ideas traveled faster and wider because books, which had been available to only hundreds of people a year, became available to the masses. "The final link between the new world we live in and the new heights of human development we've reached is the spread of ideas," writes Goldin.[9] "However knowledge is packaged—as a device, a pill or injections, or as a set of policy steps—by adopting it, less-developed societies can leapfrog the year or decades that led to its development and reap its benefits immediately."

Johan Norberg reminds us of Thomas Robert Malthus, who in 1780 pessimistically argued that humanity would always suffer from famine and poverty. Although Malthus accurately described the times, "He underestimated [humanity's] ability to innovate, solve problems, and change its ways when Enlightenment ideas and expanded freedom gave people the opportunity to do so."[10] Over time the world's population did grow, but the supply of food grew more quickly. The result was a massive decline in major famines and malnourishment. According to Norberg, the population is now four times larger than it was 100 years ago, but the death toll from famine is just 2 percent of what it was 100 years ago. "Democracy is one of our most potent weapons against famine," argues Norberg, because a free press and the free flow of ideas make people aware of problems, and people are then free to implement ideas to solve them.

Peter H. Diamandis is the founder of more than a dozen space and high-tech companies. He's a graduate of the Harvard Medical School and has degrees in molecular biology and aerospace engineering from MIT. "Using almost any metric currently available, quality of life has improved more in the past century than ever before," writes Diamandis, chairman and CEO of the X-Prize Foundation and co-founder of the Silicon Valley think tank Singularity University.[11] As billions of people join the global conversation, says Diamandis, "Their ideas—ideas we've never before had access to—will result in new discoveries, products and inventions that will benefit us all."

McCloskey may have said it best: "Our riches did not come from piling brick on brick, or bachelor's degree on bachelor's degree, or bank balance on bank balance, but from piling idea on idea."[12]

The Growing Value of Changing Minds

Ideas cannot build upon one another without advocates to argue for them and evangelists to spread them. In a world built on ideas, the persuaders— the ones who can win hearts and change minds—have a competitive edge.

Deirdre McCloskey conducted an impressive research project to prove that old-fashioned rhetoric—persuasion—is responsible for a growing share of America's national income. She calls persuasion—changing behavior by changing minds—"sweet talk."

McCloskey began by exploring the employment categories in the *Statistical Abstract of the United States*, a list of 250 occupations employing more than 140 million civilians. First, she eliminated those jobs where "sweet talk" played a small role in day-to-day activities: home appraisers, firefighters, construction laborers. Although workers in these occupations may have had to be persuasive to get their jobs or—in the case of firefighters—must give urgent instructions to save lives, their earnings are less dependent on rhetoric.

McCloskey then identified those occupations in which at least 90 percent of work time is devoted to persuasion: lawyers, public relations specialists, counselors, social workers, etc. She assigned a lower, but still high, figure of 75 percent to managers and supervisors. In other words, 75 percent of their income is derived from their ability to persuade others. "In a free society the workers cannot be peremptorily ordered about and beaten if they do not respond. They need to be persuaded."[13]

In the category of 50 percent persuaders, McCloskey included loan officers, HR professionals, writers and authors, teachers, college professors, and others. Police and patrol officers, detectives, and investigators came in at 25 percent, as did the 7.6 million doctors, dentists, nurses, speech pathologists, and healthcare workers.

McCloskey tallied up the workers and multiplied the number of employees in each category by the percentage of sweet talk that made up their incomes. By doing so she reached the following conclusion: *Persuasion is responsible for generating one-quarter of America's national income.*

McCloskey performed the calculation for three separate years and found that the share barely budged. It's important to note that in nearly every category, McCloskey interviewed people who said the percentage of their income derived from persuasion was higher than the number she assigned. *One-quarter is on the low end.*

Economist Gerry Antioch, who works for the Australian Treasury Department, wanted to see if he could replicate McCloskey's findings. He reached a similar conclusion. In fact, Antioch found that persuasion made up an even higher percentage of income than McCloskey's original research indicated. "Persuasion is now 30 percent of the U.S. economy," according to Antioch.[14] "Persuasion is the common thread in almost all voluntary transactions. Sellers persuade buyers, politicians persuade voters, and lobbyists persuade politicians. And non-government organizations are increasingly persuasive in policy deliberations. Persuasion's footprint in the modern economy is substantial and growing."

While McCloskey and Antioch's calculations were done using U.S. data, the economists agree that persuasion plays an equally large role in most modern economies. Here's the key. As automation continues to replace the labor we once did by hand, persuasion as a share of national income is only getting larger. McCloskey expects sweet talk to make up 40 percent of America's labor income in the next 20 years.

Periods of great enrichment come at the expense of great disruption. In 1840, nearly 70 percent of the U.S. labor force worked on farms; today less than 2 percent of Americans work in agriculture. Manufacturing's share of the labor force has dropped from 40 percent in 1950 to under 20 percent today. Income from manufacturing continues to fall as robots replace workers and automation takes over repetitive tasks once handled by humans. The main task of the jobs that are left—and the new ones created—is to change minds.

As McCloskey explains, "Nothing happens voluntarily in an economy, or a society, unless someone changes her mind. Behavior can be changed by compulsion, but minds cannot."[15]

"Occupations that depended on sweet talk were fewer in the olden days. In future days they will be more and more numerous," says McCloskey. "A coder who only knows technical skills might start at $40,000 to $80,000 in Silicon Valley. A coder who can speak to the client can easily command $120,000 and up." McCloskey hasn't met Qureshi but wouldn't be surprised by the engineer who sweet-talked his way to a quarter million dollars a year.

No matter what form technology takes in the future, the value of communication skills will only go up. As McCloskey says, "In free societies, sweet talk rules." Words and ideas created the modern world. Words and ideas will make you a star in your field. Persuasion—sweet talk—affords the greatest opportunity to leapfrog from where you are today to where you want to be.

3

ARISTOTLE WAS RIGHT AND NEUROSCIENCE
PROVES IT

*At least as far out as I can see, the human brain and
the human heart will be valued.*

—AVINASH KAUSHIK, data analytics expert, Google

Avinash Kaushik found nirvana in the workplace. His road to happiness spanned 10 years, three countries, and half a dozen job titles. He was searching for "joy," for his passion and skills to intersect at a company that valued both. Kaushik found such a company at Google and Google found its voice in Kaushik.

Kaushik is one of the world's leading experts in the field of data analytics. He's written two internationally bestselling books and hosts a popular blog called Occam's Razor. Kaushik's a big deal in the analytics field. He also landed a big deal at Google. As the company's digital marketing evangelist, Kaushik plays two important roles. He meets with leaders who run the world's largest brands, helping them understand the full power of Google's data so they can create successful businesses. Kaushik has a second important job. He teaches 4,000 Google managers, leaders, and sales and marketing professionals how to be more persuasive presenters. Visualizing data brings him joy. He says there is "something magical" about making sense of the complexity hidden in data and illustrating its implications to Google's customers.

"My job is to change the way Googlers tell stories," Kaushik told me during one of my visits to the Google complex in Mountain View, California.[1] Kaushik's team of 75 people holds workshops to spread the gospel of data visualization and storytelling to Google professionals who, combined, are responsible for generating billions of dollars in annual revenue.

"Avinash, when people think of Google, they think of search. They think of data. They think of artificial intelligence and machine learning. What role does storytelling play?" I asked.

"Storytelling is a powerful way to get our clients to think differently," Kaushik said. "If we can show people how to unlock data to make money, grow a business, or make them more successful, we'll have made a heart-and-mind connection that drives action."

The world is awash in data, and nowhere are the numbers more striking than at Google, an Alphabet company. Every second of every day people perform 40,000 search queries on Google, or 1.2 trillion searches a year. Every minute of every day people view nearly three million video streams on YouTube, a Google subsidiary. The amount of data that Google collects can help brands move faster than they would have been able to at any other time in history. But if the mountains of data overwhelm Google's clients, the data is worthless. That's where Kaushik and his storytellers step in. "The size and the scope of the change we drive is so big that it's best done with stories," says Kaushik.

Where most salespeople and marketers are proud to deliver "insights," Kaushik prefers "out-of-sights." An insight, by definition, is in sight of the audience. It's information that the listener already knows. For example, it would not be a groundbreaking revelation if Kaushik were to tell retailers that fewer people are seeing their ads in print newspapers these days. However, showing them that 70 percent of in-store purchases are influenced by what their shoppers see and read on mobile devices might fundamentally change how those retailers run their businesses. A "Googler" is taught to always open presentations with an out-of-sight, a big, transformative idea that radically alters a customer's perspective.

"In the first two to three minutes of a presentation, I want people to lean forward in their chairs," says Kaushik. Charts, tables, and graphs on a slide do not elicit a lean-in moment. Stories do because stories are emotional. Stories trigger a megadose of neurochemicals in the human brain, which makes presentations irresistible.

Google engineers build products that change the way humans and machines interact. From search engines that predict what you're looking for, to cars that drive themselves, Google is at the leading edge of artificial intelligence and machine learning. And yet one of its most influential employees is a big-data guy whose most powerful tool is more than 2,000 years old. The tool is *rhetoric*—the art of persuasion—and the philosopher is Aristotle.

The rest of this book is dedicated to helping you understand and apply the tools of persuasion to stand out in the modern world. But it's worth a short digression to explain how Aristotle—the father of persuasive theory—is also credited for inventing the building blocks of our modern digital age: logic.

Aristotle, Father of Persuasion and the Modern Computer

The digital revolution traces its roots to 1847, when mathematician George Boole introduced an obscure discipline called mathematical logic. Boole demonstrated that all variables are either "true" or "false," "on" or "off." The subject was considered too abstract for any practical applications at the time. But as we know, ideas build on ideas and that's exactly what happened to Boole's equations and formulas. In the 1930s, MIT graduate student Claude Shannon applied Boole's algebra to electrical circuits, laying the groundwork for modern computers. Scientists credit Boolean logic for ushering in the information age, but Boole himself owed credit to Aristotle for inventing logic in the first place.

Aristotle believed that our ability to speak, write, reason, and change people's ways of thinking could unleash human potential. Since he believed that the mark of an educated person in a free society was the ability to persuade others, Aristotle developed tools to help people be more effective when speaking in public. First, he said, a persuasive argument required a logical structure. The formula he invented became known as a syllogism:

All men are mortal.

Socrates is a man.

Therefore, Socrates is mortal.

If we replace the object of the argument—Socrates—with anyone else, the argument retains its validity. Boole built on Aristotle's concept, replacing the words with a mathematical formula:

$$x = x * y \text{ (Everything in the set } x \text{ is also in the set } y).$$

Chris Dixon, a partner at the venture capital firm Andreessen Horowitz, wrote a detailed essay on Boole's connection with Aristotle.[2] In his piece—"How Aristotle Created the Computer"—Dixon writes that Aristotle's logic set the stage for "artificial neural networks" that both reason and learn. If Aristotle is, indeed, the father of the modern computer, he was a pretty smart guy because he also gave us the secret for competing against the machine. Aristotle provided a formula, a set of tools to distinguish humans from computers. The philosopher's formula allows us to build emotional intelligence, develop empathy, and create meaningful connections with other people. Aristotle believed that without human connection, we have no community. Without community, there can be no happiness. And if we're not happy, we will fail to flourish.

Pathos: The Tool to Outwit Smart Machines

By inventing logic, Aristotle gave humans the tools to build smart machines. He also gave humans a tool to outsmart those machines. He called the tool "rhetoric."

Aristotle defined rhetoric as the art of using written and oral language to persuade people to better their lives. Aristotle believed that success in a civilized society required both wisdom *and* eloquence. And eloquence, he argued, came down to a system, a formula for reaching hearts and changing minds. Aristotle's techniques form the bedrock of public speaking today. Every inspiring speech, PowerPoint presentation, or pep talk has—at its core—the strategy Aristotle introduced more than 2,000 years ago.

Aristotle didn't consider persuasion to be manipulative. In fact, he considered it shameful *not* to study the art of persuasion. Scott F. Crider, an English professor who has taught Aristotle to college students for 25 years, holds that the Greek philosopher was optimistic about the human capacity to discern the truth among arguments because truth is stronger than falsehood. "So, if all other circumstances are equal yet truth, or justice is less persuasive than falsity and injustice, the fault must be in the theater, the audience, or both," says Crider.[3]

"Rhetoric is ultimately the art of happiness," says Crider.[4] Aristotle called audiences "judges" because they are constantly weighing arguments and judging which one will bring them the most happiness. The end goal of persuasion is to use language to encourage both parties to flourish, to find happiness, and Aristotle said there are two means to achieving the goal. The first step in persuasion is articulating the theme of the argument itself. Second, the speaker must prove that their argument is solid and logical.

The theme of your argument is what you want the other person to do: An entrepreneur's theme might be that a venture capitalist should invest in an idea, a manager's theme might be that a team should give priority to one product line over another, and a salesperson's theme might be that customers should adopt a new service.

A theme gives an argument its direction and sets the goal of a conversation, but it's Aristotle's second step that gives an appeal its persuasive power. A speaker must back up the argument using three rhetorical proofs: logic, credibility, and emotion. Persuasion requires that my argument follow a logical structure (Logos). It requires that you trust me based on my character and credibility (Ethos). And it requires that I make an emotional connection with you (Pathos).

Logical reasoning is critical, but it is only one-third of the formula. Persuasion cannot occur in the absence of Ethos and Pathos. Ethos refers to the credibility of the speaker. Aristotle believed that audiences found a speaker to be trustworthy if the speaker had three characteristics: wisdom, virtue, and goodwill. If a speaker was prepared with a well-structured argument, they would be seen as wise. If a speaker was seen as a moral and virtuous person, they would be considered reliable and credible. Very importantly, a speaker who clearly wanted what was best for the audience was seen as a person of goodwill. A "snake oil salesman" conjures up the least trustworthy kind of person because peddlers in snake oil only want to separate you from your money. They don't have your best interest at heart; only theirs. They are considered unethical because they don't have Ethos.

Aristotle's work is considered the first real discussion of human psychology because Pathos—emotion—makes up such a sizable portion of his formula. In the absence of emotion nothing else matters, according to Aristotle. In fact, he saw lack of emotion as a serious personality defect. After all, when you see an injustice carried out, it's natural to feel angry. When you experience the death of a parent, it's natural to grieve. Aristotle believed emotion *should* guide our decisions, as long as the emotion we experience is the *appropriate* one.

Martin Luther King Jr.'s "I Have a Dream" speech on the steps of the Lincoln Memorial in 1963 beautifully blends all three rhetorical proofs. Without an appeal to emotion—both indignation at the status quo and hope for a brighter future—the speech would have fallen flat and certainly wouldn't be considered one of the greatest speeches of the twentieth century. As Thomas Paine, Alexander Hamilton, and Thomas Jefferson successfully did years before, King galvanized a movement, in this case the growing civil rights movement. Our most significant historical events were triggered by writers and speakers, thinkers and leaders who mastered the art of rhetoric—specifically, the appeal to emotion—to move hearts and convince minds that something had to change.

The most persuasive document in American history is the Declaration of Independence, which the country celebrates on every Fourth of July. Thomas Jefferson, an attorney, was chosen to write the document because he was skilled at delivering information in a logical structure while also eliciting the right emotions for the cause. He was a master of the persuasive arts, combining all three of Aristotle's rhetorical proofs in a document that was written to be read out loud on street corners.

The television miniseries *John Adams* captures the power of Jefferson's appeal. "This is altogether unexpected," Adams (played by Paul Giamatti) says to Jefferson. "Not only a declaration of *our* independence, but the rights of *all* men. This is well said, sir. Very, very well said."

Today's best trial lawyers have learned from Jefferson's rhetoric that persuasion isn't simply a recitation of facts. Persuasion requires connecting words *to a broader theme* that inspires people to embrace a big, bold vision, much like Kennedy did when he inspired people to reach for the moon. It's instructive to remember that Jefferson left explicit instructions that only three of his achievements were to be inscribed on his tombstone "and not a word more." They were: "Author of the Declaration of Independence [and] of the Statute of Virginia for Religious Freedom and Father of the University of Virginia."

In Jefferson's mind, two of his three greatest lifetime achievements involved writing. Left off his tombstone is the fact that Jefferson served as the third president of the United States and, while at it, acquired the Louisiana Territory, doubling America's size overnight for less than three cents an acre.

Ideas matter and Jefferson knew that communicating ideas persuasively could change the world.

While the world has changed since Aristotle first gave us rhetoric more than 2,000 years ago, and since Jefferson penned the Declaration of Independence more than 200 years ago, the human brain has not changed. And that's why what worked then, works now.

As humans we are wired to seek emotional connections with one another. Ideas built upon ideas unleashed the age of automation we experience today. Yes, the pace of change is rising exponentially, sparking fear and anxiety for many people who see their world changing daily. They watch as entire job categories are eliminated and entirely new ones are created. How do we compete? How do we remain relevant? How do we flourish and thrive? Of course we all need to be experts at our jobs and flexible enough to adapt to this fast-changing landscape. But that is not enough. The answer is in persuasion and, more specifically, Pathos. Facts *alone* don't spark movements; emotions do. Facts don't inspire people to look to the stars; emotions do. Facts don't excite; emotions do. Facts don't encourage people to seek out innovative solutions to challenging problems; emotions do. Pathos—emotion—is the key to winning the future. And now science proves it.

Emotion Is the Fastest Path to the Brain

In the last decade we've learned more about emotion and its role in persuasion than we've known since our ancestors began drawing stories on cave walls.

For example, neuroscientists label words and images that evoke strong reactions as "emotionally competent stimuli." These are words, pictures, or objects that trigger fear, joy, hope, and surprise. "Emotionally arousing events tend to be better remembered than neutral events," says molecular biologist John Medina.[5] In the presence of a powerful emotional stimulus, the brain releases a rush of chemicals that acts as a mental Post-it note, flagging a piece of information as something that's critical to remember. Using fMRI, or non-invasive imaging techniques, scientists know how emotion triggers this surge, where the chemicals are produced in the brain, where they're sent to in the brain, and how they make us feel. In one of Medina's scientific papers, he writes:

> In the presence of emotionally competent stimuli, norepinephrine is released from neurons that arise from the lateral brain stem tegmentum and the locus caeruleus. This is a big deal. Neurons that originate from these areas project to an astonishingly wide variety of regions in the brain, including the hippocampus and the amygdala. After norepinephrine arrives at its target cells, the hormone binds to β-adrenergic receptors.[6]

In plain English, emotion grabs our attention and emotional memories are unforgettable.

Medina is just one of many neuroscientists and researchers who study the impact of emotion on persuasion. Throughout this book you'll hear from the world's leading experts in the fields of communication, memory, and human behavior. For example, at Claremont Graduate University, Dr. Paul Zak is studying which neurochemicals are in play when a person tells another person a story. He's found that stories trigger a rush, provided by chemicals such as oxytocin, dopamine, and cortisol. Zak is even identifying which parts of the story provide the rush. "A compelling story with an emotional trigger alters our brain chemistry, making us more trusting, understanding, and open to ideas," says Zak.[7]

Princeton University neuroscientist Uri Hasson is experimenting with images that would allow us to look at the brain patterns of people who are engaged in conversation. Hasson discovered that a specific type of dialogue results in "neural coupling," where scans show similar patterns of activity in the same regions of both the speaker's and the listener's brains. Hasson has concluded that an emotional story is the only kind of dialogue that triggers this kind of mind-meld between two brains.

According to a study published in the *Harvard Business Report*, the rise of AI doesn't make emotion less important. On the contrary, researchers conclude that in the age of automation, emotion is more important than ever to sustain a successful career. The research finds that highly skilled workers command higher incomes because of three capabilities: ability to perform rote tasks quickly, their experience in evaluating data to determine a course of action, and their savviness in helping clients navigate the course. "AI and machine learning will quickly surpass our abilities on the first two capabilities," according to the research.[8] "Those who want to stay relevant in their professions will need to focus on skills and capabilities that artificial intelligence has trouble replicating—understanding, motivating, and interacting with human beings."

In chapter 10, you'll learn more about Pathos. Specifically, you will learn about a formula for evoking emotion that has been used for centuries and that you can use today to promote your ideas. For now, keep in mind that Pathos is the most effective tool we have as humans to outwit smart machines. You simply cannot persuade, motivate, inspire, and relate to people without it.

4

THE HUMAN CAPACITY TO DREAM BIG

There's one thing only humans can do, and that's dream,
so let us dream big.

—Garry Kasparov, chess champion who lost
a match to IBM's Deep Blue

Hell Week. The name alone underestimates how tough it really is. Five and a half days of brutal training on four hours of sleep. It's the ultimate test of endurance, determination, and mental toughness. Only one of every four candidates will make it to the end. Most quit on the first night as they shiver waist-deep in the cold ocean off Coronado Beach in San Diego. If they can run, swim, and paddle their way to the finish line, their reward is another 20 weeks of strenuous training. The few who make it become Navy SEALs, the most advanced warriors the world has ever seen.

Despite its physical demands, Hell Week is not a fitness test. The best athletes often fail to make the cut. It tests a person's mental strength. It also gives instructors an opportunity to identify leaders who can inspire, motivate, and communicate with clarity, all while covered in mud and sand and approaching hypothermia. Teamwork is essential. Building trust and cooperation among teammates is a unique and desirable skill, and it explains why many Navy SEALS successfully transition from the battlefield to the boardroom.

In business and combat, effective leaders have a clear vision and the ability to show individuals how their contributions help the team achieve its success. In the SEALs, communication skills matter. They matter a lot. The penalty for poor communication is letting the bad guy get away. The penalty is a failed mission. The penalty is death.

From officer to commander and from captain to admiral, mastering the art of persuasion is a critical skill that allows leaders to climb the SEAL ranks. In the modern military a leader cannot simply tell soldiers to take a hill. They must be persuaded. Anyone—even the most loyal soldier— will begin to question their purpose while sitting in 120-degree heat in the desert, unshowered and loaded down with 75 pounds of gear.

According to former Navy SEALs Leif Babin and Jocko Willink in their book *Extreme Ownership*, "Combat leadership requires getting a diverse team of people in various groups to execute highly complex missions in order to achieve strategic goals."[1] Babin is a highly decorated officer who saw combat in two tours in Iraq. "You can't *make* people listen to you. You can't *make* them execute," he writes. "To implement real change, to drive people to accomplish something truly complex or difficult or dangerous—you can't *make* people do those things. You have to *lead* them."[2]

After surviving Hell Week himself a few years earlier, Babin returned to Coronado Beach in San Diego as an instructor. Babin learned a valuable lesson in leadership when he assembled seven-men boat crews for training purposes. The crews worked together to lug 200-pound boats up 20-foot sand berms and over miles of beach. On the water, they'd race. The person assigned to lead the crew was responsible for receiving orders, directing the team, and motivating the other six members.

The crews had incentives to win. First, they wanted to impress the instructors. Second, they could earn a few minutes of rest. During the exercises, one boat won nearly every race. "Boat Crew Two had a strong leader, and each of the individual boat crew members seemed highly motivated and performed well. They compensated for each other's weaknesses, helped each other, and took pride in winning," Babin observed.[3] Morale was high and smiles were broad on Boat Crew Two. Boat Crew Six came in dead last in nearly every race. The team members were angry. They yelled at each other. They worked independently with little concern for the greater good. The instructors came up with an idea. They swapped boat-crew leaders, but not teams. The leader of the winning boat took over the losing team and the leader of the losing boat went to the winning team.

In the very next race, Boat Crew Six—the ones who were usually last—crossed the finish line in first place. It wasn't a fluke. The crew went on to win most of the next races. Babin's revelation: "There are no bad teams, only bad leaders . . . leadership is the single greatest factor in any team's performance."[4]

Military leaders who deliver clear and persuasive mission briefs—the who, what, when, where, why, and how of a combat operation—are often elevated to higher positions. Even though elite SEAL team commandos train on state-of-the-art technology developed at DARPA, the defense department's top-secret research center, the technology is worthless in the absence of a leader who can inspire his team to action.

Elite military leaders have something extra—they can persuade subordinates that they're capable of accomplishing 20 times more than they ever imagined.

Storytelling Isn't a Soft Skill; It's the Equivalent of Hard Cash

Five hundred miles north of the SEAL training, teams of entrepreneurs participate in another type of boot camp. They get more hours of sleep than the SEAL candidates, but not by much.

Twice a year the famous Silicon Valley seed accelerator Y Combinator invests $120,000 each in about a hundred startups. Admission is a hot ticket. The firm only selects 3 percent of the founders who apply. In exchange for roughly 7 percent of a company's equity, Y Combinator gives entrepreneurs and founders advice, guidance, and an inside track to a powerful alumni network. Since 2005, Y Combinator has invested in 1,500 startups with a combined valuation of $100 billion. The most famous alumni include Airbnb, Reddit, Stripe, and Dropbox. More than 50 of its companies are each worth more than $100 million.

For three months, young, ambitious, driven founders work with advisors to refine their products and ideas. They're preparing for the big event—Demo Day. It's often the most consequential day in the life of the entrepreneurs who take part. It's the day they show off their products and pitch their ideas to a group of investors who can take their company to new heights. The Demo Day presentation is a story, a narrative of the founder's story and vision of the future. Storytelling is at the heart of Demo Day, which is why Y Combinator looks for founders with great ideas and great storytelling skills to match.

"Anytime you try to sell something to somebody, you're selling a dream. You're asking them to become part of your story," Geoff Ralston says.[5] Ralston built one of the first web mail services—Yahoo Mail. He went on to create Lala, a music distribution site that he sold to Apple. He also holds computer science degrees from Dartmouth and Stanford. Ralston is a computer scientist who considers soft skills to be the equivalent of hard cash. In fact, he doesn't like the phrase "soft skill" to describe an essential attribute he looks for in entrepreneurs. "Storytelling isn't a soft skill; storytelling is fundamental," Ralston told me.

> Successful companies and entrepreneurs create a narrative around their products, services, and brand. If I'm to have an impact on your life. If I want to sell you something. If I want you to use something I've created, I have to fit that into *your* narrative. I have to tell you a story that is compelling enough for you to want to be a part of *my* story because I've created a change, something new and something interesting. And that narrative is something that I want you to be a part of. That is how humans have created our civilization. We tell a common story that holds us together.

Entrepreneurs accepted to Y Combinator typically have little more than a minimally viable product, or MVP. In the language of startups an MVP is a product that has just enough core features to be functional and to prove that it works. With feedback and cash, the MVP might become the next big thing. When pitching an MVP, an entrepreneur who can craft a compelling story has a competitive advantage. In Part Three, you'll learn specific pitch and presentation tips from the actual investors who have prepared Y Combinator's most famous entrepreneurs for Demo Day.

When asked about the traits he looks for in an investment pitch, Y Combinator founder and president Sam Altman gave this immediate response: "Are they good communicators?"[6] According to Altman, if someone cannot communicate clearly, "it's a real problem."

Altman's investment will be worthless if the entrepreneur cannot motivate, inspire, hire, sell, raise money, and talk to the press. An inspiring leader who articulates an intoxicating mission will have an easier time hiring the best and the brightest. Without such a leader, Altman says, "I usually get bored." Great communicators don't put people to sleep.

After backing more than 3,200 founders, Altman has arrived at a series of questions he asks himself about the opportunity[7]:

- *Will the company build something lots of people LOVE?*
- *Will the company be easy to copy?*
- *Are the founders "forces of nature"?*
- *Does the company have a clear and important mission?*

Only the second of Altman's four questions deals directly with proprietary technology, patents, or barriers to entry. Three of the four questions are related to emotional connections. Will people LOVE the company? People might like an average product or find it useful, but love is reserved for five-star companies. The last two questions involve communication skills. Altman says finding a founder who is a "force of nature" is the most difficult factor to evaluate, and he must rely on the founder's communication skills to decide. Finally, if the founder cannot articulate a clear and important mission, he or she will struggle to persuade others to join the journey.

Y Combinator doesn't invest in average companies. It backs dreamers. Asking the right questions helps to identify them.

The right questions led to the creation of the world's most profitable and admired brand, a company that has mastered emotional appeal: Apple.

Empathy Creates Energy and Drives Profits

When Apple opened its first store in 2001, many experts thought it was a crazy idea. One retailing analyst predicted Apple would "turn the lights off" its failed experiment within two years. A headline in *Business Week* read: "Sorry, Steve, Here's Why Apple Stores Won't Work." The experts weren't just wrong; they had committed a colossal misjudgment. Fifteen years later the Apple stores were making more money per square foot than any other retailer on the planet and Apple enjoyed a market value of $750 billion, making it the world's most valuable brand.

The analysts failed to predict Apple's success because they were crunching numbers instead of considering experiences. The critics were correct that—compared to its peers—Apple stores would have to generate more money to pay for their expensive spaces in shopping malls. What they didn't realize was that Steve Jobs and his team didn't set out to sell computers. Instead they planned to introduce customers to tools that would unleash their personal creativity. They knew that if they could make emotional connections, sales would follow.

Jobs and the Apple store team began to ask questions. About their competitors: "What's their mission?" The answer was "to move metal and sell boxes." The Apple team took a different approach. They asked a more empowering question: "How do we enrich lives?" Here's what the answer looked like in 2001:

> A store that enriches lives has a non-commission sales floor. Instead of clerks or salespeople, it would hire geniuses and concierges.
> A store that enriches lives hires for empathy and passion.
> A store that enriches lives greets you as you step foot inside.
> A store that enriches lives lets you play with the products.
> A store that enriches lives is located where people live their lives.[8]

Better questions led to better innovations. The vision to enrich lives served as Apple store's true north for 15 years. In May 2017, enriching lives still remained the heart of the company's mission as it embarked on its most significant redesign since the first stores opened.

In an interview on CBS News, Apple's vice president of retail, Angela Ahrendts, said the redesign was a celebration of Apple's legacy. "Anything you do at Apple, you want to carry on the legacy," she said.[9] "Our soul is our people and our job is to enrich lives."

The Apple store makeover that Ahrendts spearheaded included "town squares" where people could gather and learn in communities. She introduced a new employee category with the title Creative Pros. These were the "liberal arts" equivalent of tech Geniuses, and they lead workshops on a host of topics ranging from photos and video to music, coding, art, and design. Ahrendts said the position of the Creative Pro was inspired by Jobs's philosophy that Apple is "technology married with the liberal arts."

In the CBS interview, Ahrendts explained that empathy was at the heart of Apple's success and served as the backdrop to the changes in the store design. "The more technologically advanced our society becomes, the more we need to go back to the basic fundamentals of human connection," she said.[10] "I don't care how advanced technology gets. I don't think there's anything that can replace looking someone in the eyes, touching their hand, that feeling . . . Empathy is one of the greatest creators of energy."

Ahrendts was the CEO of the fashion company Burberry when she received a call from Apple CEO Tim Cook. At Burberry, Ahrendts had successfully merged the company's traditional retail locations with an online sales component. The result was a tripling of the company's stock. Cook had been searching for a new leader for Apple retail and asked Ahrendts to fill the role.

"Tim, I'm not a techie. You have the wrong person," she said.[11] But Cook didn't approach Ahrendts for her technical skills. "We have plenty of people with that," he said. Cook was looking for someone who had the personal equivalent of Apple's secret sauce: the marriage of technology and liberal arts. Cook chose Ahrendts for her reputation as a leader who motivated her teams and who could empathize with the customers.

Ahrendts said she learned empathy as one of six children raised in a small Indiana town. She was raised by a spiritual mother and a philosopher father. "My dad used to always say, I can teach you anything. But I can't teach you to *feel*. I can't teach you to *care*."[12]

Brands that care have a healthy culture. They outperform their peers on customer satisfaction scores and enjoy higher rates of growth, revenue, and profits. Culture drives success at the world's most admired companies: Apple, Google, Virgin, Microsoft, Southwest, Starbucks, Zappos, and many others. Inspiring leadership is critical to each of these brands. They were founded or are currently run by men and women who believe that technology alone is not enough. They see their role as fostering community and creating experiences. Ahrendts once said that human energy has the power to unite people, build companies, and transform lives. Great leaders are great at unleashing human energy.

Five-Star Principles to Take Healthcare off Life Support

For 80 years the hospital gown has taken its place among the ugliest, most uncomfortable and embarrassing of garments. Halee Fischer-Wright, CEO of a medical group association representing nearly 50 percent of all healthcare providers in America, says that hospital employees would often joke that gowns come in three sizes: short, shorter, and don't bend over.

In her book, *Back to Balance,* Halee Fischer-Wright explains how the hospital gown got a fashion makeover in 2010 when designer Diane von Furstenberg partnered with the Cleveland Clinic to create a new gown with comfortable fabric, bright prints, and the easy access that doctors and nurses required. Dozens of hospitals around the country began to follow the Cleveland Clinic's lead, redesigning gowns to offer patients more dignity. But why? For a century, hospitals didn't seem to care. The gowns were cheap and durable. Money was behind the motivation to change— and the goal wasn't to save money, but to make more of it.

In 2001, the Institute of Medicine published *Crossing the Quality Chasm,* a report that called for extensive reform in the U.S. healthcare system. It concluded that a fundamental breakdown in communication was one of the main culprits behind a failed system.

In 2002, the Centers for Medicare & Medicaid Services (CMS) began developing the first national standards for patient experiences called the "Five-Star Quality Rating System." In 2006, hospitals had to make their ratings public, and patients were able to compare hospitals based on their satisfaction scores. That hurt hospitals that didn't keep up, but the impact was nothing compared to what happened next. CMS tied Medicare reimbursements to patient satisfaction scores. With billions of dollars at stake, hospitals had a very real incentive to improve the patient experience.

To make it easier for patients to evaluate hospitals, CMS ranks hospitals on a recognizable star system. The ratings cover 3,544 hospitals across the country. The majority (77 percent) are average, receiving three or four stars. Only 168, representing fewer than 5 percent of all hospitals in the United States, receive the coveted five stars. The five-star hospitals stand out because they're run by leaders who understand the value of clear, empathetic, and effective communication.

The ratings are based on data from the Hospital Consumer Assessment of Healthcare Providers and Systems survey (HCAHPS). The survey is comprised of 32 questions filled out by some 8,700 patients a day. At least one-third of the questions cover communication skills. For example:

- During your hospital stay, how often did doctors or nurses explain things in a way you could understand?

- During this hospital stay, did doctors, nurses, or other hospital staff talk with you about whether you would have the help you needed when you left the hospital?

- Before giving you any new medicine, how often did hospital staff tell you what the medicine was for?[13]

More than 70 percent of negative HCAHPS scores are directly related to a breakdown in communication. This is a serious problem. Poor communication leads to decreased revenue for healthcare systems and more health problems for patients. Effective communication is directly correlated to better health outcomes. "Studies confirm what instinct has told us from the very beginning," writes Halee Fischer-Wright. "When doctors have the time to do what's necessary with their patients—look patients in the eye, listen to them, learn from them, lay hands on them, empathize with them, communicate with them, give trust, and earn trust—patients are much more likely to take the steps necessary to get healthy or stay healthy. When the art of medicine isn't present, everything in healthcare becomes more of an uphill fight."[14]

Cleveland Clinic chief executive Toby Cosgrove learned this lesson when giving a talk at the Harvard Business School in 2006. A student raised her hand and told Cosgrove that her father had recently needed heart surgery. They'd considered the Cleveland Clinic, which had excellent results, but ultimately chose another hospital for treatment. "We heard you had no empathy," she said.

The student's comments alarmed Cosgrove. When he returned to the clinic, he set about tackling the problem head-on. First, he changed the motto of the hospital to "Patients First." It sounded simple, but, like Apple's vision to "enrich lives," it would serve as the hospital's north star for years to come.

Cosgrove then established the new position of chief experience officer, who was charged with improving patient engagement by marrying digital technology with human warmth. Under his leadership the Cleveland Clinic rose from the eighth percentile in patient satisfaction to one of the most admired hospital systems in the country. Cosgrove did not just improve the hospital score; he changed a culture.

"In healthcare, communication skills are key," says Dr. Adrienne Boissy, Cleveland Clinic's chief experience officer. "Illness transports many of us to a strongly emotional state, while clinicians are generally more comfortable in the cognitive realm."[15]

Leaders at the Cleveland Clinic realized that communication skills— like any other skill—improved with practice. Over time they conducted training workshops for all 43,000 caregivers (doctors, nurses, administrators). In the sessions the staff learned to follow a five-step communication model that goes by the acronym HEART. The "H" stands for "Hear the story." It reminds caregivers that everyone has a story and should be treated as a unique individual, not just as a patient.

To support the theme that "everyone has a story," the Cleveland Clinic created a video that quickly attracted millions of views online. It's titled *Empathy: Human Connection to Patient Care*.[16] It begins with a hospital worker pushing a man in a wheelchair through the hospital doors. The words on the screen read: "Has been dreading this appointment. Fears he waited too long." They pass another man walking out of the hospital. The words read: "Wife's surgery went well. Going home to rest." In the next scene we see a woman sitting in a chair connected to IVs. She has a vacant stare in her eyes. The words read: "Day 29. Waiting for a new heart." The video shows people in the elevator, waiting rooms, surgery prep, and hospital rooms. It ends with this advice for all healthcare providers: "If you could stand in someone else's shoes. Hear what they hear. See what they see. Feel what they feel. Would you treat them differently?"

The Hospital Corporation of America (HCA) is one of the largest for-profit healthcare providers in the world. It has a big footprint in the United States. It operates 170 hospitals and generates $40 billion in annual revenue. On any given day, 1 out of every 22 people who visit an emergency room will go to an HCA-affiliated hospital. When I met with HCA executives, they were exploring the role of communication in boosting patient satisfaction scores. An HCA hospital that earned high marks from 6 of every 10 patients would place near the bottom of the ratings. But a high score from 8 out of 10 patients was enough to earn the top spot among its peers. In other words, beyond dramatically improving the lives of their patients, winning over just 2 more patients out of every 10 could mean hundreds of millions of dollars in additional revenue.

On the micro level, more effective communication between patient and healthcare provider improves the patient's experience, keeps more patients healthier and happier, and generates more revenue. On a macro level, better communication skills could save the country from financial catastrophe. Economists point to the rising cost of healthcare ($3 trillion a year in the United States alone) as the most significant threat to America's long-term financial security. Direct, clear, and empathetic communication is considered the key to bringing down costs and improving the quality of care.

As it turns out, balancing technology with empathy—automation and communication—is the secret to earning five-star ratings in a host of categories, from healthcare to hospitality.

In a world of big data, it's easy to lose sight of the small things that make a big difference.

The Secret Ingredient Behind Five-Star Experiences

Harrison can scan dozens of hotels in the blink of an eye, recommend one, and make the reservation. What Harrison doesn't know is that your children want a photo in front of Cinderella's Castle at Disney World. Here's an inside secret that only experienced travel agents know: to get an unobstructed view of the castle, book a breakfast reservation inside the park before the gates open to the public.

Harrison is smart, but it's not a person. Harrison is an artificial intelligence tool, the product of machine learning. Harrison is the brainchild of Paul English, the founder of Kayak, a popular travel search engine. English's new company, Boston-based Lola, is a travel company that provides travel services through a smartphone app.

Lola stands out because it combines machine learning tools like Harrison with the personalized service of human experts. Harrison matches customers with hotel and flight recommendations—and does so blazingly fast—freeing up Lola's human travel agents to focus on making creative suggestions. English describes his new service as "human powered travel."

By the time English had launched Kayak in 2004, the Internet had already reduced the need for traditional travel agents. But they didn't go away entirely. English launched Lola with the goal of bringing human contact back to travel. English says that the human factor is a company's competitive edge in the age of automation.

In hospitality and services, emotional resonance is the single most important factor in standing out, and nowhere is that more evident than in star ratings.

Yelp has access to a massive database. The service connects consumers with local merchants hundreds of millions of times every month. Since its inception in 2004, Yelp has collected more than 120 million reviews for everything from restaurants and hotels to salons and mechanics.

The average rating on Yelp is 3.8 out of 5 stars. An average hotel is clean, but may lack some amenities and might have long wait times. Four-star hotels have more comfortable beds, a helpful staff, and nicer amenities such as pools and hot tubs. They are clean, comfortable, and convenient. They are acceptable and a little above average. But the theme of this book is not for the average or even the above average. It's for those who want to stand apart and make transformative changes in their lives and their businesses. For these people, anything less than five stars is unacceptable.

A data analyst had the clever idea of crunching the massive amounts of information that Yelp compiles—publicly available data—to gain a better understanding of the ratings system. He discovered that five-star ratings were backed by positive emotions in Yelp reviews, emotions that lower ratings lacked. For example, customers who gave five stars to hotels used phrases such as: "Can't wait to go back," "Love this place," "Made me happy," "Very friendly," or "Great service." The data analyst uncovered a trend that hospital leaders are beginning to learn and that the world's leading hotel owners have known a long time—human communication builds emotional connections, and emotion is the secret to earning the coveted fifth star.

Among the tens of thousands of hotels across America, fewer than 1 percent earn the Five Diamond award by AAA. Those hotels that earn five diamonds *and* five stars from the prestigious Forbes Travel Guide are exceptionally rare, comprising less than one half of 1 percent of all properties.

Forbes is famous for its lists. Every year the magazine ranks the richest people in America or the world's billionaires. Landing on a Forbes list is prestigious and the brand carefully guards its methodology. The same holds true for Forbes's coveted five-star ratings given to hotels and restaurants. But through interviews with hospitality leaders and publicly available information, we know much more about the most important quality that a brand must show to earn five stars from the Forbes Travel Guide.

To come up with a star rating, inspectors anonymously spend two nights at a hotel and evaluate the property on 800 objective standards. Four-star properties on the Forbes list are considered exceptional. Four-star hotels deliver a high level of service and quality. The mattresses are comfortable, the linens are soft, and the service is "professional." The staffs at five-star hotels are different. They push the boundaries of the guest experience. They are caring, gracious, and thoughtful. They show a genuine interest in their guests. They anticipate a guest's needs. They surprise and delight. Service differentiates four-star from five-star hotels and standout service requires emotional resonance.

The Sanctuary Hotel on South Carolina's Kiawah Island is 1 of only 154 hotels in the world to earn a Forbes five-star rating. The resort hires and trains employees to make emotional connections with each and every guest in each and every interaction. Employees are taught to:

Get the customer's name right. A name personalizes the interaction. Employees are trained in using memory tricks to remember those names. A customer is not a room number. A customer is "Mr. and Mrs. Johnson and their four-year-old daughter, Veronica."

Beat the greet. The first few seconds of a customer interaction sets the foundation for the rest of their experience. The Sanctuary staff are taught to take the greeting one step further, to *beat the greet*. They are the first to say hello, to start a conversation, to step out from behind a desk or to say "Good afternoon."

Anticipate needs. Employees are trained to recognize guests' needs before they realize those needs themselves. For example, a front desk employee might anticipate a family's needs based on the weather: "There's rain in the forecast tomorrow. Here are some activities your kids might enjoy indoors." A business professional will have an entirely different set of needs than a family on vacation. They might need to know where the business center is located or where the meetings are being held the next morning. A three-star employee meets needs; a five-star employee anticipates.

Daily storytelling. Employees of every Sanctuary department gather for short meetings each day. In addition to the basic information they need about the day's guests or events, they also share stories with one another. These stories reinforce the company's mission and values, and offer vivid examples of what five-star service looks like. For example, the employees heard the story of a guest whose car battery had died. A security guard tried to jump-start the battery, but it needed to be replaced. The guest was frustrated because he assumed a full day of his vacation would be wasted, waiting for a tow truck and repairs. Sensing the guest's frustration, the security guard said, "I live close to an auto repair store. I'll get the battery and have it installed. We'll put the charge to your room." The guest was so surprised—and delighted—he sent a long letter of thanks to the employee and the hotel's general manager. Such stories encourage and motivate employees to find opportunities to create their own guest experiences.[17]

When the hotel's guests rave about the place, it's rarely to say how much they enjoyed the soft sheets or the delicious food. It's nearly always about how a particular employee made them feel.

In this chapter, we've learned how a small constellation of brands and leaders stand out in a sea of average. We've seen where machines can beat humans, and where they can't. We've discovered that ideas can't sell themselves. In the rest of the book, we'll hear from men and women who have made the transition from good to great, and we'll learn about the communication skills they've developed to reach the next level.

As you read their stories, keep in mind that they share one mental habit—they're optimistic about the future and their role in a changing world. In 1997 Garry Kasparov was the greatest chess player in the world. In that year he famously lost a match to IBM's super computer Deep Blue. The event left him unsettled and anxious. In 2017, after 20 years of remarkable computer advances (today's smartphones have more processing power than Deep Blue), Kasparov is more optimistic than ever. He's been thinking about what machines are capable of doing and what humans can do better than machines. Machines can accomplish tasks better and faster, but that gives humans the opening to think of greater things. "Machines have calculations; humans have understanding. Machines have instructions; we have purpose. Machines have objectivity; we have passion . . . If we fail, it will not be because our machines were too intelligent or not intelligent enough. If we fail, it's because we grew complacent and limited our ambition. There's one thing only humans can do, and that's dream—so let us dream big."[18]

Let's meet the men and women who dream big.

PART TWO

WHO'S EARNED
FIVE STARS

5

THE SCIENTISTS

There's nothing wrong with cherry-picking the cool stuff.
—NEIL deGRASSE TYSON

Neil deGrasse Tyson gets 200 speaking requests a month. He accepts 4.

He has 10 million Twitter followers.

He is Stephen Colbert's favorite guest.

His books are bestsellers, and they have "astrophysics" in the title.

His television shows are seen in 180 countries.

Neil deGrasse Tyson is a five-star communicator because he makes learning about the stars so much fun. Tyson grew up in the Bronx, New York. At the age of nine, Tyson got starstruck, literally, when he visited the Hayden Planetarium at New York's Museum of Natural History. Tyson left the planetarium that day, but the call of the cosmos never left him. Tyson's passion led to a physics degree from Harvard, a Ph.D. in astrophysics from Columbia, and a career as a celebrity scientist. Tyson's gift is the ability to excite his audiences, unleashing their innate desire to explore a world beyond their own.

Tyson laughs easily on stage and in television interviews. In an e-mail exchange with the famed astrophysicist, I suggested that part of his appeal is tied to the passion he has for the subject. After all, passion is contagious and science proves it. Tyson agreed but said his enthusiasm runs deeper than a mere "passion" for the subject.[1] He calls his style *the manifestation of curiosity.*

Tyson manifests curiosity brilliantly. In his book *Astrophysics for People in a Hurry,* Tyson grabs the reader in the first sentence: "In the beginning, nearly fourteen billion years ago, all the space and all the matter and all the energy of the known universe was contained in a volume less than one-trillionth the size of the period that ends this sentence."[2] Tyson's method is to take a complex or abstract idea and "embed it in familiar ground." For example:

> Earth's mountains are puny compared with some other mountains in the solar system. The largest on Mars, Olympus Mons, is 65,000 feet tall and nearly 300 miles wide at its base. It makes Alaska's Mount McKinley look like a molehill.[3]

> There are more stars in the universe than grains of sand on any beach, more stars than seconds have passed since Earth formed, more stars than words and sounds ever uttered by all the humans who ever lived.[4]

On social media, Tyson's posts ground complexity in the familiar. The familiar is often a major sporting event; football games provide plenty of fodder for Tyson's unique take on physics. For example, as Super Bowl LI kicked off on February 5, 2017, Tyson played off the controversy of demoting Pluto from planethood:

> @Neiltyson: If a football were the Sun at the 50-yard line, Earth would be at the 15-yard line. Pluto, a quarter-mile away. Get over it.

In 2015, Tyson made a comment that his followers retweeted 4,000 times. He said a Cincinnati Bengals overtime victory was partly due to science:

> @neiltyson: Today's @Bengals winning OT field goal was likely enabled by a 1/3-in deflection to the right, caused by Earth's rotation.

Twitter has helped Tyson become a better a communicator. "Each of my posted tweets is an attempt at humor, communication, learning, enlightenment, etc. The instant response of followers serves as a kind of neurosynaptic snapshot of the public's response to my thoughts. This helps me tune in to what I say and how I say it for maximum effectiveness."[5]

There are many topics Tyson avoids. It's part of the key, he says, to making science fun. Instead of powering his way through the whole syllabus, so to speak, Tyson cherry-picks "the cool stuff" to make science accessible and to hook the audience into wanting to learn more. "There are many topics I don't come near, because I have yet to find a way to make them fully (or even partially) accessible," he says. For example, "Topics like spectroscopic analysis, interferometry, or Einstein's special theory of relativity. You can ask me about them. But after my attempt to explain it to you, if you look back at me confused, we will need to sit down with pen and paper."[6]

The secret to communicating science and other complex topics is not to "translate" the content—which Tyson says only serves to oversimplify and dumb it down—but to "explain with enthusiasm and, where and when necessary, link the concept to something embedded in pop culture, where we all have active receptors."

One of Tyson's most popular public presentations is called "An Astrophysicist Goes to the Movies." In it, he talks about convincing director James Cameron to change the night sky for the re-release of the movie *Titanic* in 2012. He also sparked a Twitter-storm when he pointed out the inaccuracies in the movie *Gravity*. The movie *Armageddon* "violated more known laws of physics per minute" than any other movie, according to Tyson. He joked on Twitter that the asteroid chunks hitting the Earth had incredible aim, targeting monuments in the world's great cities. By keeping one foot in pop culture and one foot in his field, Tyson inspires his audience to jump into the topic with both feet.

Tyson's books, presentations, lectures, radio shows, podcasts, and television appearances earned him the Public Welfare Medal from the U.S. National Academy of Sciences. The academy said Tyson earned the medal for his "extraordinary role in exciting the public about the wonders of science." The key word is "exciting." Tyson says exciting an audience is a critical skill for "anyone who knows anything that other people don't know, but perhaps should know."[7] And we still have so much to learn, about every topic, really, but science in particular.

Tyson believes that reframing a person's perspective—the cosmic perspective—opens their minds to extraordinary ideas and keeps them humble at the same time. And in this way, he says, science communication serves a noble purpose: "The day our knowledge of the cosmos ceases to expand, we risk regressing to the childish view that the universe figuratively and literally revolves around us."[8] In that "bleak world," he says, nations and people take up arms against each other because they're protecting their own turf or interests. When people are reminded that the world doesn't revolve around them, racial, ethnic, religious, national, and cultural problems shrink—or can be eliminated in many cases.

Earthly problems would shrink if people saw the big picture. The big picture, according to Tyson, is that we're all interconnected. In 1990, another science communicator—the astronomer Carl Sagan—convinced NASA to give the *Voyager* spacecraft one last assignment as it left our solar system. *Voyager* turned its camera back to Earth. In the photo, taken four billion miles away, the Earth appears as an almost imperceptible dot of light measuring 0.12 pixels in size. The photograph has become known as the Pale Blue Dot. The photo reminded people that we are quite small in time and space, and that Earth is not the center of the universe. Tyson says if we look at our place in the universe in the right way, it can be empowering. "Because the stuff that makes up each and every one of us is traceable to the stars, humans are special—not because we're different, but because we're alike . . . and our three-pound brains figured it out."[9]

By forcing us to think small, Neil deGrasse Tyson inspires us to dream big.

Educators who can make science accessible, entertaining, and inspiring will always be needed to engage the next generation of explorers and thinkers. According to Tyson, artificially intelligent systems will make our world better but will not replace the human capacity to inspire others to shoot for the stars. "Society did not crumble when oxen replaced humans or when tractors replaced oxen. And we survived the moment that robots replaced humans on the automotive assembly line," Tyson explained. "Meanwhile, nobody wept when computers began calculating faster than the sum of all human brain power on Earth. And all was well the day after the world's best chess player lost to a computer. Further, society did not crumble when our best player—ever—lost to a computer on the game show *Jeopardy!* And we are all quite comfortable in the fact that computers help fly our most modern airplanes. Artificial intelligence is not a cliff-face, it's a landscape on which we all live. And I am happy to be there."[10]

Getting Hired to Be an Astronaut Is 100 Times Harder Than Getting Into Harvard. So How Do You Do It?

Every few years thousands of ambitious Americans apply for one of the most selective programs in the world: the NASA Astronaut Class. In 2017, America's space agency received a record number of 18,300 applications. Twelve applicants were selected, which made the process 100 times more competitive than getting into Harvard.

The astronauts are a diverse group. Five women and seven men were chosen for the 2017 class. Some are military pilots, one is a nuclear engineer, another is a Ph.D. student, while another is a marine biologist. After two years of training, they will be assigned missions on the International Space Station or on the new *Orion* spacecraft for deep-space exploration.

If you want to become an astronaut, you'll need at least a bachelor's degree in a STEM major (science, technology, engineering, or math). An advanced degree wouldn't hurt. Nearly half of those accepted have a master's or Ph.D. If you're applying as a pilot, you'll need at least 1,000 hours of flight time. You'll also need to pass NASA's long-duration space-flight physical. If you can swim three lengths of a 25-meter pool, that's a warm-up. Next, they'll ask you to swim another three lengths in a flight suit and tennis shoes. Dry off and step on the treadmill as they place a 50-pound pack on your back and ask you to run at a pace of 12 miles per hour. Of course, none of this matters if you can't fit in a Russian-made Soyuz spacecraft, which carries astronauts into orbit. If you're not between 62 and 75 inches, forget it.

Applicants who pride themselves on their experiences, advanced degrees, and fitness levels often don't realize that NASA chooses candidates for another key skill. Without this one skill, none of the others matter. And NASA begins to evaluate the skill as soon as candidates turn in their applications. The people who stand out and are ultimately selected to become NASA astronauts are those who excel at written and verbal communication.

"When we look at astronaut selection and career trajectory, communication is critical," says Ann Roemer, a manager who oversees NASA's selection process. Astronauts are the public face of America's space program. Within days of being selected, new astronauts hold their first press conference to tell the world why they were chosen and to explain the practical benefits of the work they'll be doing. While they train and work on Earth and in space, they will speak to a wide range of audiences—from students to scientists—stirring up excitement for space exploration.

In addition to mastering their immense technical tasks, astronauts must be able to communicate clearly with Mission Control in Houston and with their international teams on the space station. In emergencies, their orders must be clear and understandable. The astronauts will also be asked to provide technical input to engineers building new equipment. They must able to "advocate and communicate" for changes or improvements, says Roemer.

Most important for the future of NASA, astronauts are those who inspire the public, lawmakers, and the next generation of explorers. An astronaut must be a good speaker. The future of space exploration rides on it. According to Roemer, "We count on them to inspire next generations about what NASA is doing today and what NASA wants to do in the future."[11]

Back to the astronaut selection process. Once NASA's selection committee reviews thousands of applications for experience, credentials, and clarity of writing, about 120 candidates are invited to Houston for a week of physicals, tests, and interviews. The top 1 percent will be called back for a second round of interviews.

During the week, selection committee members are constantly evaluating the candidates for their communication skills. A dinner with the other candidates isn't just a friendly meet and greet. Since the candidates come from diverse fields such as the military, academia, science, and medicine, NASA's hiring officials are looking for people who can communicate comfortably with people from different backgrounds.

The face-to-face interviews come next, and these are critical. The questions might sound easy, but they are used to identify those prospects who are persuasive, engaging, and inspiring. For example, the selection committee often asks, "Why do you want become an astronaut?" A skilled communicator will offer three to five specific reasons. An unskilled communicator will recite a long list of accomplishments and provide a confusing, convoluted answer. Another common question for candidates in the first round is, "Tell us about yourself, starting with high school." For this answer, the storytellers stand out. They are the ones who condense a lengthy career history and wrap it in an engaging narrative, all the while connecting their experience with NASA's ultimate goal.

Dr. Kate Rubins had the experience, the degrees, and the expertise to reach the interview process. Rubins was selected in 2009, and she trained for the next seven years. In 2016, she spent 115 days on the International Space Station, took part in 275 scientific experiments, and became the first person to sequence DNA in space.

Rubins has an impressive list of degrees and experience. After completing a bachelor of science in molecular biology, Rubins earned a Ph.D. in cancer biology from the medical school at Stanford University. At MIT, Rubins led a team of researchers who studied viral diseases like Ebola in the Congo. Rubins's fieldwork was so risky, she had to wear a biosafety level-four suit, which provides the highest level of protection against contamination. She worked with airborne viruses that can kill people and for which there are no known vaccines or treatments. She had the experience and credentials to be an astronaut, but her communication skills set her apart.

Rubins is a star at NASA because she brings science down to Earth.

All astronauts are asked to take frequent breaks from their scientific experiments on board the space station to give live interviews. Rubins is a master at delivering information in language that's familiar to her audience. For example, a class of middle school students asked her what she had to learn to become an astronaut. Rubins's answer: "We have to learn a lot of things to become an astronaut. One of the things most interesting

to me was learning about flying and all the kinds of engineering and mechanical work that we do on the space station. We have to learn a whole
lot of things. And sometimes it's a little bit hard to learn so many new
things. It's really enjoyable and fun to learn things about new things and
new discoveries."[12]

I pasted Rubins's response in a software tool that measures the grade
level of text. It returned the answer—six. In other words, the average sixth-
grader in middle school should be able to read and understand the content.

Rubins adapts her language to the audience. In a discussion with biomedical researchers at the National Institutes of Health, Rubins began
the conversation by explaining how she prepared samples for sequencing
genomic DNA in a microgravity environment. She talked about the data
she was studying from the trip, RNA expression, and epigenome telomere
shortening. These are not topics that most students—or Americans—
would care about or understand. She was able to talk to sixth-graders on
their level and to advanced biomedical scientists on theirs.

A good communicator relays scientific information that's reasonably
understandable to non-scientists; a great communicator gets her audience
to care. For more general audiences, Rubins always makes it clear that the
research conducted on the space station not only benefits a future Mars
crew but also has practical implications for improving health on Earth.
Speaking to the Associated Press, a general audience, she said: "Anything
we do on the space station helps us understand how human beings can
live in space . . . but it also has a benefit for Earth-based research. When
we do things in a remote environment up here we can understand how
these technologies might work in remote places on Earth that don't have
access to good medical care."[13] Like Neil deGrasse Tyson, Rubins grounds
the content in the familiar and connects with her audiences at their level.

Don Pettit is a chemical engineer who likes to play the popular mobile
game Angry Birds . . . in space. NASA chose Pettit for his credentials
and experience, but also because he makes science entertaining. "Angry Birds isn't just any video game. It has to do with trajectories, veloci-
ties, accelerations. You're shooting little birds as projectiles," Petitt
said as he floated weightless 240 miles above the Earth.[14] Pettit was an-

nouncing a partnership between NASA and Rovio, the company that makes Angry Birds. The game Angry Birds Space requires that players use basic physics to explore various levels. On the space station, Pettit put a "red bird" (one of the game's main characters) in a slingshot to demonstrate trajectory in space. It flew straight. Under the force of Earth's gravity, a trajectory is curved. "Astronauts have to worry about these things because if you're in a rocket and you're trying to rendezvous with the International Space Station, you go in curved trajectories. You need to know how to fire your rocket engines so you can go from where you are to where you want to be," he explained.

"We count on astronauts like Pettit to inspire the next generations about what NASA is doing today and what NASA wants to do in the future," says Roemer.[15] "People who do well can explain the science or complexity to someone like me who is not a scientist by training."

NASA's TED-Like Presentation to Announce Earth-Sized Planets

Astronauts are not the only scientists NASA relies upon to persuade the public of its mission. Since NASA is not allowed to advertise, the space agency has devised innovative methods to sell its story. The tools include marketing and social media, public relations, video and graphic design, storytelling, and persuasive public speaking.

In February 2017, astronomers using NASA's Spitzer space telescope discovered seven Earth-sized planets around a single star called TRAPPIST-1. The NASA press conference to make the announcement offered a master class in communicating complex information to a broad audience.

The presentation was notable for its brevity, language, and pictures.

Brevity

The TRAPPIST-1 presentation was 18 minutes, the same length as a TED talk. Research has shown that delivering too much information at once results in "cognitive backlog," which simply means our short-term memory bank gets full, fast. The TED conference has found that 18 minutes is just the right amount of time to have a substantive discussion without putting your listeners to sleep. NASA sticks to the same 18-minute principle.

Language

When two astronomers bump into each other in the hallway, one doesn't say to the other: "We've discovered seven Earth-sized planets in the Goldilocks Zone just 40 light-years away."[16] The astronomers might say: "The transiting configuration of seven temperate exo-planets around the ultra-cool dwarf star TRAPPIST-1, located 12 parsecs away, is well suited for atmospheric configuration."

Both explanations are accurate and both were used to announce the exciting discovery of the seven planets. But the explanations were used for different audiences. The second, more complex scientific explanation appeared in the paper distributed to the academic community. The first explanation was delivered by some of the very same scientists—for the rest of us.

Jargon has no place in a NASA press conference intended to convey information to the general public. Each of the five speakers at the TRAPPIST-1 press conference was coached on how to deliver the information. Most of the following quotes do not appear anywhere in the scientific paper—but they played a prominent role in the press conference. Scientists don't speak this way to their peers, but they do when they need to inspire the masses. For example:

> The discovery gives us a hint that finding a second Earth is not just a matter of if . . . but when.

> We've discovered not one, not two, but seven Earth-sized planets around the same star. This is the first time that so many Earth-sized planets have been found around the same star, three of them in the habitable zone. Habitable zones are also called "Goldilocks Zones" where liquid water could exist.

> At light speed we'd arrive [at TRAPPIST-1] in 39 years. A jet plane would take 44 million years.

> We've made a giant accelerated leap forward in search for life
> on other worlds . . . In this planetary system, Goldilocks has
> many sisters.[17]

Goldilocks has many sisters? These aren't the words of a scientist; they are the words of a leader who wants to ignite our imagination. And it worked.

Pictures

NASA provided high-quality photos and video animations for anyone to download, for free. The most frequently downloaded photo was not one that appeared anywhere in the scientific paper. The image showed an artistic rendering of a basketball and a golf ball floating in space. The basketball represented our sun and the small golf ball represented the TRAPPIST-1, an ultra-cool dwarf star. In fact, the 18-minute NASA presentation contained several colorful photos, beautiful animations, and gorgeous artistic renderings of what the sky would look like from the surface of these newly discovered planets.

NASA scientists are experts about space exploration and they're experts at communicating with the ancient brain. If you deliver information verbally, a listener might remember 10 percent of the content; add a picture and retention soars to 65 percent.

Scientists and astronauts want to answer the question, "Are we alone?" They want to explore the stars to benefit life on Earth. They can't do any of it if they're out of business. In order to stay in business, NASA needs to convince the public that it's relevant. It's mastered the art of persuasion to get us excited about science, stretch our imaginations, and inspire us to explore worlds beyond our own.

Science Left in a Drawer Benefits No One

"Science left in a drawer doesn't benefit anyone," says Anders Sahlman, the founder of a pitch competition for Swedish scientists.[18] In 2012, Sahlman started the Researchers' Grand Prix, an annual *American Idol*–style event for scientists. Across the country, in nine regional events at universities and science centers, scientists get four minutes to present their research to a panel of experts, journalists, and a general audience. The finalists are invited to the main event in Stockholm.

While giving their four-minute presentations, scientists are judged on their vocal delivery, the structure and content of their message, and their overall performance. The standouts can condense their research and explain it to a non-technical audience. Winners get noticed. Winners stand out and get ahead. In 2014, the winner, Andreas Ohlsson, had developed a technique for sterilizing needles used to treat premature babies. The method is now used in hospitals throughout the country. The aim is to raise the profile and status of science communication as well as showcase the breadth of Swedish research.

The winning presentations use many techniques covered in Part Three of this book. The presentations are entertaining, visual, and simply told. Stories provide the emotion, something scientists were reluctant to try at first, until they saw the results of using emotion to breathe life into their lab experiments. Speakers are encouraged to tell a short story about their research, a story with a traditional structure that's recognized across time and distance: an introduction, climax, and conclusion. Above all, the story must sell the benefit of the research and be clearly understood by people in other disciplines who know nothing about the subject.

The competition is meant to identify those scientists who can thrive in a diverse work environment—the type of cooperation complex science requires today. In science, interdisciplinary work draws together experts from different fields and academic disciplines—with different values, assumptions, and methodologies—and asks them to perform research together as a team. "Communication is more important than ever because we're asking physicists, social scientists, biologists, to work together," says Sahlman.[19] "In the past, they would work alone on individual projects and keep to their own discipline. The global scientific community is moving toward open science, open access, and open data." The scientists who can communicate successfully across disciplines are the ones who bring the most value to the team and draw the most attention to their research.

Cognitive psychologists have given this topic a lot of thought. "Humans are the most complex and powerful species ever, not just because of what happens in individual brains, but because of how communities of brains work together," according to cognitive science professors Steven Sloman and Philip Fernbach.[20] "The interdependence of knowledge is truer today than it has ever been. Many scientific fields have become so interdisciplinary that the breadth of knowledge encompassed makes it impossible to master all the knowledge required to do scientific research. More than ever, scientists depend on one another to work . . . A strong leader is one who knows how to inspire a community and take advantage of the knowledge within it."

"The cost of *not* being interdisciplinary is high," says artificial intelligence scientist Neil Jacobstein.[21] "The ability to inspire people. To ignite their imagination. To call them to action. Those are rare skills." Jacobstein chairs the AI track at Singularity University, the famed Silicon Valley think tank. Jacobstein is a popular science communicator because he makes complex topics understandable to diverse audiences who are not experts in AI. His presentations on exponential technologies that will shape our future are in high demand. Executives pay $12,000 for a seven-day program at Singularity to gain new insights from Jacobstein and Singularity co-founders Peter Diamandis and futurist Ray Kurzweil.

Jacobstein uses analogies to paint a picture of how far technology has come and how fast it's changing the future. "We all face a common problem. We are surfing in front of a tsunami wave of zetabytes of information," says Jacobstein. "Our brains did not evolve under that kind of information processing pressure. The human brain hasn't had a major upgrade for over 50,000 years."[22]

Jacobstein presents information in a way that the human brain can easily absorb, even without an upgrade. For example, he told me that technologies such as AI and cognitive systems are growing exponentially, while humans think in linear terms. "I try to start with where the listener is at, not where *I'm* at," he explains. "Most listeners have expectations about the future, that it will grow in steps—1, 2, 3, 4, 5 . . . But exponential growth is a very big difference. It goes from 2 to 4 to 8 to 16 to 32, and on. If I take 30 linear steps, we can predict where I'll be. I'll end up 30 meters away. But if I take 30 exponential steps, I'll be over a billion meters away. That's twenty-six times around the planet. It's a really big difference and it's not intuitive."[23]

Jacobstein argues that we can't shape the future if we fail to understand how quickly exponential technologies are changing the future. In a linear world, the twenty-first century will see 100 years of progress. In an exponential world, it will see 20,000 years of progress. Jacobstein's presentations help people bridge the knowledge gap.

"Currently, if you unwrap the human brain surface area it's about the size of a dinner napkin," Jacobstein explains in another powerful analogy. "Eventually we'll be able to build artificial neocortex the size of a table-cloth or the surface area of a large room. We will need that kind of processing power because of the accelerating wave of human knowledge."[24]

The power of AI adds value to our world. It expands the range of the possible, says Jacobstein, who has studied more than 360 practical applications of AI. The technology augments human skills and helps us solve complex problems quickly. It will impact every field we can think of: music, transportation, medicine, law, manufacturing, oceanography, microbiology, government, ecology, education, and even art. "AI will blow the roof off these fields," says Jacobstein.[25]

"What role do humans have to play?" I asked him during our conversation.

"Computers can learn to read human emotion, but they don't *have* human emotion. And that's a very important distinction," says Jacobstein.

"People are responsible for the state of the world. *We* are managing the world. Great communication skills empower people to lift themselves up from their current situation and to join together in a systematic effort to create a higher quality of life for everyone." According to Jacobstein, we can teach machines to read facial expressions, a kind of simulated empathy. But inspiring another human being to build the future boldly requires empathy that's uniquely human. "The most important messages are not the ones that inspire you to do something easy. The most important messages inspire you to achieve your highest potential, and that's hard. It's always hard. But it's worth doing."

6

THE ENTREPRENEURS

*Communication is the most important skill any
entrepreneur can possess.*

—Richard Branson

Katelyn Gleason believes healthcare is stuck in the pre-Internet Stone
Age. When doctors need to verify a patient's insurance, they'll ask a receptionist to call the patient. It's one of the problems that Gleason's startup,
Eligible, set out to fix. At the age of 29, Gleason was named to the *Forbes*
list of "30 under 30" entrepreneurs who are remaking the healthcare
space.

Less than a decade earlier, Gleason was an unlikely candidate to revolutionize the healthcare technology field. She was an actress, studying
theater arts at Stony Brook University, a state college in Long Island, New
York. Although she had dreams of conquering the Broadway stage, she
had to pay the bills, and so Gleason worked as a sales agent for a healthcare startup. The company was called DrChrono, a web-based service for
medical practices. Gleason's comfort on stage impressed the founders, who
asked her to join them in their pitch to enter Y Combinator, the selective
investment firm introduced in chapter 4. DrChrono won a coveted spot,
a rare accomplishment in the startup world.

Gleason didn't start the company, nor did she have prior knowledge
of the healthcare space. Yet the experience inspired her to learn more
about the field. One year later, in 2012, she started her own company from

a San Francisco apartment. She decided to pitch Y Combinator again, this time as a founder. She earned a slot and went on to raise $1.6 million. Today, Eligible has 50 employees and is one of the leading healthcare billing companies in the United States.

"She [Gleason] credits her acting experience with contributing significantly to her social skills, confidence and talent for sales," writes venture capital investor Scott Hartley in his book, *The Fuzzie and the Techie*. "Her acting work helped her understand how to craft a compelling story about the company, which is essential to convincing investors to provide support."[1]

I contacted Hartley after reading Gleason's story. Hartley's experience as an investor who has seen more than 3,000 startup pitches reinforces the theme of this book—those entrepreneurs who have mastered the ancient art of persuasion are more likely to get seen, get ahead, and get funding.

According to Hartley, "As our technology continues to improve, cultivating our humanity, in particular the softer skills that the liberal arts foster, will be the best way to ensure job security . . . Finding solutions to our greatest problems requires an understanding of human context as well as code; it requires both ethics and data, both deep thinking people and Deep Learning AI, both human and machine."[2]

Bridging the world of AI and humanity is the mission of another healthcare startup co-founded by Dr. Rajaie Batniji, an entrepreneur who combines the fuzzy and the techie.

Translating Complexity Into Third-Grade Language

After studying history at Stanford and receiving a medical degree from UC San Francisco, Dr. Rajaie Batniji was selected to attend Oxford University on a Marshall Scholarship—1 of 30 American students selected every year to study in the United Kingdom. With an acceptance rate as low as 3 percent, it's among the most prestigious scholarships for U.S. citizens.

In 2013, Batniji's friend Ali experienced a sharp pain in his abdomen. A scan revealed a life-threatening condition: his intestines had twisted upon themselves, cutting off the blood supply. Emergency surgery saved his life. Like many Americans, Ali had a long battle with his health insurance company, which refused to pay much of the bill. Batniji told his friend that the experience was typical; patients are their own advocates and it's nearly impossible to get clear answers from health insurers. The two friends decided to combine their experience and know-how to fix how Americans pay for healthcare.

Today Ali Diab is the chief executive officer of Collective Health, a company that takes the complexity out of employee healthcare plans. Batniji is the company's co-founder and chief health officer. When I spoke to Batniji, *The Wall Street Journal* had named Collective Health as the number-two "Tech company to watch in 2017."

"Trust is our primary currency," said Batniji. "And how we win trust is through communication that's accessible, simple, and familiar."[3] Collective Health's insurance material is written in language that a third-grader can read and understand. Yes, third grade—not eighth grade, or even fifth grade . . . but third grade.

"We meet people where they are," Batniji told me. "Most people don't have a sophisticated understanding of insurance terminology. We define everything at a third-grade reading level. We don't assume they know how cost-sharing works or how the plan works. We put things in accessible language for them. All of our written communication should be easily interpreted by someone even in the third grade, and that's intentional."

Batniji has a point. In 2013, a study in the *Journal of Health Economics* found that consumers do not understand insurance terms nearly as well as they think they do. The study, led by a healthcare economist at Carnegie Mellon, gathered hundreds of people with employer-sponsored health plans and asked them four questions to measure their understanding of basic terms such as "deductible" and "copay." Only 14 percent answered all four questions correctly (simply guessing at the questions would have returned an accuracy rate of 20 percent).[4]

The study, which was undersigned by 13 scholars from a dozen prestigious universities, concluded that simplified language would lead to better decisions and *better health outcomes* because misunderstanding basic terms carries such serious consequences. When individuals do not understand their options, they stick with the status quo, which may not be the best health plan for their needs.

Collective Health writes its material in language that doesn't require a Ph.D. to understand. For example, a deductible is defined as: "The amount you'll pay up-front for care until your insurance kicks in."[5] The readability of the previous sentence is set for a second-grader. There are zero adverbs, zero uses of the passive voice, and zero words that are hard to read. It's the simplest explanation for a term that confuses many consumers of health-care services.

Call center representatives (referred to as member advocates) are all coached to use simplified language, as well. For example, Batniji doesn't say: "Our dedicated member advocates are incentivized to solve every member concern they encounter."[6] Instead, he says, "Our dedicated member advocates are on hand to answer your questions when they come up." The first sentence has a readability level of grade 14. The second explanation is in eighth-grade language. In addition, words like "on hand" instead of "incentivized" are more in line with the way humans talk with one another. According to Batniji, falling back on corporate and formal language throws off the tone that members are used to hearing.

Batniji isn't a techie, but he has a competitive advantage—he knows what Aristotle taught us long ago: The human brain cannot be persuaded if it has to work too hard to understand the information. His company has achieved a rare status by marrying data, artificial intelligence, and predictive analysis with empathy and simplicity. "As a physician, we're data driven and empirical, but for data to find its way to clinical efficacy you need to combine it with humanity. We need to put our hand on someone's shoulder as they repeat back to us what we said and why they should be doing it."

At the time of our conversation, Collective Health had received $150 million in venture funding, employed 260 professionals, and handled health benefits for 77,000 people. Communicating with clarity makes all the difference.

Content, Conversation, and a $1 Billion Payday

When Unilever bought the Dollar Shave Club for $1 billion, experts cited the Southern California startup as yet another example of a business creating new ways of selling direct to consumers without the overhead of bricks and mortar. True. It was also an example of a new breed of entrepreneur persuading consumers to reconsider their brand loyalties.

On the week of the sale, I spoke to David Pakman, the former CEO of eMusic.com and a partner in Venrock, the first major investor in Dollar Shave Club (DSC). Pakman, like millions of others, first saw DSC's founder, Michael Dubin, in the viral video that put his startup on the map. In the video, Dubin calls his blades "F****** great." It attracted nearly five million views within three months of being posted on YouTube.

Pakman was impressed with Dubin's pulse of the market. Dubin had seen an opening to disrupt a category where many customers found the product to be too expensive and shockingly inconvenient (anyone who's had to ask a clerk to unlock the "razor fortress" can understand). According to Pakman, Dubin also recognized another major vulnerability of legacy consumer companies: they were broadcasting messages through traditional media while consumers were living their lives on social media. "Dubin intuitively understood how to use content and conversation as a marketing tool at a time when legacy brands were still shouting at their customers with TV ads," Pakman told me.[7]

Building a "conversation brand," as Pakman explains, means more than posting a television commercial on a company's Facebook or Twitter profile. "A conversation is knowing your customers and having a relationship with them," something that DSC did from its inception.

For example, in addition to Dubin's cheeky videos, DSC's employees have created many more videos that are funny, edgy, and, above all, use conversational language. In one video titled "Let's Talk about Number 2," Dubin introduces a product that legacy brands gingerly call "flushable wipes" or "cleansing cloths." In a video that's been viewed 3.5 million times, Dubin calls his product "Butt wipes for men." Why do you need one? "Because you're not an animal and whatever you're using now, it's primitive . . . with One Wipe Charlie, you wipe once and get on with your life." The video is short, shocking, irreverent, and shareable—the makings of a hit on social media.

Entrepreneur Michael Dubin impressed investors with his communication skills, skills that he sharpened in two jobs: news producer and stand-up comic.

As a producer for digital news properties, Dubin learned to write content that resonated with an audience. "When you're launching a new business and sharing a new idea, if you can get people to remember it, there's obviously a better chance at success," Dubin said.[8] He was also a student of improvisational comedy at the Upright Citizens Brigade in New York City. Dubin once credited his eight years of improvisation classes for helping him to plan, write, and present a business case as well as connect to people through his humorous videos. "People tend to remember things when they're musically presented, and comedy is a form of music," according to Dubin.

According to Pakman, "If you're a brand in this age of splintered attention on social media, you have to be good at reaching people conversationally and you have to have good content that they want to see, otherwise they choose not to listen to you."[9] Dubin's experience as a communicator in the digital age helped him to create content that people wanted to see and, more important, wanted to share with their friends.

In five years, Dollar Shave Club earned a 5 percent market share in a category that had been dominated by one brand—Gillette—for 115 years. According to Pakman, "Gillette was blithely unaware of what their own customers thought of them. They had no idea because they never talked to them."[10]

Pakman says the big lesson of DSC's success story is to see social media as a tool to build content and conversation. For the better part of the past 100 years, consumers had a few newspapers and magazines to read and a few television channels to watch. It's the environment in which Gillette thrived for 115 years. But times have changed and so have our viewing habits. "With the Internet and mobile phones, our attention has shifted from the legacy of one-way broadcast media to the conversational forms of social media," says Pakman.[11]

Entrepreneur Michael Dubin had the right skills at the right time to take advantage of the social media trend, a trend that rewards authenticity, shareable content, and two-way conversations between brands and their customers. DSC's social media platforms (Instagram, Facebook, Twitter) feature stories of actual customers, invite customers to give a constant stream of feedback, and encourage an ongoing relationship with the brand.

Michael Dubin, Rajaie Batniji, and Katelyn Gleason are five-star entrepreneurs whose soft skills helped them stand out against entrenched competitors.

Every year in the United States alone, entrepreneurs start 600,000 businesses. Only 5 percent of these businesses receive venture capital funding. Venture capitalists are highly selective because they write big checks averaging $2.6 million to seed-stage companies. They are also well aware that many of their bets will fail, and only invest in 1 of every 400 pitches they see. According to America's top investors, entrepreneurs who have mastered the art of persuasion are more likely to overcome the immense challenges they'll face: selling ideas; growing revenue; attracting customers; recruiting, retaining, and motivating the best employees; and raising more capital.

Seven "Winningest" VCs Identify the Communication Skills That Will Set You Apart

The *New York Times* partnered with CB Insights to publish a list of the top 20 "winningest" venture capitalists in the world.[12] Many of them have made notable remarks on the role that communication skills play in an entrepreneur's ultimate success.

Bill Gurley: "The great storytellers have an unfair competitive advantage."

Bill Gurley of Benchmark Capital (Grubhub, OpenTable, Uber) defends the use of PowerPoint decks during investor pitches. He says it helps VCs evaluate how well an entrepreneur can communicate his or her ideas. Gurley wrote an article called "In Defense of the Deck," where he states: "Investors are not solely evaluating your company's story. They are also evaluating your ability to convey that story."[13]

Gurley says that communicators who can deliver a compelling narrative have several advantages. They are going to "recruit better . . . be darlings in the press . . . raise money more easily . . . close amazing business developer partnerships, and they are going to have a strong and cohesive corporate culture."

Chris Sacca: "Storytelling is at the core of everything we do in this space."

The influential investor Chris Sacca manages a portfolio of over 80 startups and mature enterprises through his holding company Lowercase Capital. He's known for seed and early investments in Twitter, Uber, Instagram, and Kickstarter. He says founders must become the best storytellers. "It's how you raise money. It's how you recruit people to your company. It's how you retain them. It's how you talk to the press. It's the cornerstone of everything we do in this business."[14]

Jeff Jordan: "Every great founder can tell a great story."

Jordan is the former CEO of OpenTable. As a general partner at venture capital firm Andreessen Horowitz, he led the series B round for Airbnb. Jordan, too, looks for entrepreneurs who have one mythical quality—the ability to tell a compelling story that draws in the listener. "Every great founder can really tell a great story," Jordan once said. "It's one of the key things in a founder that you can convince people to believe."[15]

The bottom line for Jordan: if an entrepreneur doesn't have the ability to craft a compelling message around a powerful narrative, it makes it much more difficult to attract investors, employees, and press coverage.

Alfred Lin: "Culture is the thing that is actually going to be very, very important to scale the business as well as your team."

Before making the transition to venture capitalist at Sequoia Capital, Lin built Zappos alongside CEO Tony Hsieh. Zappos created an extraordinary culture around "delivering wow through service." In a class at Stanford University, Lin said a major part of a leader's role is to keep the culture and the mission of the company front and center—and to communicate it often. When a leader makes culture a daily habit, the company will be rewarded in many ways—from financial performance indicators, to customer loyalty, to employee retention. "I think you can have the smartest engineer in the world but if they don't believe the mission they are not going to pour their heart and soul into it," says Lin.[16]

Fred Wilson: "Get people engaged in the conversation as soon as you can."

Fred Wilson, founder of New York City–based Union Square Ventures (Twitter, Etsy), once said that, when it comes to investor pitches, he wants an entrepreneur to use a "hook and reel 'em in" method. Grab their attention early with a bold or audacious statement. Above all, it's "a bad idea" to waste time on a long backstory. Wilson doesn't want to hear about your journey from the time you graduated. Get to the point and get to it early.

Wilson also recommends simplicity. For example, entrepreneurs pitching VCs often create presentations—pitch decks—that consist of 20 slides or more. Wilson believes the ideal pitch deck for a new idea should have 6 slides. In a blog post, he wrote: "Like many things in life, less is more in fundraising slides. You can explain your business in mind numbing detail or you can inspire an investor and let them imagine. Guess what works better?"[17]

Michael Moritz: "Burning a message into a person's skull is a rare art. In order to do that, it must be memorable, clear, vivid, and have an element of emotion associated with it."

When I interviewed the famed Sequoia Capital investor behind Google, Yahoo, PayPal, Airbnb, LinkedIn, and other notable companies, we talked about how great leaders inspire others. For Moritz, clarity is everything. "You cannot lead an individual—let alone a team or an organization—without being able to clearly communicate the direction in which you want to go," Moritz told me.[18]

Mary Meeker: "I grew up believing that one person could make a difference."

Meeker is known for an annual presentation on the state of the Internet (the Internet Trends Report). She's also played a major role as a former Morgan Stanley analyst who helped the firm snag IPOs such as Google, Netscape, and Priceline. Today, as a partner at the Silicon Valley venture capital firm Kleiner Perkins Caufield & Byers (KPCB), she sits on the boards of Lending Club, Square, and DocuSign.

Meeker agrees with legendary KPCB venture capitalist John Doerr that great leaders articulate powerful mission statements. Doerr once told

Stanford business students that he'd rather invest in missionaries than mercenaries. Mercenaries, he explained, have "a lust for money." Missionaries have "a lust for meaning."[19]

Missionaries, according to Meeker, consistently communicate their big ideas in ways that attract and excite listeners. In one interview Meeker said, "The powerful mission statement to me was Google's—to organize the world's information and make it universally accessible and useful. We were involved in that IPO, and I had to ask myself: 'Are we in?' We could have said no. But I remember thinking, 'Oh my God, they may be able to do this.'"[20]

Meeker's observation that inspiring leaders infuse their companies with intoxicating purpose speaks to a critical communication skill that separates the great entrepreneurs from the merely good.

The Dreamer Who Changed Tim's Life

Tim struggled with finding his purpose throughout high school and college. He moved from achievement to achievement with no real meaning in his life or career. "It tore me apart," he said. After 15 years of searching for his place in the world, Tim met an entrepreneur named Steve Jobs. Tim recalled their first meeting: "He wanted to empower the crazy ones— the misfits, the rebels and the troublemakers, the round pegs, and the square holes."[21] Tim had found his home and for the first time felt "aligned with myself and my own deep need to serve something greater."

Apple CEO Tim Cook told that story to MIT graduates at the university's 2017 commencement ceremony. "Technology is capable of doing great things," he said. "But it doesn't *want* to do great things. It doesn't want anything. That part takes all of us. It takes our values and our commitment to our families and our neighbors and our communities, our love of beauty and belief that all of our faiths are interconnected, our decency, our kindness. I'm not worried about artificial intelligence giving computers the ability to think like humans. I'm more concerned about people thinking like computers without values or compassion, without concern for consequences." Science, says Cook, is a search in the darkness, while the humanities are the candles that show us where we've been and what lies ahead.

Tim Cook met a dreamer and it changed his life. "We should all dream, and encourage others to do so, too," says billionaire entrepreneur Richard Branson. "Dreaming is one of humanity's greatest gifts; it champions aspiration, spurs innovation, leads to change, and propels the world forward."[22]

Branson believes that big dreamers can change the world, but he also says dreams need a strong persuader to advocate for them. Branson maintains his own personal blog and Twitter handle and writes every word himself. Much of his advice revolves around his insights on communicating ideas. Branson is a vocal supporter of teaching students to speak and write well beginning in grade school. He's adamantly convinced that it's nearly impossible to be a successful entrepreneur today without the ability to persuade others. After 50 years in entrepreneurship, Branson has identified communication as the one skill great entrepreneurs share: "I believe that communication is the most important skill any entrepreneur can possess. Communication makes the world go round. It facilitates human connections, and allows us to learn, grow and progress."[23]

Overseeing a holding company of some 400 companies and 70,000 employees gives Branson a unique perspective on the skills that are required for entrepreneurs to thrive in today's age of technological acceleration.

Oil Made the Country Rich; Communication Will Keep the Country Strong

The rulers of Dubai and Abu Dhabi in the United Arab Emirates (UAE) are seeing the trend toward globalization and are wasting no time in preparing the entrepreneurs of tomorrow. On a visit to several universities in the UAE, I was struck by how openly the country's rulers talked about how entrepreneurship—not oil—will drive the future.

Dubai is a city of contrasts. Sand dunes and Bedouin tents surround the world's tallest buildings; camels share the road with luxury cars. In 1958, oil was discovered under the Emirates of Abu Dhabi. Today 6 percent of all the world's known oil reserves lie beneath Abu Dhabi alone.

On the week of my visit to the UAE, the crown prince of Abu Dhabi,

Sheikh Mohammed bin Zayed, spoke at a conference of 3,000 young people and told them that the country's riches are not found in the ground but in the talent of the people who will lead the country when the last drop of oil is gone. "You have to be better than us . . . there is no option," he stated.[24]

As the region shifts from oil to a knowledge-based economy, it will need a new generation of engineers, scientists, and professionals who have the skills to remain globally competitive for the next 50 years. "We should know about other cultures, customers, and traditions because, 25 years from now, you will have to deal with other countries to make our own Emirati companies profitable," he said.

Education is the government's number one priority, precisely to wean future generations off government jobs. In order for the UAE to thrive, it needs to help its citizens become more self-reliant and less dependent on the government for income. Students are encouraged to study a wide range of subjects and to pursue callings, not careers. Entrepreneurship classes are springing up across the region to prepare job creators, not job seekers.

Since students are learning to compete with the best and the brightest around the world, they are taught public speaking in primary school and more advanced techniques in the art of persuasion at the high school and university level. At one university in Sharjah, I met entrepreneurship students working on an impressive range of applications: games, online marketplaces and learning platforms, food delivery services, a dashboard solution for the restaurant and hotel industry (hospitality is a fast-growing field of study in Dubai), and an online app for monitoring and controlling energy consumption. Their final grade was based on a three-minute pitch they were required to make in front of members of the ruling family.

Students in the UAE are reminded that communication in the form of storytelling is an ancient art form that traces its roots to the very place where they live.

Al hakawat is the Arabic word for "storyteller." Thousands of years ago, a tradition began where, after evening prayers, men would gather around an open campfire, share a drink that resembles today's Turkish coffee, and tell stories. The tradition was handed down from generation to generation. Today, reciting poetry in the desert is a popular pastime. I was told that if you want to do business in the Middle East, start your conversation with a story. If your host starts with a story, listen to them intently and don't switch the topic abruptly.

In Part Three, you'll learn that storytelling is as old as civilization itself. In the book *One Thousand and One Nights* (known in popular culture as *The Arabian Nights*), the protagonist Scheherazade tells stories to save herself from execution. The earliest known manuscript dates back to the ninth century. The spoken word holds a special meaning for the Emirati people and holds the key to their future progress.

Oil made the country rich; communication will keep the country strong.

Communication skills are worth their weight in gold in Dubai and around the globe. Surveys of international companies find that entrepreneurial-minded people (EMPs) are good for business. Human resource directors are looking for EMPs because they bring valuable ideas and insights to help companies maintain their edge in innovation. But how can you distinguish an EMP from an average employee? One study of 17,000 working adults found that those who score highest in "persuasion" are the ones who will bring the entrepreneur's mind-set to an organization. "Unquestionably entrepreneurs need to excel at persuasion—the ability to convince others to change the way they think, believe or behave—to recruit a team or get buy-in from investors and stakeholders," according to the report.[25]

According to Thomas Friedman in *Thank You for Being Late*, the age of acceleration gives a single individual with a single idea more power than ever to shape the world around them. At no time in our Earth's history has the power of one been so amplified. "One person can now help so many more people," writes Friedman. "One person can educate millions with an Internet learning platform; one person can entertain or inspire millions; one person can now communicate a new idea . . . to the whole world at once."[26]

Historians often look back at monumental events in humanity's progress and say the past was a time when heroes walked the Earth.

Heroes still walk the Earth. They are entrepreneurs and innovators, dreamers and doers who are developing ideas to solve our world's greatest challenges. They don't fit in; they stand out. We find them irresistible because we need heroes to believe in. They tell their stories and tell them well. When we listen to them, we believe their story is *our* story, and their dreams might make *our* dreams possible.

7

THE PROFESSIONALS

If we want people to accept our original ideas,
we need to speak up about them.

—Adam Grant, Wharton professor

Sharon didn't need to wear incontinence products, but she did . . . for a month. She wore them to work, at night, and while delivering important presentations.[1]

Sharon worked in product design for one of the largest retailers on the planet. The company sold millions of adult incontinence products every year. Sharon joined the team and asked a simple question: "Has anyone worn these things?" Not one person raised their hand. "Well, that's not right," she said. And that's how Sharon transformed an entire product category that's forecasted to grow by 48 percent over the next two years due to the world's aging population. Incontinence products generate $7 billion a year in sales, and Sharon's employer had a large share of that market.

Sharon noticed that the products had ruffles on the bottom and looked nothing like an undergarment that she—or any adult man or woman—would want to wear. Sharon recalls thinking, *They look like diapers for kids*. They looked that way because they were—diapers for kids, but made to fit an adult.

"I wore them every day for a month, switching the brands we sold for a few days apiece," Sharon told me. "I wore them when I interviewed people for jobs. I gave presentations in them. Did I feel self-conscious? You bet I did. I wore longer jackets and sweaters and wanted to cover up my backside. They didn't fit well. I was taping them together so they wouldn't fall inside my pants."

Sharon presented the results of her experiment to senior managers and convinced them to completely redesign the products. Sharon's pitch was irresistible. "We know a lot about underwear at this company," she began. "We are one of the few retailers that sell both incontinence products and men and women's clothes, including underwear. If we bring the two groups together—apparel and product design—we can reinvent the category." The company took her advice. Sharon's presentation triggered a complete reevaluation of the product. Today, adult incontinence products across most major brands look and feel far different than they did several years ago. Fashion models are even being hired to pose for ads that show off the improved look and comfort.

"I was the catalyst for a stronger voice," Sharon told me. "We need to stand up for our shoppers and make changes that are the right thing to do."

Sharon knew next to nothing about adult underpads when she started with the team. Sharon doesn't have an MBA. She doesn't have advanced degrees from elite universities. But she has a uniquely human quality that places her in high demand: empathy. The word "empathy" is defined as feeling another person's emotions by sharing their experiences. It had never occurred to anyone on Sharon's team to share the experiences of the people they were selling products to.

Incontinence is one thing, but could Sharon's empathy transfer to a completely different department? It could and it did.

"Has anyone used these things?" she asked. Once again, nobody on the team raised their hand. Nobody had pricked their finger to draw blood. *Here we go again*, Sharon thought.

Sharon's employer sold 100 million units a year of blood glucose monitoring kits, used by those with diabetes to measure the amount of sugar in their blood. It's an important market—for the company and for those who have the condition. About 9 percent of the U.S. population has diabetes and nearly 1.5 million new cases appear every year. The ability to test sugar levels regularly and to read the results easily is a matter of life and death. And that's why Sharon was concerned. Although the company was selling millions of units, hundreds were being returned. One vendor said, "What does it matter? Who cares if a few get returned?" Sharon responded angrily, "There's a six-year-old child using that test kit to monitor her diabetes. She could live or die based on the reading that comes off the meter. Why can't the girl understand it?"

Sharon didn't have diabetes, but she started lancing her finger with the blood test. "I had to interact with the product at a human level," she said. She soon realized that the meters were not easy for children to read. Today, thanks to Sharon's input, advocacy, and personal experiments, the glucose monitoring kits are much easier to read, especially for children. Once again Sharon completely reimagined a large and important product category: "If you can't understand that there is a person on the other end of the data, you have completely missed the boat."

"Persuasion is a huge part of my success," said Sharon. "The days are gone where you command someone to do something and they do it. That whole directive management style is gone. You have to coach, inspire, instill, and persuade people to get to where you want them to go."

Sharon is indispensable and has proven her value at four companies—from retail to food service. In each company she climbs the ladder much faster than her peers and is sorely missed when she leaves. One company promoted Sharon four times in less than a decade. Some of her peers had not been promoted once in the same time period. Today she's the director of research and development for a major food brand that carries 1,000 labels in America's grocery stores.

"What sets you apart?" I once asked Sharon.

"Passion and empathy," she said. *"The people who stand out, stand up for customers."*

Sharon is a business professional whom Wharton psychology professor Adam Grant would call an original. According to Grant, an original is a person who "champions a set of novel ideas that go against the grain but ultimately make things better."[2] Originals have radical ideas, but those ideas are meaningless if a person cannot advocate for them. "If we want people to accept our original ideas, we need to speak up about them," says Grant.

Sharon is also a person Emory neuroscientist Gregory Berns would call an iconoclast. An iconoclast, says Berns, is "a person who does something that others say can't be done."[3] Berns argues that most people will never be iconoclasts because they cannot overcome two fears: (1) the fear of uncertainty (iconoclasts take risks that challenge the status quo) and (2) the fear of speaking up and selling novel ideas. "You can have the greatest idea in the world, completely novel and different, but if you cannot convince enough other people, it doesn't matter," writes Berns.

Sharon convinced enough other people that product design mattered.

A Civil Engineer Channels Steve Jobs to Win a Big Contract

Matthew is a civil engineer and project manager in a major American city.[4] He works for a firm hired by states and cities to build roads, bridges, buildings, and sewage and water treatment plants.

Matthew is one of 300,000 civil engineers in the United States. He has the basic requirements: an engineering degree, licenses, and apprenticeships. Matthew's credentials helped him to land a job as a staff civil engineer, but he wanted to stand out and advance his career. He focused on building the one skill that computers can't replace and degrees don't measure—the ability to persuade people to support his ideas.

As Matthew grew in confidence as a public speaker, he got one promotion after another, each accompanied by a significant boost in pay. Matthew started as a technical engineer, a job he describes as "sitting at a desk calculating formulas." As his presentation skills got stronger and stronger, he rose to project engineer, project manager, and business development manager. The average staff engineer in the United States takes home a yearly salary of $60,000. A project engineer earns anywhere from $65,000 to $90,000. A project manager's salary is substantially higher and can range from $100,000 to $250,000. As Matthew's speaking skills improved, so did his salary and influence.

Let's hear from Matthew on the role that persuasion plays in his day-to-day routine.

(1) We have to perform engineering analysis or evaluate options for our clients. Then, we give formal and informal presentations to recommend a proposed solution.

(2) We need to market our services to get new clients or expand our client base. The best way is to make presentations about successful or innovative projects at our professional association conferences.

(3) We almost always work as a team, so as a leader I have to explain our project goals, critical issues, or challenges, and inspire/motivate our team to action to get the project done on time and on budget.

(4) The fourth and most important type of presentation is to win a new infrastructure project with a city or state. In a typical bid, up to 10 firms submit a 25-page proposal. A selection committee reduces the number of candidates to three or four firms who are invited for in-person interviews and presentations. We're often not the lowest-priced firm because we don't want to compromise on our quality, so the strength of our presentation makes the difference.[5]

As Matthew got better at communicating his ideas, he increased his exposure in the industry and raised his value. Matthew's boss remembers one presentation in particular that left an impression on their clients. It was novel, different, persuasive, and, ultimately, successful.

Here's how Matthew wowed his boss and earned a major contract for his firm. Many cities in America have pipes, bridges, and roads that are in dire need of upgrades. In the presentation, Matthew had to explain how the engineering team might fix a 100-year-old drinking water main that had sprung a bad leak under a set of train tracks used to transport more than 15,000 people a day. The pipe was four feet in diameter. It required a completely new lining yet had to maintain a maximum flow of water.

Matthew, who was obsessed about learning all he could from great communicators, had watched a lot of Steve Jobs's presentations on YouTube. He recalls watching a video of the Apple co-founder introducing the first Macbook Air. Jobs walked onstage with a manila office-sized envelope. He pulled a laptop out of the envelope and proclaimed, "Today we're introducing the world's thinnest notebook." Matthew stole a page from the Jobs playbook and did something similar. He put the new carbon fiber lining material into a manila envelope and did a big reveal. Matthew said the solution to the problem is "the world's strongest, thinnest pipe lining system." Matthew's presentation was a hit and his firm won the bid.

Matthew sent me a copy of the winning presentation. He skillfully used several techniques that you will learn in Part Three. One of the most effective tools of persuasion is to use the classic narrative structure of dividing the story into three parts or "acts": the set-up describes the current situation; the conflict highlights the problem your customer faces; and the resolution proposes your idea or solution. Matthew followed the three-act structure, which we'll cover in detail in chapter 11.

First, Matthew showed slides with historical photographs of men installing the water main in 1870. Next, he explained the problem: how to repair 3,000 feet of pipe under a public transportation system that carries thousands of people a day. To make part two as clear as possible, he even had a slide that read: "The challenge." To add some tension to the challenge, he showed photos of tree-lined streets in one of the city's most historic neighborhoods. Any project would have to minimize surface disruptions to the streets and driveways, he argued. The big reveal from the manila envelope kicked off part three, the solution. By the time he'd finished, the clients' decision-makers—who had been leaning toward a lower-priced firm—changed their minds and awarded the contract to Matthew's company.

Even before the clients made their final decision, Matthew's boss could see the presentation was "astounding," the best presentation he had seen in his entire career. Matthew had only been in the industry for five years and he was making a name for himself in the company and among his peers.

"If I can tell a better story, I can win the new projects," says Matthew. "If the story also demonstrates how we're uniquely qualified because we have a solution to a critical (or unknown) issue that the client is unaware of, our chances of winning go up significantly . . . even if we charge a higher price than our competitors."

Matthew stands out because he's made the transition from being a good communicator to a great one. Bestselling author Thomas Friedman calls the pace of change in the modern world the "age of acceleration." Friedman argues that the words we use to describe technology are too weak for the transformations they bring. Data isn't moving to *cloud*, it's experiencing a "supernova," says Friedman. "The supernova is vastly expanding and accelerating the power of flows. The flows of knowledge, new ideas, medical advance, innovation, insults, rumors, collaboration, match-making, lending, banking, trading, friendship-forging, commerce, and learning now circulate globally at a speed and breadth we have never seen before."[6]

This is the world in which Michael, Sharon, and millions of other professionals are trying to leave a mark. The empowering news, according to Friedman, is that the modern world "amplifies the power of one." One person can inspire, educate, or entertain millions of people over the Internet. One person can communicate an idea that advances a field or changes the world. Here's the irony professionals face in the modern world: to stand out in the age of acceleration, they must improve their skills of persuasion. According to Friedman in his book *Thank You for Being Late*, middle-class jobs require more knowledge and more education. "To compete for such jobs you need more of the three R's—reading, writing, and arithmetic—*and* more of the four C's—creativity, collaboration, communication, and coding."[7]

Standing Out in the Age of Acceleration

Hart Research Associates conducts the most comprehensive surveys of college students and prospective employers. Every two years the research firm asks detailed questions of more than 300 employers across a range of categories. In a recent Hart survey, employers made a surprising admission. Over 93 percent of employers said that when making hiring decisions, a job candidate's ability to think critically and communicate clearly outweighs their choice of college major. According to the report, "Employers are highly focused on innovation as critical to the success of their companies. They report that the challenges their employees face today are more complex and require a broader skill set than in the past."[8] A job candidate's major, even if it aligns with their chosen industry, doesn't guarantee success in communication and critical thinking.

Employers who responded to the Hart survey say that the decline in written and oral communication skills is a major hurdle to being hired and promoted. Eighty percent of employers say colleges should place more of an emphasis on these skills. Unfortunately, study after study shows these skills to be in short supply, and the supply is dwindling year after year. There exists a growing gap between what employers expect to see in job candidates and the skills those candidates have to show.

"Strong communicators have a competitive edge," says Susan Vitale, chief marketing officer for iCIMS Insights, a company that sells talent recruiting software to large companies.[9] According to one iCIMS study, about 90 percent of college seniors are confident in their interviewing skills, but more than 60 percent of recruiters say graduates' interview skills leave much to be desired. For starters, hiring experts recommend that job candidates need to become much more familiar with the company and the industry.

"Candidates think they're doing homework, but there's a difference between rattling off facts that they learned from a company website and crafting narratives around their experience," Vitale told me. "Today there is more information available about businesses than ever before. It's not enough to know when the company was founded, who the CEO is and where their headquarters are." Vitale recommends that job candidates clearly explain the value they bring to the company, as well as how their experience will benefit the customer and help advance the company's position in the market.

Vitale also points to a growing trend that underlines the importance of communication skills. Hiring managers are increasingly saving time by asking for short 90-second videos of prospective candidates. They often use these videos to decide whether a candidate deserves an in-person interview. If a candidate cannot speak well or enunciate clearly, dresses too casually, or records the video with an unprofessional background, it could prevent a follow-up interview, even if the candidate looks good on paper.

In an iCIMS survey of 400 HR and recruiting managers in the United States, 63 percent said that, given two candidates of equal qualifications, the one who has better "oral communication skills" would be the one they'd choose to hire.

Craig knows exactly what it means to be hired and promoted for communication skills. Five years ago, Craig graduated with a degree in economics and business from a public university.[10] He sent out dozens of resumes with no response. Craig was entering a tough job market. The U.S. economy continued to struggle in the aftermath of the 2008 housing crash, and the unemployment rate stood at 8 percent. Employers were not in a hiring mood, especially for entry-level grads with little to no practical experience.

A San Francisco software firm looking to beef up its marketing department was the first company to call Craig back for an in-person hiring interview. One hitch remained. The startup scene in San Francisco was a close-knit community. Craig knew someone at the company who told him that the other top candidate for the same position was good friends with the hiring manager. Craig decided to master the art of persuasion to differentiate himself. In doing so, he went from being a good job candidate to a great one.

"I studied their competitors, I studied their product, I created a product pitch," Craig told me. Craig spent eight hours rehearsing his pitch and crafting answers to potential questions. He walked into the interview on a Thursday and received a $45,000 job offer the following Monday. The company didn't want to risk losing him because, in the words of the hiring manager, "You can explain our product better than our salespeople." Craig's first assignment upon starting the job was to show the existing sales team how to pitch the company's product.

After 18 months at the startup, Craig realized that he wanted to grow as a leader and move up in his career. He decided to complement his current experience with technical skills. He enrolled in a coding bootcamp, a three-month intensive course, to learn software engineering. Upon completion of the program, Craig sent out 80 to 90 resumes. Not one company called back. "I didn't look fantastic. The others in the class had a four-year computer science degree and four years of experience. I didn't have any of that. I knew my biggest advantage would be communication skills," Craig said.

Then Craig got his chance. A company in the business-to-business software space invited Craig to their San Francisco headquarters for an in-person interview. The hiring managers asked the types of questions that are becoming increasingly common at companies such as Google and Tesla: behavioral interviews. Instead of relying on brain teasers such as "How many golf balls can fit inside a school bus?" (a real question asked by tech companies), they now ask questions that measure how people think, collaborate, and communicate. For example, Tesla CEO Elon Musk says he's identified the single best question to ask a job candidate: "Tell me the story of your life, the decisions you made along the way and why you made them."[11] Musk is looking for people who can clearly explain the problems they've faced and how they solved them.

Craig practiced for the interview, rehearsed several key stories from his life, and learned everything he could about the company. After eight hours of study, he knew the company inside and out and, once again, could articulate the company's products even better than its own sales staff. Craig nailed it. He landed a job on his first interview for double his previous salary.

The company has since rewarded Craig with two promotions in under two years. He was making over $120,000 when a competitor came calling. They had heard that Craig had a unique ability to speak to internal teams of engineers and to translate their language into conversations their key customers could understand. Craig liked his second company, but he didn't want to pass up an opportunity to weigh his value in the marketplace. Once again, Craig wowed his interviewers. They were impressed with Craig's "cross-functional" communication skills—the ability to lead engineers with clear directions and then to translate engineering language for the customer. The competitor offered Craig a job with a 40 percent higher salary. Craig's employer found out and matched the 40 percent hike. They also gave him an international assignment. They told Craig they could not afford to lose a "world-class communicator." Just five years out of college and Craig was being groomed for senior leadership positions.

CEO recruiter James Citrin wouldn't be surprised at Craig's success. Citrin works at Spencer Stuart, a leadership consulting firm, where he has been involved in more than 600 searches for CEOs, board directors, and top corporate leaders. In an interview for the *Los Angeles Times*, Citrin was asked how to land a job, keep a job, and get promoted. Citrin offered a two-part solution. "First, develop the skills where you add value and leadership such as problem solving, communicating, and analytical skills. Then a person should study some of the disciplines related to where the world is going."[12] According to Citrin, communication is the foundation—the base skill—the competency upon which a great career is built. "You need to have the whole package," says Citrin. For Craig, communication was the base skill and coding was the extra competency. And today, there's no limit to what Craig can accomplish in his career.

The McKinsey Edge

A senior managing director at McKinsey, the world's most influential consulting firm, took to the stage to kick off the company's annual gathering of consultants. The event is referred to as Values Day and is meant to reinforce the firm's mission. All consultants—new and experienced—are expected to attend. The managing director spoke first. He had worked at the firm for 20 years and, as the former head of the firm's technology practice, had advised some of the world's most valuable companies. The theme of his speech was "storytelling," and he began with five personal stories from his consulting career, each story meant to highlight a particular habit that the firm valued.

The managing director's slides were all photos. His first slide was a black-and-white photo showing a small group of about a dozen people, all men, meeting around an office table in 1940. It was the company's first effort to arrange an annual meeting to talk about the company's values. The photo was effective because it stood in sharp contrast to the present day, which saw *6,000* employees (many of them women—indeed, McKinsey is now recognized as one of the top 10 companies for women) from 100 offices attending Values Day. Although the managing director lived in a world notable for its endless tables, charts, and bullet points, he wanted his consultants to know that their competitive advantage was not the data alone, but in how they told the *stories* behind the data and connected with clients on an emotional level. And emotion was best transferred through photos, not charts and graphs.

He told personal stories, case studies, and stories of consultants who had succeeded—or failed—in their projects. He delivered a 20-minute presentation with no text, no bullet points, no charts, and no graphs. It's an extreme example. The managing director did not expect his consultants to deliver a client proposal made up of all photographs, but he wanted them to know that presentation skills would have a profound effect on their careers at McKinsey. The way they had learned to deliver presentations in business school (most had MBAs from the top schools) had to be radically reconsidered.

New consultants enter the firm armed with the skill to create PowerPoint decks with more than 100 text-heavy slides. Unfortunately, that is the least effective way for the brain to process information. And that's why senior leaders at McKinsey go to great lengths to retrain new consultants and to coach their existing ones.

Quoting a screenwriter named Robert McKee, the McKinsey managing director told his audience, "Storytelling is the currency of human contact."[13] He was on to something. In Part Three you'll learn why delivering information in a logical sequence is only one component of persuasion. Without the emotional attachment of a story, an idea will fall on deaf ears.

After the speech, one McKinsey consultant told me that in his first week at the firm he proudly showed off a lengthy PowerPoint deck that he intended to present to a client. His boss said, "You're not done. I only want to see two slides for every twenty slides you currently have. And the language must be simpler. If a fifth-grader cannot understand your idea, it's too complicated."

As you might imagine, earning a job at McKinsey is hard. Very hard. The consulting firm hires less than 1 percent of the 200,000-plus applicants it considers every year. Only 25 percent of the firm's consultants will be promoted to engagement managers, 25 percent of those will be elevated to associate partner, and 25 percent of those will become full partner. In simple terms, about 1 of every 100 people who pass the selective process to even join the firm will become full partners.

Partners get a cut of the revenue and can easily make upward of $1 million or more per year. The others don't do badly, either. A McKinsey associate can start at $160,000 and climb into roles that pay in the mid-hundreds of thousands. The key is to stand out. But how does one stand out among a group of MBAs from the best schools in the world who all have above-average GPAs and are all extremely bright? Four words: the art of persuasion.

McKinsey consultants receive an evaluation after every project. The goal is to get a rating of "distinctive" because it means that you stand out from the crowd. You stand out from the MBAs, the Ph.D.s, the people who have specialized experience in a hot area, and the people who put in long hours. You have all those things, too. But you also have the "extra" that Thomas Friedman recommended. That's how a consultant earns the mark of distinction.

Distinctive consultants are the most persuasive.

A McKinsey career is intense from day one and doesn't let up. McKinsey consultants are on a job hunt every week—an internal hunt. Each consultant receives a weekly e-mail that previews new projects. Those candidates without the most direct industry experience must persuade the project leader to give them an opportunity. Good projects and good results are a ticket up the ladder.

New consultants quickly discover that when a senior leader asks them for a project update, what they really mean is: "Tell me what really matters on this project in 30 seconds." In *The McKinsey Edge*, a former consultant writes that speaking in shorter sentences is the sign of a more mature leader. "When you reach the C-suite level, make your presentation as simple as possible. C-levels and top performers in every field believe that if you sound complicated you will be complicated . . . Talking to someone using fewer words takes practice. By concentrating on convincing people faster and with fewer words, you are building a unique skill."[14]

McKinsey's 6,000 consultants are spread across 100 offices around the world. The company is considered a launching pad for aspiring leaders. McKinsey mints more CEOs than any single company anywhere in any industry. One of every 690 McKinsey consultants will become the CEO of a publicly traded company. The second-best CEO training ground—another consulting company—will see only one of every 2,150 consultants become CEOs.

McKinsey is truly a CEO learning lab, and it teaches future CEOs that clear and concise communication is an enormous career advantage.

Students of Communication Climb the
Career Ladder

Claire is a member of the millennial generation (those born between 1980 and 1995).[15] She received a bachelor's degree in economics and Middle Eastern studies. Upon graduation she was hired by a large financial insurance company as a business consultant, selling a suite of products to financial advisors. Financial services have changed dramatically in the last few years. As insurance, investment, and retirement products are increasingly seen as commodities, much less emphasis is placed on "pushing products," and more focus is paid to helping advisors grow their businesses. In a world of low-cost index funds, advisors must persuade their clients that they bring value to the relationship. If they can't show value, they're out of business. Claire's job is to sell products to advisors to help them stand out.

Claire's firm holds a yearly internal competition where young sales professionals are invited to present new ideas in a 10-minute presentation. Managers score participants based on the creativity of the idea and how effectively the professional can explain it. This is where Claire shines. Although she acknowledges that she's not a naturally comfortable speaker, she is a student of persuasion. She reads books, watches TED talks, and analyzes the many presentations she sees at financial conferences.

In Claire's first competition, she presented to managers twice her age and in front of an audience of 100 of her sales peers. "People remembered my presentation even months later," she told me. "This kind of recognition from several bosses several levels up the totem pole simply would not have happened if I could not deliver an effective presentation." Claire's presentation followed many of the strategies you'll learn in Part Three. She set a clear theme and agenda at the beginning, focused on three ideas, circled back to her main point, and closed with a strong statement. Although she received compliments for the structure of the presentation, Claire says the "greatest accolades" were reserved for the stories she told.

I first heard from Claire in November 2016. Seven months later, I received a follow-up e-mail. "I was just promoted to a business development role, which means I'm tasked with bringing in new prospects. This is going to have a positive impact on my earning potential!"

Mike, another millennial, is one generation removed from the farm.[16] Where his father and grandfather worked with their hands growing corn and tomatoes, Mike's career value is based on his ideas and his ability to successfully communicate those ideas.

Today, at the age of 25, Mike's career is soaring. Shortly after college, Mike landed a job as a field sales rep for a mid-sized U.S.-based pharmaceutical company. Mike had a good start to his career. He enjoyed a salary of $60,000 and focused on the company's drugs for the cardiology division. After his first year, Mike received an opportunity. All sales reps had to return to home base for advanced training. Part of the program was aimed at building the presentation skills for each salesperson. Mike, along with the others, had to deliver a 10-minute presentation to the rest of the class of about 20 field agents. "This was a pivotal point in an employee's career because senior managers watch the presentations and begin to identify those professionals who should be fast-tracked to higher positions," Mike told me.

After the training, the company's HR department posted an open position for a corporate sales trainer. Mike was a little-known sales rep at the time, but he decided to apply. He didn't think he had a chance against peers who had been at the company for a longer period of time, but it would give him a chance to begin making a name for himself. Mike's superiors remembered him from the advanced sales training course and offered to consider him, along with 12 others who applied. Mike would later learn that there was a shortlist of just two people who were expected to win the position, and he wasn't on it. Until, that is, he gave a presentation to decision-makers (each of the candidates had to deliver a 6- to 10-minute presentation as part of their final interview). Mike practiced the presentation dozens of times to build up his comfort with the material. No doubt his body language and presence reflected his confidence.

Although Mike's stage presence was strong, it was one slide in particular that caught everyone's attention. On the first slide, Mike showed a photo of a tractor. He talked about his family's background and the values he learned on the farm. He made the analogy to pharmaceutical sales and building relationships with doctors/prescribers: first, a rep plants the seeds of the relationship, he nurtures those relationships, and eventually he enjoys the bounty of the harvest. At the end of his six-minute presentation,

Mike returned to the tractor slide and brought the conversation full circle. "Building a sales territory is about trust, belief, and accountability. The same values I learned from my dad and grandfather. As a sales rep you must trust in your training, believe in your product, and hold yourself accountable."

After Mike ended his presentation, a vice president and chief decision-maker in the room turned to a colleague and said, "Who is that and where has he been hiding?" Mike got the job.

Although the role came with a solid jump in salary to $105,000, Mike took the job for another reason. He was looking at the long term. His ultimate career aspiration was to be the CEO of a $1 billion company. "A CEO has to have a vision and communicate it effectively," Mike told me. "In my role as a corporate sales trainer, I create content, teach new hires about the business and its vision, and give several presentations a week. It's the best CEO training I can imagine."

One thing worth noting is that Mike's previous boss—who encouraged Mike to try out for the new position—was not a fan of Mike's "tractor" opening. It was "out of the ordinary." Mike politely listened to his boss's advice, but he didn't take it. He wanted to be extraordinary, otherwise he'd never stand out. Three stars wasn't good enough. Mike was a student of persuasion and he knew that the brain craves novelty. When the human brain detects something it hasn't seen before, it triggers a release of dopamine in the brain's reward center. A neuroscientist once told me that our brains are hardwired to look for something new, something brilliant, something "delicious." If Mike had given an ordinary presentation, one of the two candidates ahead of him on the shortlist would have won the job. But Mike wasn't satisfied with an average career—or even a good career. Mike wanted a great career, and he knew that extraordinary presentation skills were his secret weapon.

Dr. David Deming is a Harvard research professor whose papers on social skills in the labor market help to explain why Mike, Claire, and the other professionals in this chapter are finding uncommon success in the age of disruption. While many people fear that automation, big data, artificial intelligence, and machine learning will replace humans in a wide range of positions, Deming argues that the most dire predictions are overblown. "One reason is that computers are still very poor at simulating human interaction," writes Deming.[17]

Deming studied U.S. job growth between 1980 and 2012. He found that jobs requiring high social skills grew into a larger share of the economy, and wage growth for those categories soared as well. By "social skills," Deming doesn't mean idle cocktail party chatter. He defines social skill as the ability to lead teams, collaborate with diverse groups of employees, and persuade peers and customers to take action. "Skill in social settings has evolved in humans over thousands of years. Human interaction in the workplace involves team production, with workers playing off of each other's strengths and adapting flexibly to changing circumstances. Such non-routine interaction is at the heart of the human advantage over machines."

Deming says that jobs requiring communication, collaboration, and persuasion will continue to experience outsized growth in the decade to come. "Think about a job like management consultant. You have to have strong analytical skills, for sure. But you also have to do many different things—analyze data, put together presentations, talk to clients, and write persuasively," Deming explained as we discussed his research.[18]

Deming advises today's professionals to acquire a broad and diverse set of skills. "We can build a machine or a software program to do almost any one thing better than a human. But computers are mostly still inflexible," Deming says. "Humans understand when to change course and can flexibly adapt to changing, unpredictable circumstances. We have a diverse toolkit that can be applied differently to different problems. It is a great idea to be good at two things that rarely go together—like being a great coder and an excellent communicator."

The Human Factor

The Harvard Extension School at Harvard University was established in 1910 to equip adult learners with skills they need for professional development and personal enrichment. "Even in the most technical fields today, soft skills are in high demand," school officials declared.[19] Program administrators say "communication skills" is the number one most desirable quality for employers, even those looking for IT professionals.

"I've believed in the importance of soft skills in the tech sector for a long time," said Ben Gaucherin, who oversees the IT department at Harvard University. Gaucherin said that STEM programs (science, technology, engineering, math) are too narrowly focused on technical skills. Yet in his experience, "The people who will thrive are the strong technologists who are capable of translating their expertise into terms that nontechnical people can understand."[20]

In a report called "The Human Factor," Burning Glass Technologies concluded that employers have a hard time finding candidates with soft skills. Burning Glass is an online jobs posting platform used by 40,000 companies.[21] Over a one-year period the company collected 25 million unique job posts to analyze the most commonly requested skills. Most of the technical positions fell under information technology (IT), healthcare, and engineering. The study found that the phrase "soft skill" is grossly inaccurate. Communication should be considered a "baseline skill" because it's critical for success in technical jobs and "notoriously" lacking in job candidates. "When employers demand a skill that's out of proportion to the traditional definitions of what a job requires, it's likely that skill is both important and hard to find," concluded the study.

The study of millions of job postings found that writing and communication skills are scarce, and yet serve as the foundation of career success. "These skills are in demand across nearly every occupation—and in nearly every occupation they're being requested far more than you'd expect based on standard job profiles, even in fields like IT and engineering."

In a survey conducted by Gartner, a technology research firm, 485 chief information officers (CIOs) were asked to name the top three leadership traits that propelled them to the highest position in their companies. Technical skill ranked twelfth on the list. Innovation and organization skills didn't make the top three, either. CIOs said that having a deep knowledge of the business was the number one attribute that helped them succeed. But the second-most important trait to be a successful CIO is "communication skills to influence decisions."

Andy Bryant chairs Intel's board of directors. He has long history of experience as a controller and a finance chief at companies like Intel and Ford. Bryant feels the frustration of technical managers and CIOs who ask the board for money to pursue a project and leave empty-handed. In many cases, he says, those professionals need to improve their skills of persuasion.

According to Bryant, a CIO or technical manager who lacks communication skills enters a budget request meeting and the conversation goes like this:

> CIO: If you don't give me this, we will die. It's over.
> Board member: Wow, that's a big statement.
> CIO: Look, I need X dollars. If you don't give me X dollars, we're going to be breached. When we're breached, the penalties will be enormous.
> Board member: OK, if we give you X dollars, then we won't be breached?[22]

No sensible CIO will answer the last question affirmatively, and as a result, they'll lose their request. Instead Bryant recommends the following approach. The CIO should act as an educator, explaining what their department does, the problems they solve, the potential data breaches the company faces, and both the inexpensive and the expensive solutions that are available. By setting up the conversation in this way, the CIO isn't demanding money. Instead the CIO is teaching, and people would rather be educated than be sold something or feel as though they're being held up for ransom. From the most technical fields to the most artistic ones, persuasion sets professionals apart.

The Rare Art of Burning Messages Into People's Brains

Earlier we met Michael Moritz, billionaire investor and chairman of the famed Silicon Valley venture capital firm Sequoia Capital. He has spearheaded investments in Google, Yahoo, PayPal, LinkedIn, and Airbnb.

I caught up with Moritz to discuss a book he had co-written with Sir Alex Ferguson, the former manager of Manchester United Football Club.

The book was titled *Leading* and revealed the qualities that Moritz and Ferguson believed would take someone from an entry-level position to the top of their profession.

As a journalist at *Time* magazine in the late 1970s, Moritz became increasingly interested in how one person can shape an organization and inspire others to achieve the seemingly impossible. Moritz recalls his first meetings with the legendary CEO of Chrysler, Lee Iacocca. At the time, most experts had given up on the company and predicted its demise. Moritz watched as Iacocca reinvigorated the company and turned it into one of the most iconic brands in corporate history. "That was the beginning of my belief in the power of an individual to shape an organization and to lead."[23]

But what, exactly, is the one skill people need to lead? According to Moritz, persuasion is fundamental. Nothing else happens without sharpening and refining the ability to persuade another person to take action. "You cannot lead an individual—let alone a team or an organization—without being able to clearly communicate the direction in which you want to go," Moritz told me. "It doesn't matter whether it's the 45-minute second half of a soccer game or the next five years of a company. The leader has got to be able to clearly enunciate where he or she wants to go."

According to Moritz and Ferguson, a business professional who stands out distills complexity into simple words, directions, and instructions. Speaking of his co-author, Alex Ferguson, Moritz said, "His directions tended to be short and concise because barely anyone, whether they work in a hospital or a steel mill, can remember more than three instructions. Long-winded monologues do not strike the target in the way that brief talks relaying precise and concise instructions do."

Moritz recalls the day when two Stanford students walked into his office and delivered the most concise business plan he had ever heard. Sergey Brin and Larry Page told Moritz, "Google organizes the world's information and makes it accessible." That pitch helped Google receive its first major funding. Moritz and the Google guys were on their way to becoming billionaires. To this day Moritz believes that if a young professional cannot explain their business or idea in one sentence, it's too complicated.

Moritz reminds us that learning to master the art of persuasion is hard work. It's a skill that successful professionals refine over time. They work at it. "It's why poetry is so much more difficult to write than prose," he says. "Most people—most listeners—don't concentrate, or they tune out, or they have short memories. So burning the message into their skulls is a rare art. In order to do that, your idea must be memorable, clear, vivid, and have an element of emotion associated with it."

A business professional who wants to enter the leadership ranks must learn the art of burning the message into people's skulls. Let's meet some of the leaders who excel at this.

8

THE LEADERS

All leadership takes place through the communication of ideas to the minds of others.

—CHARLES COOLEY, American sociologist

Ke Jie had a "terrifying" experience that triggered a surge of anxiety across Asia. Jie is the number one Go player in the world. Well, he was, until May 2017. In that month he lost to a better player—Google's AlphaGo, a machine built in the company's Deep Mind lab.

When Garry Kasparov lost a chess match to a supercomputer named Deep Blue in 1997, it shocked people across the western world. But according to a *New York Times* article shortly after the match, the event was met with a yawn across much of Asia. After all, chess was one thing—surely no machine could beat a human grandmaster in the game of Go. It's one of the oldest games ever invented—about 2,500 years old—and the most complex. It's said a player can take more potential positions on a Go board than there are atoms in the universe. After Kasparov's loss to a machine, one astrophysicist predicted that it would take a hundred years for a computer to beat a human at Go. It only took 20 years for it to happen. And that's why it was so "terrifying."

On the same week that Google's modern machine beat a player at an ancient game, Google's CEO Sundar Pichai relied on the ancient art of persuasion to launch a suite of modern tools.

Sundar Pichai is one of the smartest technologists on the planet. He has a mathematical mind and can remember every phone number he's ever dialed. Pichai received his bachelor's degree in metallurgical engineering from the highly competitive Indian Institute of Technology (IIT). The school admits less than 2 percent of its 500,000 applicants (for comparison, Harvard admits 6 percent of its applicants). Pichai also earned advanced degrees from Stanford and Wharton in material sciences, engineering, and business. He enjoyed a meteoric rise at Google from the year he joined in 2004. He convinced the company to release Chrome, the world's most popular browser, and went on to lead the company's Android division, as well as Search and Maps. He became Google's CEO in 2015. Pichai's world revolves around big data, machine learning, and artificial intelligence, but his hallmark as a leader is making the complex simple to understand.

Pichai was born in Chennai, in South India, a city where the ancient meets the modern. It's home to the largest IT park in Asia and one of the oldest dance forms known to civilization. High-rises stand next to ancient temples. Restaurants serve nouveau cuisine along with traditional dishes. It's a city where contemporary musicians tap into the music of the culture—thousands of years old—to create innovative beats and rhythms.

Persuasion, too, occurs at the intersection of the ancient and the modern. Pichai is an effective communicator because he uses brain-friendly presentations to sell ideas to contemporary audiences.

Google's CEO Doesn't Use Bullet Points, and Neither Should You

Once a year, Pichai kicks off Google's developer's conference, known as Google I/O. He begins with an explanation of how Google's technology is enhancing our lives and a vision of how Google will create the future. Pichai's presentation is a master class in public speaking because he follows the age-old rules of persuasion.

Visual storytelling plays an important role at Google, where employees are trained to present ideas in a bold, fresh style. Since stories are best told with pictures, presenters avoid text and bullet points. Pichai's slides are remarkably uncluttered. Just as professional ad designers avoid filling up an entire page with text, Pichai doesn't clutter his slides with extraneous words or numbers.

One researcher concludes that the average PowerPoint slide contains 40 words. In Pichai's presentation at the 2017 Google I/O, he didn't reach 40 words until slide 12. Instead he used photos, videos, and animations. When text did appear, Pichai used the fewest words possible. For example, his first slide had seven logos of primary Google products (Search, YouTube, Android, etc.) and the following text: *1 Billion+ Users.* Pichai explained that the Google products each attract more than one billion monthly users. Slide number five contained the most words—five. Only one sentence was on the slide—the one line that reinforced the theme of Pichai's presentation: "Mobile first to AI first."[1] It represented a major shift in the company's direction. Instead of placing a priority on developing tools for mobile devices, as Google had been doing for several years, the company would focus on creating artificial intelligence systems that connect people everywhere—at home, in the car, at work, or on the go.

Cognitive scientists say it's impossible for us to multitask as well as we think we can. The brain cannot do two things at once and do them equally well. When it comes to presentation design, we can't retain text on the screen *and* listen to the speaker. And that's why pictures are almost always more memorable than words alone on a slide.

University of Washington biologist John Medina has done extensive research into persuasion and how the brain processes information. His advice is to burn most PowerPoint decks and start over with fewer words and more pictures. "We are biologically incapable of processing attention-rich inputs simultaneously," writes Medina.[2] A common mistake, says Medina, is to communicate too much information at once. It may sound counterintuitive, but the neuroscience research is clear: when it comes to slide design, less is more.

Slide design guru Nancy Duarte recommends following a three-second rule. If viewers do not understand the gist of your slide in three seconds, it's too complicated. "Think of your slides as billboards," says Duarte.[3] "When people drive, they only briefly take their eyes off their main focus, which is the road, to process a billboard of information. Similarly, your audience should focus intently on what you're saying, looking only briefly at your slides when you display them." When is the last time you saw a billboard sign with a list of bullet points? Bullet points are the easiest design to create on a PowerPoint slide, and the least effective.

In his book *TED Talks*, Chris Anderson writes that traditional PowerPoint presentations with headlines followed by multiple bullet points on each slide is a sure-fire way to lose the audience's interest. "When we see speakers come to TED with slide decks like this, we pour them a drink, go and sit with them at a computer monitor, and gently ask their permission to delete, delete, delete."[4]

Pichai's Google slides obey the TED rule—delete, delete, delete.

Google Revisits the Past to Move the World Forward

Google is building the most advanced tools on the planet, but its top leaders are schooled in the ancient art of persuasion. Prasad Setty is one of them. A former McKinsey consultant and mechanical engineer, Setty also traces his roots to Chennai, India. As vice president of people analytics at Google, Setty's role is to use data-driven insights to keep Googlers happy and productive.

"We spend an inordinate amount of time doing hardcore science and analytics, but how do we ensure that it's memorable? How do we ensure that we can communicate better so that our messages resonate and stick?" Setty asks Google employees.[5] He believes that communicators need to ask themselves the following questions: What do you want your audience to know, what do you want them to feel, and what do you want them to do?

According to Setty, in the area of communicating science, people tend to fall short on those questions. "Instead of telling people what they should know, we like to tell people what we did. We like to use a lot of high-falutin' jargon. It takes a Ph.D. to understand the work that another Ph.D. does. We don't even think about emotions when we communicate science and analytics. It's as if in our quest for objectivity and rational thinking, we try to strip away all emotion from our speech. And that becomes less memorable."[6]

Setty works in Google's HR department, what the company calls "People Operations." In 2012, HR researchers launched an ambitious project to identify the habits of the most effective teams within the company.

The three-year study was code-named Project Aristotle.[7] The researchers reached the conclusion that Aristotle was right. The Greek philosopher's techniques are just as effective today as they were when he first introduced them.

Julia Rozovsky led Project Aristotle. Her team interviewed more than 200 employees, analyzed 180 teams, and looked at 250 attributes. Rozovsky was confident they'd be able to pinpoint the ideal combination of talents and skills that would make up winning teams. After all, she had assembled a scientific dream team: Rhodes scholars, engineers, data experts, and Ph.D.s. In an astonishing admission, Rozovsky said, "We were dead wrong."

Project Aristotle found that *who* is on a team matters less than *how* team members interact with one another. Not surprisingly, a leader who makes an emotional connection with his or her team is the catalyst to successful interactions. The researchers concluded that successful teams have the following traits:

> *Psychological safety:* The team members feel confident taking risks. They are secure in speaking up and comfortable being vulnerable in front of one another.
> *Clarity:* The team members have clear goals and roles.
> *Impact of work:* Team members know their work matters and can see how it supports the greater good.

Psychological safety was, by far, the most important quality found in winning teams. "The safer team members feel with one another, the more likely they are to admit mistakes, to partner, and to take on new roles," said Rozovsky. Individuals on psychologically safe teams were more likely to "harness the power of diverse ideas, bring in more revenue, and they're rated as effective twice as often by executives."

Googlers love data, but they want to put the data into action. The results of the study were shared throughout the company, and a "toolkit" of skills was distributed. Over the course of a year, 3,000 employees across 300 teams began using the new tools. Teams around the world that adopted the new framework saw immediate results.

As employees sent their feedback to the research group, some common themes began to emerge. First, "psychological safety and emotional conversations were related," according to Charles Duhigg, who wrote a piece for *The New York Times Magazine* about the experiment. "The behaviors that create psychological safety—conversational turn-taking and empathy—are part of the same unwritten rules we often turn to, as individuals, when we need to establish a bond. And those human bonds matter as much at work as anywhere else. In fact, they sometimes matter more."[8] Duhigg says that Project Aristotle is a reminder that not everything can be quantified and optimized. Effective workplaces are often built on experiences and emotional interactions with leaders and teammates. Successful leaders make people feel like winners.

Duhigg interviewed a manager named Matt who took a keen interest in Project Aristotle. Matt was passionate about his work at Google but was leading a team that didn't cooperate well. Armed with the study's findings, Matt encouraged his colleagues to open up to each other, especially at the beginning of team meetings. Matt went first, revealing that he was undergoing treatment for cancer. The team was stunned. What came next was extraordinary. One by one, they began to share personal stories. They began to speak openly and honestly with each other. Matt agreed to do a better job at showing each of the team members how their work fit into the greater whole. The team members, in turn, agreed to have more frequent dialogue and to make others feel secure in sharing their ideas.

Many meetings at Google now start with sharing stories and experiences—the emotional component of team building that bonds people together. Leaders who tell stories and show vulnerability encourage others to speak up. Leaders who clearly communicate goals and roadmaps enjoy the confidence of the team. And leaders who show individuals why their roles matter and how they connect to the big picture inspire people to do their best work.

During the years that Google was collecting data to create the perfect teams across its global enterprise, a psychiatrist turned CEO in Los Angeles was arriving at some of the same conclusions. And he was using the results to change the face of healthcare.

See, I Care

Dr. David Feinberg is equally comfortable talking about Starbucks customer service as he is about Medicare reimbursements. It's part of what makes Feinberg a rock star in the healthcare field. He's a successful leader because he's constantly looking outside of his industry for creative ideas and studying the art of persuasion to motivate his staff.

Feinberg is the president and CEO for Pennsylvania-based Geisinger Health, a system of 12 hospitals and 30,000 employees. Prior to joining Geisinger, Feinberg transformed the UCLA medical system into one of the most admired hospitals in the country.

When Feinberg assumed his role as chief executive at UCLA, the hospital wasn't known for patient satisfaction.[9] In fact, it ranked near the bottom. When Feinberg had accepted the position, one survey found that two out of three patients would not recommend the hospital to a friend or family. Under Feinberg's leadership over the next seven years, patient satisfaction soared. Today, UCLA medical center ranks in the top 1 percent of all hospitals in America.

What made the difference? David Feinberg walks the talk—and walks and walks. At UCLA, Feinberg would spend two to three hours a day visiting with patients, even leaving a card behind with his cell phone number. He knew his approach was working when he walked into a patient's room and found several cards other hospital leaders had left behind . . . with their personal phone numbers.

Feinberg hasn't stopped walking at Geisinger. The day before one of my phone conversations with Feinberg, he had spent 30 minutes in the waiting room of a Geisinger clinic (1.5 hours from his office) just to observe how patients were being checked in. He was so impressed with what he saw, he praised the staff and wrote a personal note to the head doctor at the clinic. On any given day you can find him talking to the cooking staff in the kitchens or nutritionists in the cafés or nurses in the hallways. And you can always find him asking patients about their experiences and helping the staff perform their duties in a patient's room. "You've got to walk the shop floor," says Feinberg.

When Feinberg walks the shop floor, he's evaluating how well the staff implements a communication program he helped to develop at UCLA. The program is titled: CICARE (pronounced see, I care). The acronym is one of the most effective communication techniques ever devised to train employees to offer exceptional service to every patient (or customer) every time. At Geisinger, UCLA, and other top-performing hospitals, the framework guides every interaction with colleagues, patients, visitors, and others. The acronym stands for:

CICARE. Program Acronym Description

Connect	Make a great first impression, greet patient by name when possible.
Introduce	Introduce yourself, your name, and your role.
Communicate	Explain what you're going to do.
Ask Permission and Anticipate	Ask questions like "May I come in?" "May I examine you now?" Also, anticipate needs and concerns.
Respond	Respond to a patient's needs or requests promptly and positively.
End with Excellence	Close the loop, communicate next steps, and manage up by explaining who the patient will be meeting next.

When Feinberg introduced the framework at UCLA, he had no idea that it would catch on around the country. In one of his first staff meetings at Geisinger, Feinberg asked the staff if they had a communication training program. A young doctor suggested they study CICARE, which he had learned at Stanford. The doctor didn't know he was speaking to the person who developed it. Stanford's CEO had worked for Feinberg at UCLA and brought the method along with him to Palo Alto. It was simply the best communication training method that any hospital had ever invented, and it took a five-star communicator to create it.

The Chief Storytelling Officer

"Storytelling is my most important tool as a leader," Feinberg told me. "I think of myself as the chief storytelling officer."

In his first meetings as CEO at UCLA, Feinberg noticed that empathy wasn't on the agenda. The meetings began with statistics, tables, charts, and revenue graphs. No discussion of patients and no stories. Feinberg discovered what Google had uncovered: teams were less engaged in the results of their jobs when they didn't see how their work impacted the big picture, in this case the patients.

Feinberg changed the meeting agenda. Everyone had to get personal and share their own stories of good and bad patient experiences. Feinberg went one step further, inviting patients to speak at the beginning of monthly meetings or reading patient letters. "In the healthcare business, our stories are better than what you're seeing in Hollywood. These are real-life people who are struggling and when we get it right, it feels really good," says Feinberg.

By the end of Feinberg's eight-year tenure as head of UCLA's health system, he had completely turned around the hospital. UCLA is consistently named one of the best hospitals in the nation. He literally took it from worst to first. Feinberg, however, was disappointed. "Although UCLA went from the 38th percentile in patient satisfaction to the 99th, that means 85 people out of 100 would recommend us. But we've failed miserably with the other 15 patients and their families."[10]

Could Feinberg's success be replicated in another part of the country? It could and it was. In his first year at Geisinger, patient satisfaction scores increased across all departments. The health system has seen its best physician retention rates on record. Employee engagement is higher than the year before. Once again, it's not enough. Feinberg is never satisfied and it drives his excellence. "When I tell you those results are better, I'm comparing us to other healthcare organizations." Feinberg doesn't want to be the best of a mediocre group; he wants to create the best experience in any industry. "I want to be the example of the right way to treat people—with dignity, respect, kindness and caring."

Just as Google discovered that employees want to feel as though they are part of something bigger, Feinberg has found ways to make employees feel as though they are part of something remarkable.

For Feinberg, helping people find their purpose began at UCLA with an empowering mission statement: "Healing humankind one patient at a time by alleviating suffering, promoting health, and delivering acts of kindness." Feinberg proudly points out that, at the time, UCLA was the only medical center in America that put "kindness" in its mission statement. The Gallup organization conducted a study on the best and worst hospital experiences. It concluded that one of the top two success factors was "a clear mission, vision and values."[11] The other success factor? "Strong and visible leadership." Mission statements don't mean much if the leader doesn't walk the talk.

Google and UCLA Health are two companies in two very different fields. One builds artificial intelligence; the other implants artificial hips. But the leaders at both organizations had the same challenge—how to develop winning teams. Leaders at both companies reached the same conclusion. Relying on the art of persuasion to strengthen emotional bonds makes teams more productive, engaged, cooperative, and, ultimately, successful.

Inspiring Leaders Wear SCARF

David Rock applies hard data to teach leaders the soft skills that will transform their businesses.

In a highly regarded paper for the management magazine *Strategy+ Business*, Rock argued that the human brain is a social organ. "Just as the animal brain is wired to respond to a predator before it can focus attention on the hunt for food, so is the social brain wired to respond to dangers that can threaten its core concerns before it can perform other functions." Those "other functions" form the foundation of high-performance workplaces: engagement, cooperation, productivity, enthusiasm, creativity. Rock introduced an acronym to explain how the ancient brain can help a leader build winning teams. The acronym is SCARF.[12]

Status

We don't like to be compared unfavorably to others on a team. It triggers our threat response. Advanced imaging machines find that threats to social status activate the same brain regions associated with pain and suffering. And we gain a great deal of pleasure when we feel valued. "As humans, we are constantly assessing how social encounters either enhance or diminish our status," writes Rock. For years economists believed that the only way to increase "status" was to give people promotions, bonuses, and higher salaries. That's part of it, no doubt. Rock says the less costly alternative is to heap praise on those you want to influence—genuine and specific praise. According to Rock, "The perception of status increased when people were given praise."

In my research for *The Storyteller's Secret,* I interviewed CEOs who own and run five-star hotels around the world. They reached the top of their field because they understand psychology and human behavior. I was impressed by how many of these five-star leaders use the power of story to transform the hospitality industry.

To understand how storytelling builds five-star experiences, you must first understand the psychology of self-esteem. Inspiring leaders make people feel good about themselves. If you can raise a person's self-esteem, you'll earn their admiration and loyalty. Five-star hotel managers often incorporate stories into their daily staff meetings. The results are stunning, and magical. Managers of average hotels hold tactical meetings to give employees the information they need to perform their tasks. Five-star hotel meetings feature managers asking employees to share stories about great customer experiences. These are usually stories one employee shares about another—or a manager shares about a team member.

Sharing stories among employees on a team serves an educational purpose, offering examples of great service. Stories also serve a psychological purpose. They improve morale and bring out the best in people's behavior. Employees who play the hero of a story receive public praise and are held up as role models for the rest of the team. Raise a person's self-esteem and you'll hit a bull's-eye in human relations.

Certainty

People hate not knowing. Uncertainty triggers a deep-seated threat response in the brain's amygdala. It's one of the reasons why you'll sit through a very bad movie until the end—the movie might be crummy, but you need to find out what happens to the protagonist. According to Rock, "Not knowing what will happen next can be profoundly debilitating because it requires extra neural energy." That extra neural energy impedes memory, energy, and performance, and leaves people disengaged. Rock's solution: share more. Communicate plans, explain why decisions are made, and make sure everyone knows how their individual performance connects to the team and to the larger picture (much like the findings in Project Aristotle at Google).

Leaders at CME Group, the largest futures exchange in the world, learned that changes related to modern technology often leave employees anxious, confused, and demoralized. When I visited CME in Chicago, I saw an open pit of about two acres where thousands of traders once stood shoulder to shoulder. They would wear colorful jackets and shout buy and sell orders while giving hand signals. But on that day the pit stood empty. There was only the soft glow of dozens of computer monitors with one or two people sitting quietly in front of them.

The pits were part of financial history. For more than 160 years, people traded commodities in face-to-face transactions: gold, silver, and oil. Cattle, corn, and pork bellies. You may remember seeing the trading floor in the movie *Trading Places* or as a colorful and animated backdrop for CNBC.

As computer trading began to rise, the number of transactions in open outcry pits began to fall. CME Group decided to close their pits down permanently in Chicago and New York. The news brought a wave of nostalgic memories. "I miss the roar," one trader said. Story after story showed the narratives of traders who reminisced about the past, the culture, and the friendships they'd lost. Television news reports showed photographs from 1874, when railroads brought wheat and corn and cattle and hogs to the Chicago stockyards. Farmers would trade these commodities, buying and selling and hedging their bets against rising or falling prices. In other words, the stories really tugged at people's emotions.

In reality, the transition to electronic trading had been happening for years. Most traders were already doing business behind a computer screen from the comfort of home. Although 60 full-time employees lost their job when the pits closed for good, a wave of new technology created jobs that hadn't existed before. Each day there are dozens of positions available at CME Group, from HR to accounting to marketing to analytics. Changes, however, raise uncertainty, and employees felt it.

An internal employee questionnaire served as a wake-up call for senior leaders.[13] Employees said they were confused. Some of their feedback was:

- How do our initiatives impact the goals and visions of the company?

- What is the vision?

- We are told to do things, but we don't know why.

- We don't have a sense of purpose.

After seeing the results, leaders determined they had to do a better job of communicating change. Leaders were failing to clearly articulate their vision for the company and connect their employees' day-to-day roles to the successful completion of that vision. Remarkably, one of the most effective tools at building trust and engagement between leaders and employees at the CME Group proved to be one of the oldest communication techniques we know—the sharing of personal stories.

The CME Group uploads hundreds of hours of videos on the internal corporate intranet. Employees in 11 offices around the world can watch the videos for training and quarterly financial updates. The videos receive about 500 views each. After the survey results showed the need for more communication, new videos were produced, titled "Meet Your Senior Leadership." Leaders answered questions such as "What do you do in your free time? Tell us about your family. What are your favorite books?" The videos quickly became the most popular on the site, attracting four times as many views as financial updates. One employee said, "PowerPoint doesn't engage me. The videos do."

The CME Group learned that change requires more communication than usual. Employees want to know what they're expected to do and why they're doing it. Presentations now take into consideration the emotional aspects of the message.

Autonomy

People want to feel as though they have control over their lives, and that extends to their work. One of the primary reasons people make the decision to run a franchise or jump from one company to another is to improve work-life balance. "A perception of reduced autonomy can easily generate a threat response," says Rock. Simply increasing the perception of autonomy increases pleasurable feelings in employees and reduces stress. Team managers are more successful when they give people permission to make choices.

I recall visiting Zappos headquarters in Nevada. Tony Hsieh built Zappos from a small e-commerce site selling shoes out of a San Francisco apartment into the gold standard for online customer service. I met some of the happiest employees I had ever seen in any company, in any country. I quickly learned that they loved the company because Hsieh gave them autonomy. They were empowered to do what they thought was the right thing for the customers. For example, there were no scripts or time limits for the call center operators. In fact, early in the Zappos history when Hsieh was generating buzz for the company, he would play a game with reporters. In the presence of the reporter, he would call Zappos and order something that the company didn't deliver, like a pizza. The employees didn't know it was the CEO on the line, but they still went above and beyond to help Hsieh find a solution to his request. It never failed to impress.

Today customers who call Zappos to order shoes or clothes will not feel pressured to get off the phone. Hsieh once told me that an employee spent a couple of hours on the phone with a customer. Hsieh did not ask the employee why she had spent so much time with one person. Instead he asked, "Was the customer happy?" Brands that have best-in-class customer service empower their employees to do what's in the best interest of the customer. Zappos.com views its call center employees as an extension of its marketing arm. Every unscripted conversation can help earn customer loyalty. Employees are encouraged to write personal thank-you notes after a call. These simple notes make yet another emotional connection with Zappos customers.

On my visit I saw that Zappos shared everything with employees, partners, and vendors—the good and the bad. Daily briefings and call statistics were posted on a whiteboard for all to see—employees and guests like me. Transparency ruled. At one point, even Tony Hsieh's condominium in downtown Las Vegas was part of the tour. The next time you think you're a transparent leader, ask yourself if you're willing to open up your home to anyone who asks for a free tour. Hsieh walked the talk.

Relatedness

Every time you meet someone new, the ancient brain kicks into threat and survival mode. It quickly tries to make the distinction between friend and foe. "Fruitful collaboration depends on healthy relationships, which require trust and empathy," writes David Rock.[14] According to Rock, when people make a strong social connection, it triggers a release of oxytocin, a neurochemical that increases bonding behavior.

Gino Blefari believes in serendipity. He was born in the Berkshires, a small mountainous region in western Massachusetts that is dotted with villages and towns. The Berkshire name appears everywhere. There's a Berkshire cleaners, Berkshire plumbing, Berkshire printing.

Blefari's working-class Italian family moved to Sunnyvale, California. Blefari became the first person in his family to graduate from college. He enrolled in a real estate course in a local community college and began his career as a real estate agent in the mid-1980s. In 2002, he founded his own residential real estate firm, Intero. By the end of his first year, Intero had closed $24 million in sales. By the end of 2003, sales had grown to $5.5 billion. Intero was named the fastest-growing residential real estate company in the country. Within one decade it became the seventh-largest real estate firm in North America. At the time, there were 80,000 real estate companies, and the six that beat out Intero had been in business for decades.

On May 17, 2014, Blefari's life came full circle when he sold Intero to Berkshire Hathaway, where Blefari is now the CEO of Berkshire Hathaway HomeServices, one of America's fastest-growing real estate brokerages.

Real estate is a field where social bonding is a key component of success. Buying a house is an emotional decision. Customers "fall in love" with a property, even if it exceeds their budget. In real estate the most successful agents and leaders are masters of emotional bonding. Gino Blefari is one such leader.

In our first lunch meeting I had come armed with questions for Blefari. By the end of the lunch I had only asked a few of my questions. Instead, I was answering Blefari's questions. He asked me about my family, my background, my hopes, and my dreams. Later I learned that Blefari had asked me those questions for a reason—he was establishing trust, a critical tool for real estate leaders whose primary job is to recruit, retain, and motivate top performers.

Blefari stands out as leader because he focuses on helping his agents become better leaders themselves. "If you help people grow personally they're going to serve their customers better," says Blefari. "Trust, respect, and integrity are everything in that relationship."[15]

Fairness

Neuroscientist Matthew Lieberman says, "We evolved over millions of years to become a deeply social species."[16] Lieberman's research shows that our brains are wired to watch for threats in our social standing. We all have a need to belong and when we feel as though our status in a group is being undermined, our brain reacts as though our bodies are experiencing physical pain. We simply don't like being treated in a way we perceive as unfair. "The cognitive need for fairness generates a strong response in the limbic system, stirring hostility and undermining trust," says Lieberman.

In his SCARF model, David Rock picks up on Lieberman's research to show that fairness is served by transparency. "Leaders who share information in a timely manner can keep people engaged and motivated, even during staff reductions. Morale remains relatively high when people perceive that cutbacks are handled fairly—that no one group is treated with preference and that there is a rationale behind the decision."

The SCARF model works because each of its components is based on how our brains were created to increase social bonding. Whether inspiring leaders in any field realize it or not, they wear their SCARF proudly.

Why We Know a Lot About Indra

We know a few things about Indra. We know she grew up in a city in India with no running water. Her mother would wake at 3:00 a.m. to make the trip to the reservoir, where residents were allowed to fill pots, pans, and buckets from the tap. Indra was given three containers of water a day so she could drink, bathe, and wash her clothes.

We know that she came to America with $50 in her pocket and worked from midnight to 5:00 a.m. for $3.85 an hour to help pay for college.

We know that on the third Wednesday of every month, her daughter's school held a mother's breakfast at 9:00 a.m. Indra could never go because she was working, and she felt guilty about it. She asked her then 11-year-old daughter if it bothered her, and her daughter responded, "No, because you're following your dream."[17] Today PepsiCo CEO Indra Nooyi gives the same advice to young professionals—follow your dream.

We know all these details about Nooyi's life because she's a leader who believes that storytelling and communication are the keys to motivating employees through the most significant change she's seen in her career. "The pace of change is enormous," Nooyi says as she explains that every aspect of PepsiCo's business is transforming. From what people eat to how they eat, everything about the food and beverage business is ripe for change and disruption. "The challenge of a leader is to look around the corner and make the change before it's too late to make the change," she says.[18]

The job of a leader is then to get the entire team or organization to do what they don't think needs to be done, because they don't see the future. Yet, leaders must drive people to accomplish the vision. Motivation is key. "It's not about motivating a small group of startup employees who have the same thinking as you do. We have 260,000 employees. When you decide to zig and zag, you've got to tell them what you'll be doing, why you're doing it, how it's going to impact them and why they've all got to come along on the journey."

Leaders, she says, must be lifelong learners, and one of the best investments is to improve communication skills, the earlier the better. "You cannot over invest in communication skills, written and oral communication. As a leader, you constantly have to mobilize the troops. Learn how to motivate people—small groups, medium-sized groups, large groups—and how to write in a way that's pithy and to the point."[19]

When Nooyi was enrolled in a master's program at Yale University, she expected to pass the courses easily. She had an MBA from India's top management school and received degrees in physics, chemistry, and math. At the time Yale required that students pass a communication/public-speaking course in order to enter the second year. She flunked. Nooyi took the course again during the summer. She didn't like to fail at anything, so this time she concentrated on being the best. "It made a huge difference," Nooyi said about the experience.

Indra Nooyi failed her first course on communication, but she dedicated herself to becoming great at it. Today she credits the skill as a crucial ingredient for her success.

David Foster Wallace, the late American essayist and novelist, once wrote that real leaders have "a mysterious quality" that inspires the rest of us. Wallace arrived at this definition of leadership: "a real leader is somebody who can help us overcome the limitations of our own individual laziness and selfishness and weakness and fear and get us to do better things than we can get ourselves to do on our own."[20]

Wallace said that a real leader's "authority" comes from the power we give that leader, and we give them power because of the way they make us *feel*. We like the way we feel in the presence of a great leader. We like the way they persuade us to work harder, to push ourselves, and to dream bigger than we ever imagined.

9

THE TED STARS

Presentation literacy isn't an optional extra for the few.
It's a core skill for the twenty-first century.

—CHRIS ANDERSON, curator, TED talks

Richard Turere is a 12-year-old boy who made peace with lions. He also has a style that makes audiences fall in love with him and his ideas.

Turere lives in Nairobi, Kenya. His family raises cattle on a ranch adjacent to a wildlife preserve. That part of the preserve isn't fenced, so lions from the preserve on the hunt for zebras frequently killed the family's livestock. At least, the lions used to attack the family's cows until Richard came up with a solution. Turere discovered that lions are afraid of moving light. He assembled spare electronic parts and built a device that flashes lights, tricking the lions into thinking someone is walking around with a torch.

The organizers of the TED talks conference learned about Turere's invention and invited him to present the story at TED's annual conference in Vancouver. A few problems came up, though. First, Turere, painfully shy, was daunted by the fact that he'd be speaking to an audience that would also hear from Tesla CEO Elon Musk, U2's Bono, and Google co-founder Sergey Brin. Turere had never even been on an airplane. TED worked with the young inventor to craft the story, design the slides, and rehearse his delivery. Turere lit up the stage and received a generous—and well-deserved—standing ovation.

The average TED talk receives about 400,000 views. Turere's presentation, titled "My Invention that Made Peace with Lions," has been viewed more than *2 million* times at the time of this writing.[1]

There are more than 13,000 TED talks available to view online, including the smaller, independently organized TEDx talks. Not all TED talks are good. An invitation to share your idea on a TED stage is no guarantee that the presentation will connect with an audience or go viral when the video is posted to the TED site. Those TED talkers who do stand out and become stars have specific qualities and practice specific habits. As 12-year-old Richard Turere proves, the techniques can be mastered by anyone at any age.

Ideas That Ripple Around the World

Chris Anderson, TED's "curator" or owner, is a strong advocate for the teaching of presentation literacy beginning in grade school. It's a skill anyone can build and it's a skill that's required today, more than ever. "At a time when the right idea presented the right way can ripple across the world at the speed of light, spawning copies of itself in millions of minds, there's huge benefit to figuring out how best to set it on its way," writes Anderson.[2] "As a leader—or an advocate—public speaking is the key to unlocking empathy, stirring excitement, sharing knowledge and insights, and promoting a shared dream."

In 2006, the TED conference began to make its talks available online, for free. It provided a platform for people with ideas and allowed them to share those ideas instantly with millions of people. It amplified their voices and launched a revolution in public speaking. TED talks are widely considered to be the gold standard of speaking and presentation. It's hard to score an invite to speak at a national TED conference, and it's even harder to deliver presentations that will be embraced by millions of people around the world. Videos are posted online along with transcripts, which has given researchers a mountain of data they can use to analyze which talks stand out and which ones don't. Researchers using high-tech data analysis tools have discovered that those TED speakers who make memorable connections with their audiences are actually using classic rhetorical techniques. The best TED speakers separate themselves from an already distinguished group. The TED stars all practice five presentation habits.

1. Replace bullet points with pictures

TED organizers select speakers carefully and work with them to craft the best presentations possible. One guideline that must never be broken involves slide design. There are no bullet points allowed on a TED slide. Ever.

For example, Richard Turere's seven-minute presentation included 17 slides, more than two slides per minute of discussion. Every slide was a photograph that complemented the narrative. Seventeen slides in seven minutes would be far too many to include in a typical business presentation because they would likely overwhelm its audience with charts, tables, graphs, and text. But the TED organizers worked with Turere to create a presentation that stood apart. TED talks are a global phenomenon for a reason. They aren't your average presentations.

People love pictures because they are a communication tool that dates back as far as humans roamed the planet—back to the cave drawing. Each of the concepts in this chapter will be explored in greater depth in Part Three, but for now keep in mind that study after study confirms that pictures are far more impactful—and, ultimately, memorable—than text alone.

2. Make the audience laugh

Even at the young age of 12 and during his first visit to the United States, Turere understood the power of humor to connect people across culture and language. He said his first idea to scare the lions away was to put a scarecrow near the cowshed. "But lions are very clever. They see the scarecrow on the first day and go back. But the second day they say, 'this thing is not moving. It's always here,'" he said as the audience laughed.[3] The scarecrow trick didn't work and Turere had to move on to other options. Neuroscientists believe that when our brain perceives a joke, it releases a rush of "feel good" chemicals: dopamine, serotonin, and endorphins. Humor is also powerfully contagious. Laughter is a social signal. It's like your peers are saying, "It's okay to like this speaker." One of the guidelines that TED issues to all its speakers is this reminder: laughter is good.

The actor Shah Rukh Khan didn't need to be reminded to make his audience laugh. Khan began his now-famous 2017 TED talk by telling his audience he's a 51-year-old movie star who hasn't used Botox . . . yet. Khan is Bollywood's biggest star and the eighth-highest-paid actor in the world. His popularity reaches far beyond the already massive box office in India. His 80 movies have garnered hundreds of millions of fans around the world. He has 24 million followers on Twitter alone.

Khan is such a skilled performer, it's instructive to see which public-speaking technique he brought to the TED stage. It's easy to spot right out of the gate: humor. He opens his presentation with the Botox joke and goes on to elicit six laughs in the first minute of his presentation. Comedy writing workshops tell students to aim for four to six laughs per minute in a tight stand-up routine. Khan is on the higher end of the range, bringing the house down with his humor. Among the other lines that had the audience erupting in laughter:

- I sell dreams, and I peddle love to millions of people back home in India who assume that I'm the best lover in the world. If you don't tell anyone, I'm going to tell you I'm not, but I never let that assumption go away.

- I've also been made to understand there are lots of you here who haven't seen my work, and I feel really sad for you. That doesn't take away from the fact that I'm completely self-obsessed, as a movie star should be.[4]

Beneath the humor, Khan had a serious subject to address. He tied in the joke about being a self-obsessed movie star with a lesson that humans should be obsessed with taking care of each other and the Earth for future generations. "Humanity is a lot like me," he said. "It's an aging movie star, grappling with all the newness, wondering whether she got it right."

The only TED star to top Khan's sense of humor is Sir Ken Robinson. Robinson's not an actor, he's an educator. And while he's not a star on the big screen, his TED talk has more laughs per minute than many Hollywood comedies. At 45 million views, Robinson's talk, "Do Schools Kill Creativity?," is the most popular video on the TED website.

Neuroscientists who study persuasion largely agree that laughter is an emotion that can help consolidate memories. Some of Robinson's humor comes in the form of funny short stories or anecdotes, while other forms of humor are self-deprecating. For example, Robinson says, "If you're at a dinner party, and you say you work in education—actually, you're not often at dinner parties, frankly, if you work in education. You're not asked . . ."[5]

Humor almost always leads to engagement because it's one of our most primal and engrained emotions. While you don't need to be a stand-up comic to be a hit on the TED stage, a little humor will help you stand out. "If they're laughing, they're listening," says Robinson.

3. Share personal stories

Dan Ariely's story isn't funny. In his senior year in high school, an explosion left Ariely with third-degree burns over 70 percent of his body. Ariely's dreams were wiped out in an instant as he spent the next three years in a hospital, underdoing countless surgeries and reconstruction.

In the hospital, Ariely experienced intense pain as the nurses ripped the old bandages from his body as quickly as you would pull a Band-Aid off a cut on your finger. Unlike one Band-Aid, however, Ariely's procedure took up to an hour and had to be done each day. Ariely tried to convince the nurses to remove the bandages more slowly—a process that might take longer, up to two hours, but with less pain. The nurses' response? They knew it was better to rip the bandages off quickly and patients should keep quiet.

After Ariely left the hospital and enrolled in a university, he began his research into human behavior, psychology, and economics. He chose a research subject close to home: how people experience pain. Through a series of experiments he discovered that his intuition was correct. Although the nurses meant well and strongly believed that ripping bandages off quickly would minimize the pain, Ariely found that they should have focused on shrinking the intensity of the pain by removing bandages slowly over a longer duration. Ariely's experience and research as a behavioral economist led him to write the bestselling book *Predictably Irrational*. He's also a TED star who has been invited six times to share his ideas on a TED stage.

Dan Ariely first talked about his burn unit experience at TED 2009. The video of the presentation went viral and introduced Ariely's ideas and research to a global audience. Since then his combined talks have generated more than *15 million views* and have made Ariely one of the world's best-known and most-admired behavioral economists. Ariely's famous for explaining the hidden reasons why humans do the things they do, but the reason for his TED talk success isn't such a hidden secret. According to TED curator Chris Anderson, "The stories that can generate the best connection are stories about you personally or about people close to you. Tales of failure, awkwardness, misfortune, danger or disaster, told authentically, hasten deep engagement."[6]

As you'll learn in Part Three, the ancient brain is wired for story. Today neuroscientists in the lab are using science to prove what we've known for thousands of years—stories are the best tool we have to develop deep, meaningful connections with those we wish to persuade.

Shonda Rhimes—the powerhouse creator of hit television shows like *Grey's Anatomy* and *Scandal*—gave a personal, revealing presentation at TED 2016. It has since topped 3 million views. In the talk, Rhimes talks about the things that scared her—activities you would expect a powerhouse television producer to have conquered. She decided to begin saying "yes" to the things that scared her.

"So a while ago, I tried an experiment," Rhimes began. "For one year, I would say yes to all the things that scared me. Anything that made me nervous, took me out of my comfort zone, I forced myself to say yes to. Did I want to speak in public? No, but yes. Did I want to be on live TV? No, but yes. Did I want to try acting? No, no, no, but yes, yes, yes."[7]

Rhimes said "a crazy thing" happened. The very act of doing what scared her made the act less scary. "My fear of public speaking, my social anxiety, poof, gone. It's amazing, the power of one word. 'Yes' changed my life."

In an essay to celebrate the one hundredth anniversary of *Forbes* magazine, Rhimes talked about the role of storytelling in nurturing connections between humans. "In a world of unlimited voices and choices, those who bring people together and tell a good story have power."

Rhimes and Ariely have power because they can share stories that amplify their ideas. Storytellers on a TED stage have launched bestselling books and careers as well as powerful social movements. Facts don't launch careers; stories do. Facts don't launch movements; stories do.

4. Make presentations easy to follow

The best TED talks are contagious for a reason—they are crafted and delivered by experienced speakers who have mastered the skills necessary to persuade their audiences.

Skilled TED speakers use humor, tell stories, and structure the argument so that it's easy to follow and easy to remember. They rely on two specific techniques to do so: headlines (which you'll learn more about in chapter 12) and the rule of three.

STATE ONE HEADLINE

"Beautiful slides and a charismatic stage presence are all very well, but if there's no real takeaway, all the speaker has done—at best—is to entertain," writes Chris Anderson.[8] Many speakers do not plan their presentation around a central theme. They open PowerPoint or whichever presentation tool they're comfortable with and write bullet points on each and every slide. No theme, just bullets. The best TED speakers design presentations around a central theme and they repeat the theme throughout the talk. For example:

- "Why We Love, Why We Cheat"— Helen Fisher
- "Averting the Climate Crisis"— Al Gore
- "What You Can Do to Prevent Alzheimer's"— Lisa Genova

I call the theme the "Twitter-friendly headline," because out of 2,460 TED talks, not one has a theme that is longer than a 140-character tweet. And most are a good deal shorter.

Neuroscientists have recently discovered that sharing the theme up front makes a presentation easier to follow. A presentation where the theme is stated clearly near the beginning is far more memorable and impactful than one that buries the theme in the middle, saves it for the end, or never states it at all. Stating your theme at the beginning frames the rest of the content.

Human rights attorney Bryan Stevenson delivered a TED talk that elicited the longest standing ovation in TED's 30-year history. In the first 40 seconds, he mentions the word "identity" three times and states the theme: "Today I want to talk to you about the power of identity." Stevenson follows up on his theme with the next technique in the TED arsenal, the triad or rule of three.

USE THE RULE OF THREE

On the first day of TED 2017, a special guest appeared via satellite. The speaker's name had been a well-guarded secret leading up to the event. When Pope Francis appeared on the screen, he lit up social media. It was the first time a pope had given a TED talk. Conference organizers spent more than one year planning and took several trips to Rome to pull it off.

Pope Francis himself decided what he wanted to say and how he wanted to say it. Since Pope Francis got the same amount of time as every other TED speaker—18 minutes—he chose three messages:

1. We all need each other. "We can only build the future by standing together."
2. Equality and social inclusion should be part of scientific and technological progress.
3. We need a revolution of tenderness, a movement that "starts from our heart."[9]

Pope Francis did not randomly select three messages. He chose three for a reason. Pope Francis once said that he learned public speaking at seminary and one of the elements of persuasion he remembers best—and applies to every speech—is the rule of three.

The rule of three is a classic public-speaking tool with roots dating back to Aristotle and his contemporary Greek orators. Today, neuroscientists have proven what those orators knew instinctively—the average person can carry three or four ideas in short-term (working) memory. Pope Francis sticks to three ideas, as do many other TED stars:

- Leila Hoteit gives us three lessons on success from Arab business-women.
- Stuart Russell reveals three principles for creating safer AI.
- Mona Chalabi says there are three ways to spot a bad statistic.
- Ramsey Musallam, a chemistry teacher, gives us three ways to get students excited.

Many of the best TED speakers have discovered that the simple rule of three—sometimes called the "Triad"—forms the foundation of persuasive speaking and writing.

5. Promise your audience that they will learn something new

My analysis of the 25 most-viewed TED talks of all time shows a clear trend. Every one of them holds the promise of teaching the audience something they didn't know before. The content is packaged in a way that's new, novel, or surprising. For example:

- Do schools kill creativity? Watch Ken Robinson's TED talk to find out.
- There are 10 things you didn't know about orgasms. Mary Roach will explain.
- Great leaders inspire action with one question. Simon Sinek lets us know how they do it.
- What are the invisible forces that guide our behavior? Tony Robbins reveals what they are.
- There's a way to speak so people want to listen. Julian Treasure tells us how to sound more beautiful.
- Surprising new science explains why people are happy even when things don't go their way. Dan Gilbert decodes our "psychological immune system."

Learning is addictive, thanks to an almond-shaped bit of gray matter in your temporal lobe—the amygdala. When you receive new information, the amygdala releases dopamine, which acts as your brain's natural "save" button. It explains why we get a buzz out of learning something new. We are natural explorers. Robert Ballard discovered the *Titanic* in 1985.

He received a standing ovation from a TED audience for his presentation, "The Astonishing Hidden World of the Deep Ocean." When I interviewed Ballard after his TED Talk, he said, "Your mission in any presentation is to inform, educate, and inspire. You can only inspire when you give people a new way of looking at the world in which they live."[10]

When you give people a new perspective, you are tapping into millions of years of adaptation. If our primitive ancestors had not been curious to explore the world around them, we would have been extinct long ago. The need to explore, to learn something new, to be attracted to something that stands out is wired deep in our DNA. Give your audience something new and delicious to chew on.

TED talks are viewed more than three million times a day because people are hungry for ideas. Your ideas matter today more than ever. And today, more than ever, the tools exist to amplify your voice across the globe. The ability to inspire people to look beyond their circumstances and to imagine worlds that have yet to exist is a gift that should be shared, nurtured, and sharpened. In Part Three, you will learn concrete tips and techniques to share your ideas persuasively. One great idea can light the world. Let's shine a light on yours.

PART THREE

HOW TO GET FROM
GOOD TO GREAT

10

THE PATHOS PRINCIPLE

*People are dying because we can't communicate in ways
that allow us to understand one another. That sounds
like an exaggeration, but I don't think it is.*

—ALAN ALDA, actor, host, *Scientific American Frontiers*

Bill coached track at the University of Oregon. One day he received exciting news. A wealthy alum had donated $1 million for a new polyurethane track. Bill's enthusiasm was short-lived, however, when he realized that his runner's shoes failed to gain traction on the new surface. During breakfast one Sunday morning, Bill gazed over to the kitchen counter and paid attention to the waffle iron. He saw the appliance every day but had never looked at it in this way. It had a gridded pattern that Bill thought might grip the track better than existing running shoes.

Bill brought the iron to the garage, poured urethane in it, and heated it. It failed. The chemical glued it shut. He bought another waffle iron and tried another chemical. It failed. Bill didn't give up, although he gave up on using a real waffle iron. He punched holes in a sheet of stainless steel to mimic the waffle pattern, and made a rubber mold from it that he sewed to the bottom of a pair of running shoes. The first student athlete who tried them out "ran like a rabbit." In that moment in the kitchen, Oregon running coach and Nike co-founder Bill Bowerman transformed the way people would run for generations.

You've probably heard of the Nike "waffle story." It's a famous business narrative, but Nike co-founder Phil Knight gave the story its soul.

In 1980, Nike went public. Knight accompanied a group of executives to New York for the so-called dog-and-pony show, when company leaders persuade investors that their vision and brand is worth backing.

Knight closed the presentation with Bowerman's story. "I talked about his brains, bravery, his magic waffle iron," Knight recalls in his autobiography, *Shoe Dog*.[1] The story had a point. "I wanted to let those New Yorkers know that though we hailed from Oregon, we were not to be trifled with. The cowards never started and the weak died along the way. That leaves us."

Knight repeated the story to bankers in Chicago, Dallas, San Francisco, and Los Angeles. Twelve cities in seven days. The story acted as a metaphor for the spirit of innovation that defined the brand.

Today the Nike campus itself is a celebration of the company's stories and history. Buildings and roads are named for Nike's "founding fathers." The youngest employees hunger for tales of the company's origin and Nike executives are there to tell them. Senior executives are designated as corporate storytellers. They tell the story of Phil Knight selling running shoes out of the trunk of his Plymouth Valiant. They tell the story of the magic waffle iron. They tell the story of Steve Prefontaine, the legendary Oregon runner who died in a car crash and whom Knight speaks about with almost spiritual reverence.

At Nike, the heroics of the past inspire the innovations of the future.

"As Nike gets even bigger, its storytellers feel that their mission becomes even more critical," according to a *Fast Company* feature on the Nike storytelling culture.[2] The company's corporate campfire storytelling program began years ago with an hour-long presentation to new employees. Today Nike's story pervades every aspect of the company culture. New employees go to a week-long "Rookie Camp" at Nike headquarters in Beaverton, Oregon. They spend one entire day in Eugene to connect with the past: they see the track where Bowerman coached and the site of Prefontaine's fatal car crash. "We're connecting what we're doing today back to Nike's heritage," one training manager said.[3] "Because when people understand why we exist, what our foundation is, and who we are today, then they understand that all of our products are still rooted in improving an athlete's performance. It's no different from how it was when Bill

Bowerman was in his workshop, tinkering and crafting shoes for his athletes."

When visitors arrive on the Nike campus, they notice that all the buildings are named after a company founder or an athlete whose name helped to build the brand. Bowerman's original waffle iron is even on display in one of the buildings. Phil Knight would have it no other way. He wants people to really know the men and women who elevated Nike to more than a brand. "I don't see buildings. I see temples. Any building is a temple if you make it so," writes Knight.[4]

Stories are the single best linguistic tool we have to persuade, and Phil Knight knows it. Knight has added the secret sauce in a great leader's toolkit: Pathos. According to Aristotle, Pathos is the act of persuading an audience by appealing to its emotions, and stories are the most direct way we have for making the appeal. By remembering the stories of the past, Nike employees are inspired to build the future.

If I Understood You, Would I Have This Look on My Face?

Alan Alda is a six-time Emmy Award winner best known for playing Hawkeye Pierce in the classic television show *M*A*S*H*. Alda's interest in science led him to host the award-winning PBS series *Scientific American Frontiers*. Eleven years of interviewing scientists on the program convinced Alda that people with the best ideas are often terrible communicators. He created the Alan Alda Center for Communicating Science at Stony Brook University to address what he considers an urgent need.

Alda writes: "You run a company and you think you are relating to your customers and employees and that they understand what you're saying, but they don't, and both customers and employees are leaving you. You're a scientist who can't get funded because the people with the money just can't figure out what you're telling them. You're a doctor who reacts to a needy patient with annoyance . . . but it doesn't have to be that way."[5]

According to Alda, the missing ingredient in communication is empathy or what actors call "relating." Alda argues that when people fail in the art of relating and communicating with one another, it can have serious consequences for careers, communities, and our planet:

> An accountant would tell me about the tax code in a way that made no sense. A salesman would explain an insurance policy that didn't seem to have a basis in reality. It wasn't any consolidation when I came to realize that pretty much everybody misunderstands everybody else. Maybe not all the time, and not totally, but just enough to seriously mess things up. People are dying because we can't communicate in ways that allow us to understand one another. That sounds like an exaggeration, but I don't think it is. When patients can't relate to their doctors and don't follow their orders, when engineers can't convince a town that the dam could break, when a parent can't win the trust of a child enough to warn her off a lethal drug, they can all be headed for a serious ending.[6]

Alda's quest to understand how we can relate to one another led him to James McGaugh, a prominent neurobiologist in the field of learning and memory. The professor at UC Irvine has spent a career studying why some memories are vivid and indelible, while others are forgettable.

McGaugh asked Alda, "Do you remember your first kiss?"[7] Alda most certainly did. Most people do. In fact, you can probably recall where you were, the details of the location, even the smells in the air. "We remember things that are tied to emotion," McGaugh says. "All Nobel prize winners know exactly where they were and what they were doing. They say it's 'etched' in my mind. It's 'welded' into my brain. Whether it's highly joyful or frightening, the memories stick because they arouse our emotions."

Emotion is the brain's ancient mechanism to help us remember key events and forget some of the rest, because, after all, not everything is equally important. If you remembered everything with equal intensity, you'd have a hard time functioning. Some memories are made to be stored. Others, not so much.

McGaugh says that emotion helps us to remember things, but a "little stress" can sear the memory into our brains.

A little stress. Now, where can we find that? As it turns out, the key is to tap into something that comes naturally to all of us. It's natural because it lies deep within our DNA. It's a tool that triggers the rush of brain chemicals that was critical for social bonding in primitive society and continue to bond us today.

The tool is storytelling, and by including tension, conflict, and hurdles within a story, you'll add a little stress that keeps your listeners glued. Stories are irresistible because we're wired to think in story, process our world in story, and share ideas in story. Master the ancient art of storytelling and you will stand out in the modern world.

Stories Align Our Brains

"Storytelling is amazing," says Princeton researcher Uri Hasson, whom we first met in chapter 3. He should know. Hasson runs a research team at Princeton University that uses fMRI machines to scan the brains of people engaged in storytelling—both telling and listening to stories.

Let's imagine for a moment that I'm about to tell you a true story. It's about my father, Francesco Gallo, who was a prisoner of war in World War II. He spent five years in a stark camp in Ethiopia, surviving on rice and water. The lessons he imparted stick with me to this day—approach life with grit, perseverance, and hope.

Now, let's imagine for a moment that tiny electrodes are placed on our scalps. You and I are both hooked up to Hasson's brain scans, along with four other people. All of us—you, me, and the four people—are connected to the machine.

Hasson takes your scan before I begin telling my story. The scan shows movement in your brain waves because the brain is always working, even when you're sitting in the dark in silence. The key is that your brain waves are doing something very different from the waves of the others who are also waiting. No two brains in the room are in sync.

I begin talking, and as my story unfolds, Hasson sees movement in the scans—your brain waves and the waves of the others are going up and down in the brain region that processes sound, the auditory cortex. Suddenly, something amazing begins to happen. "The subjects lock to the story," according to Hasson. In other words, your brain waves begin to move up and down *together* and blood flows to the same regions of your brain and the brains of the other participants. You are in sync with the other listeners and you are all in sync with me, the person telling the story. Hasson calls it "neural entrainment," or brain alignment between speaker and listener.

To prove that it's the story itself causing the alignment, Hasson records my story in Russian and plays it back to non-Russian-speaking listeners. He sees movement in the auditory cortex because the brains of the listeners are processing sounds, but the scans do not show alignment. Only a story, a comprehensible narrative, can trigger alignment among all the listeners. In addition, "only when we use the full, engaging, coherent story do the responses spread deeper into the brain into higher-order areas, which include the frontal cortex and the parietal cortex, and make all of them respond very similarly."[8]

Recently, biomedical engineers at Drexel University used a more advanced tool called fNIRS (functional near-infrared spectroscopy) to study the brains of two people having natural conversations with one another in less formal settings than a lab. The technique uses light to measure neural activity and to give researchers a view of blood flow to different parts of the brain. The study was based on Hasson's work but intended to give a more accurate measure of what's happening when two people tell each other stories. The researchers' conclusion confirmed Hasson's experiments—a listener's brain mirrors a speaker's brain when the speaker is telling a story about a real-life experience.

In study after study, neuroscientists using the latest technology are confirming what we've known intuitively for centuries. The human brain is wired for story. Since humans began to communicate with one another, we've told stories. Anthropologists believe that when our ancestors gained control of fire, it was a major milestone in human development. Fire cooked food, which gave us protein to build larger brains. Campfires also extended the day. Instead of hunting and gathering as they did during daylight hours, our ancestors sat around the light exchanging stories. Stories informed others in the camp of potential threats, taught new ways of building tools, and sparked imagination.

Okay, now we know that Pathos—emotional appeal—is an essential component of persuasion. We also know that stories are the best tool we have for making such an appeal. But are all the stories the same, or do some carry more weight than others?

According to Hasson's research, stories that highlight the common ground between two people trigger more alignment in brain activity between speaker and listener. If I can find common ground with you, my listener, I'll have more success at persuading you to see the world from my point of view.

Finding Common Ground

Jack's parents were Pingtan performers in China. Pingtan is a 400-year-old performance art that's a combination of music and storytelling. It's a verbal art form in which the artists use vivid words and images to evoke emotion from the audience. Jack was influenced by watching his parents master the craft. He fell in love with the art of storytelling and pursued a career as an English teacher. In China, Jack was only earning $12 a month. Although the meager salary was his only means of paying the rent on his one-bedroom apartment, Jack left his teaching job to start an online commerce company, one that would connect small businesses to customers around the world. Today, the company he founded, Alibaba, is the world's largest virtual shopping mall and Jack Ma is the richest person in China and one of the 30 wealthiest people on the planet.

Employees who worked for Ma in the early years of Alibaba remember him as "a captivating speaker" who could fire up his listeners. His vision was contagious. Author and former Alibaba consultant Duncan Clark wrote a book about Jack Ma. He credits Ma's storytelling skills—no doubt influenced by his parents—as a critical component of his success. "With tales of overcoming challenges and defying the odds, Jack regularly drives some in his audience to tears, even hardened business executives," writes Duncan.[9] But Ma doesn't just tell any story. He tailors the story to his audience to build an emotional connection. Ma quotes from recent movies popular in a particular country and even draws on the heroes and stories that his audience would recognize. "To audiences in China, Jack often draws on stories from his favorite martial arts novels, or Chinese revolutionary history."[10] When an American colleague asked Ma how he would tell the story in America, Ma said he wouldn't. "For me to motivate you, I would talk about George Washington and the cherry tree," he said.

"Jack is a master at appealing to people's emotions," writes Duncan. "He had a well-honed stable of stock stories, mostly from his childhood or Alibaba's own infancy. A close inspection of all of his speeches reveals he has essentially been giving the same speech for seventeen years. Yet by subtly tweaking his message to match the mood and expectations of the crowd, he somehow manages to make each speech feel fresh."[11]

Ma tells the stories of his own struggles to inspire others to pursue their dreams, despite the obstacles that might be in their way. He openly tells the story about failing the college entrance exam . . . twice. He tells the story of getting 1 out of 120 points on the math portion of the college exam. He tells the story about being rejected by Harvard . . . 10 times. He tells the story of being turned down for 30 jobs, including one at KFC. He tells the story of being 18 months away from bankruptcy. His stories of failure carry an important lesson—the value of persistence. "Giving up is the biggest failure," Ma says. "Never give up. Today is hard, tomorrow will be worse, but the day after tomorrow will be sunshine."[12]

Humble origins make for good stories. If you've overcome adversity in your life, in your career, or in your business, it's important to share that story because we are hardwired to love rags-to-riches stories. And we love them because we *need* to hear them. Psychologists say struggle is part of the human experience, that we are hardwired to find meaning in hardship. Stories of success over adversity, or triumph over tragedy, ignite our inner fire because struggle is a part of nature. Stories of success despite overwhelming odds inspire us all to be our best selves. Remarkably, Jack Ma says he was inspired by a story and a fictional character: Forrest Gump. The character, played by Tom Hanks in the 1994 movie, didn't let a low IQ stop him from chasing dreams or accepting challenges. He never saw himself as disadvantaged. Gump was the perennial optimist. Ma once said he got his story, his dream, from the movie. Every time Ma got frustrated, he would watch the film. It taught him to never give up. That's the power of story. Stories elevate our spirits and bring us hope. Jack

Ma's charisma has been referred to as "Jack Magic." Now you know that the real magic is Jack's ability to weave a story that captures the imagination.

The Key to Our Hearts

If you want someone to hand over the keys to their heart, tell them a story. If you want them to hand over the keys to a new car, stories work, too.

In 1997, Phil Wall visited a children's home in Johannesburg, South Africa, and met an 18-month-old girl named Zodwa. Zodwa's mother, suffering from HIV/AIDs, had abandoned the girl nine months earlier. Phil and his wife, Wendy, sought to adopt the girl in a process that lasted eight months, but the adoption fell through when Zodwa's grandmother came forward and offered to take care of her.

Phil and Wendy were crushed, but they bounced back and turned their disappointment into action. Determined to help other children, Phil and Wendy began a charity to transform the lives of orphans. "We decided to spend our life helping young kids in Africa with no mommies or daddies," Phil Wall told me in a phone conversation from his office in Wimbledon, England.[13] Today, WeSeeHope supports 150,000 children a year and has raised $20 million for the cause.

Phil Wall tells his personal adoption story because it establishes common ground with his audience—potential donors. "People find something within themselves that resonates with another person's story," Wall said. "I talk as a parent to other parents about the child I felt I let down. When I tell them I want to change the lives of hundreds of thousands of kids who don't have a mommy and daddy, people find something in my story they can relate to."

Wall isn't in the charity business; he's in the relationship business.

In 1998, Wall and his wife took the $7,000 they were saving for a house and borrowed another few thousand. They were asked to speak about the charity to a large audience. After the presentation, they distributed 1,300 envelopes to members of the audience. In each envelope they had placed a $10 note. They issued a challenge. The people holding the envelope could give it back, keep it for themselves, or come up with creative ideas using their talent, skills, or networks to turn the $10 into $100. Over the next five months the $13,000 distributed to 1,300 people raised $2 million for WeSeeHope.

One particular response sticks in Wall's memory. He received a phone call out of the blue from a person who had received the $10 envelope. The caller said, "I'll take your $10 and, in return, give you the keys to one of my cars." The car was an Aston Martin DB7, a luxury sports coupe, and it fetched $43,000 at auction.

"The heart of the human spirit is story and purpose," Wall told me. "One of the greatest deficits in western society is a deficit of meaning. When people are captivated by a story and see themselves in your story, they are very giving and generous."

Stories Ignite the Human Spirit

Disagreement is part of all scientific research, but on the subject of persuasion, there's a near-unanimous consensus among neuroscientists: Stories are the single best vehicle we have to transfer our ideas to one another. Stories trigger a release of neurochemicals that force us to pay attention to a speaker, empathize with them, understand them, and get excited about their ideas. Humans not only crave stories, we need to hear them. Stories are irresistible, and storytellers are alluring.

One day, while I was leading a communication course for a group of business professionals, I met Ethan, a manager for a mid-sized company.[14] Ethan wanted to advance his career and move from project manager to business development executive, a role that requires confident presentations. Ethan's boss had suggested that he take the class to improve his ability to win more and larger deals.

Ethan's company faced a challenge. In Ethan's particular part of the country, competitors were winning projects by coming in with artificially low bids. Unfortunately, in a move that tarnished all companies in the region, the lowest bidders would mark up costs in the middle of the project to make up for the low bid they used to land the work. Selection committees didn't trust contractors, but were also under pressure to look for the lowest bids.

Ethan's company prided itself on its open and transparent process.

It could provide evidence (Logos) that an initially higher bid would save clients money in the long run. But the facts alone were often not enough to persuade potential customers.

If we look at the triad of appeals that Aristotle said was the foundation of persuasion, Ethan registered high on Logos: the evidence to support his argument. He struggled with communicating the other two-thirds of the formula: Ethos and Pathos.

Ethos is the character of the speaker. Ethan had character. He was a man of integrity and honesty. But he was an introvert, quiet and shy. He had character, but people didn't know it. He also lacked Pathos: emotional appeal. In class Ethan didn't volunteer any information about himself other than his title and job description. He responded to questions with one-word answers. The class tried their best to get Ethan to open up, but it was difficult to get more than a few words out of him.

After two days of hearing his classmates tell their stories, however, something clicked. Ethan found a personal story to make an emotional appeal. He stood in front of the class and introduced us to his new "pitch." First, he began by acknowledging the clients' concerns. Second, he told a personal story to find common ground. Ethan decided to begin his pitch like this:

> Construction is serious business. It can be financially risky, there are safety and health hazards, and time constraints. You want to make sure your project is in capable hands. We've passed out our qualification package. In it you'll find our resumes, certifications, past projects, and recommendations. I'm here to tell you the story behind the package, the underlying driver that my father taught me. My passion outside of construction is sailing. I'm a life-long sailor. My father was a lifelong sailor. I was 14 years old and there was a tropical storm on the island where we were living. We boarded up the house and prepared to get hit. The storm veered away from land and remained out over the ocean. We never got a direct hit. But I was a hotshot sailor. I had been competing since I was eight years old, traveling the country, and I was very good at it. Actually, a little cocky about it. We had a dinghy by the harbor. I told my parents

I'd go check on the boat. The wind was howling and the waves were large. It was a dumb thing to do, but I convinced my buddy to go out with me on a sailboat. We had fun for a while, until we took a big wave over the bow, and the boat sank. We had to swim in. Someone had seen it and called my dad. I made it to the beach, where my dad was waiting with a towel. He handed me the towel and in a booming French accent said: "You may be a hotshot sailor, but you have a lot to learn about seamanship." I was disappointed because I had disappointed my father. What I didn't know at the time—but I do now—was the lesson he had taught me: all the talent, knowledge, and experience that you have must be backed by discipline, judgment, and commitment. Otherwise, you can get into a lot of trouble.

If you've watched *America's Got Talent* or similar shows around the world, you'll have a sense of how the class responded to Ethan's story. When a performance is better than expected, the camera pans to the audience and judges, who are stunned and pleased. The class reacted the same way after Ethan delivered his story. Jaws dropped, students turned to each other with a smile, some clapped in the middle of the pitch, and one woman pointed to goose bumps on her arm. Ethan had dropped the shield, revealed an intriguing aspect of his personality and background, and earned the admiration of his peers. Every person has a story.

You might have noticed that Ethan's story has "a little stress." He includes dramatic tension when he talks about taking the boat in stormy waters. Stress will make a story more memorable and help to strike an emotional chord with the audience. Neurobiologist Larry Cahill can prove it.

Cahill also studies memory at the University of California, Irvine, with Dr. James McGaugh. Cahill is famous for his "ice water" experiment. In the experiment, people sat down and watched a series of slides while a researcher measured their emotional response. The slides were photographs that triggered various emotional responses by featuring snakes, guns, or flowers. After a participant watched the slides, their hand was stuck in a bowl of ice water, a technique scientists use to trigger the stress hormone response.

Cahill tested their memory one week later. Those who had put their hands in ice water remembered the emotional slides much more vividly than the control subjects. Stress hormones helped to solidify the memories consolidating in their brain. The lesson? Arouse emotions by adding a little stress. It takes just a small amount of emotion to enhance the power of a story.

Three Kinds of Stories You Can Tell

There are three kinds of stories that you can—and should—incorporate in any conversation or presentation intended to move people to action. They are:

- Stories about personal experiences
- Stories about real customers or clients
- Stories about signature events in the history of a brand or company

Stories about personal experiences

Personal stories about a successful outcome after an adverse event, a triumph over a tragedy, are powerful. Using struggle and success as rhetorical tools allows us to make deeper, more meaningful connections with each other.

For example, I once met with a senior director at Walmart. Her challenge was to share the culture of Walmart at the monthly orientation sessions for new employees. These meetings were quite large. Walmart received 10,000 applications a month and employed more than two million people. All new hires were required to watch this manager's keynote—from associates to managers to executives at the corporate office in Bentonville, Arkansas.

The manager had plenty of facts and figures about Walmart, but we decided that a personal story would help her relate to new associates. During our conversation, the manager turned me to and said:

"You know, Carmine, our slogan—save money, live better—really means something."

"Oh? Tell me about it," I said.

"My brother-in-law was diagnosed with ALS. I helped my sister care for him as his health deteriorated. The monthly costs for his care began to pile up, so I suggested to my sister that we shop at Walmart to save money—this happened before I even worked for Walmart. We saved $300 a month on the very same supplies we had been using. With that $300 a month, we bought a wheelchair-accessible van, which gave my brother-in-law more freedom. He even used the van to attend my nephew's college graduation, which my nephew will never forget."

Once those of us in the room wiped the tears from our eyes, I asked if she had a photo of her brother-in-law. "If you tell that story and show photos of your brother-in-law, nobody will ever forget the company's mission and what it means to the lives of every one of your customers."

At the next orientation session she delivered the story, along with photos. Immediately after, a new employee approached the manager and said, "That was one of the most inspiring presentations I've ever heard."

"I only have one complaint," the manager told me a few weeks later. "I can't keep up with the requests for lunch. My next communication challenge is to learn how to let people down gently," she joked.

"At Walmart, we love stories," Walmart CEO Doug McMillon once said at a company shareholders meeting. "There is just something about them. We enjoy telling them. We remember hearing them. We repeat stories and pass them down. We also write them. Together, we're writing our company's story."

Stories about real customers or clients

KPMG, the fastest growing of the Big Four accounting firms, discovered that storytelling gives employees purpose. The company conducted an internal study of thousands of managers and employees and found that "A workforce motivated by a strong sense of higher purpose is essential to engagement."[15] KPMG made storytelling a key part of its management training to help everyone understand the brand's long history and influence. "We recognized that just telling people from the top down about their higher purpose would not succeed," said Bruce Pfau, KMPG's vice chair of human resources.[16] "We encouraged everyone—from our interns to our chairman—to share their own stories about how their work is making a difference." After creating a storytelling culture at KPMG, turnover plummeted, morale skyrocketed, and profits soared.

Stories about signature events in the history of a brand or company

I once had the opportunity to have lunch with San Francisco 49ers football legend Dwight Clark. "It's funny, Carmine. I caught five hundred and six passes in my career with the Niners, but everyone wants to hear the story of The Catch," Clark told me.[17]

The Catch has its own Wikipedia entry. It's one of the most famous plays in professional football history. When Clark caught Joe Montana's pass in the NFC conference championship on January 10, 1982, it sent the 49ers to the Super Bowl, which they won. The team went on to dominate the 1980s with four Super Bowl victories. Clark now sketches out the play as his signature on autographed footballs. Dwight Clark is an individual, but also a brand. "The Catch" is his signature story, literally.

What's your signature story? Every person has one. Every company, startup, or brand has one, too.

Seven Elements of Impactful Signature Stories

"Signature stories represent a critical asset that can be leveraged over time and which can provide inspiration and direction both inside and outside the firm," write David and Jennifer Aaker, marketing professors at the Berkeley-Hass School of Business and the Graduate School of Business at Stanford.[18] "Signature stories are a powerful way to gain awareness, communicate, persuade, change behavior, and precipitate discussion. They are almost always far more efficient and impactful than simply communicating facts or features."

In a paper about signature stories, the Aakers use the following example: "A Nordstrom customer in the mid-1970s walked into the Fairbanks, Alaska, store and asked to 'return' two worn snow tires. It was an awkward moment. Nordstrom, which had evolved from a shoe store to a department store, had never sold tires (although another company once did at this store's site). Despite that fact, the salesperson that had been on the job only a few weeks, relying on a customer-first culture supported by a generous return policy, had no doubt what to do. He promptly took back the snow tires and refunded what the customer said he had paid."

Nordstrom is known for its generous return policy, and it empowers employees to make the right decisions for its customers. Nordstrom leaders—as well as executives in many companies such as Nike, Accenture, KPMG, Southwest, and others—use stories to reinforce the values of their company cultures. Memos, e-mails, PowerPoint slides, or binders full of training material cannot replace a compelling signature story.

David and Jennifer Aaker say an impactful signature story includes the following seven elements:[19]

1. *It's a story.* A signature story is just that—a narrative with a beginning, middle, and end (a resolution).
2. *It's intriguing.* According to the Aakers, an intriguing story is "thought-provoking, novel, informative, interesting, entertaining."
3. *It's authentic.* The characters, settings, and challenges must feel real. A story that doesn't ring true will be perceived as fiction and may harm the speaker's credibility.
4. *It includes details.* Small, vivid, or important details enhance the authenticity of the story. In the Walmart story, I provided one key detail—the speaker saved $300 a month. The audience doesn't need to know every item on the list and how much she saved on each product. Too much information that's not relevant to the central narrative would have diluted the story's emotional impact.
5. *It reveals a surprise.* In a movie, this is the twist. It's the M. Night Shyamalan moment when the audience says, Whoa, I didn't see that coming.
6. *It introduces empathetic characters.* The listeners should be able to see themselves in the shoes—or context—of the hero.
7. *It has conflict and tension.* This is the stuff all great narratives are made of. If there's no struggle or conflict, it makes for an uninteresting story. An empathetic hero overcoming a meaningful hurdle—and succeeding in the end—is irresistible.

Incorporating these seven elements in a story is not as daunting as it might appear. They can be checked off in one or two words. For example, I'm a fan of the California wine industry because it's full of stories and storytellers—mavericks, pioneers, and entrepreneurs who are passionate and creative. Wine and storytelling pair perfectly. Here's a signature story from the Stag's Leap Wine Cellars in Napa Valley, California. The elements of a signature story are in brackets:

In 1976, a blind wine tasting was held in Paris. At the time, it was inconceivable to most international wine critics that a California wine could beat—or even match—the quality of French wines [details, intriguing].

Because it was "blind," the judges didn't know what they were tasting. The scores were tallied [tension builds]. To everyone's shock, a bottle of the Stag's Leap Wine Cellars 1973 Cabernet Sauvignon from Napa won the first prize [surprise, twist].

Some of the judges couldn't believe it. They were furious. They thought they had been tricked. They demanded to see their scorecards [conflict]. The event may have been buried and lost to history if it had not been for a *Time* magazine reporter in attendance [twist]. George Taber was the only journalist to show up for the contest because "everyone knew French wines were going to win, so why bother?" At one point, a French judge—a famous chef—tasted a white and said, "Ah, back to France!" The judge didn't know it, but he was sipping a Napa Valley chardonnay. Taber knew and realized the story would shock the wine world. Taber wrote a short story about the shocking results. The event—known as The Judgment of Paris—brought international recognition to the winery, its pioneers, and Napa Valley, helping it attain its status as a world-class wine region [empathetic characters and a full story with a beginning, middle, and happy ending].

The story can be delivered in about 60 seconds. One of the challenges with storytelling is keeping the audience's attention without putting them to sleep with a long, ponderous story. Details are vital, but it takes practice and feedback to keep your stories compelling and brief.

Stag's Leap Wine Cellars trains its team members to tell the story. The company also redesigned its tasting room as a visual complement to the story. The room has a story wall with key dates, bottles of the award-winning wine, the actual scorecards from the Paris tasting, and the *Time* magazine article, among other items. Clearly, not every story will have a room to go with it. If you're telling a story in a presentation, simply include photos or videos to complement the narrative.

A signature story will help you, your product, and your brand stand out. It's a differentiator because no two brands share the same story. What's yours?

Five-Star Principles:

- Persuasion cannot occur in the absence of Pathos, an appeal to the audience's emotion.
- Stories are the best linguistic tool we have to build Pathos because humans are wired for it.
- There are three types of stories you can use in your next pitch or presentation: (1) stories about personal experiences, (2) stories about customers, clients, or other people, and (3) signature stories about your brand or company.

11

THE THREE-ACT STORYTELLING STRUCTURE

*The great storytellers have an unfair
competitive advantage.*

—BILL GURLEY, venture capitalist

Brian had lost 20 pounds. He survived on ramen noodles and dry cereal. Brian's mother urged her son to buy milk. He said he'd struggle through it because someday "It'll make a better story." He was right. Today Brian Chesky is the CEO of Airbnb, the apartment-sharing company that is worth $30 billion. Chesky and his co-founders pioneered the sharing economy. Chesky is also a storyteller who uses the power of narrative as a competitive advantage.

Author Brad Stone calls Airbnb an upstart: a newly successful person or company that bucks the established way of doing things. Stone has covered the tech industry for 20 years. He believes today's upstarts have a critical skill that separates them from the previous generation of entrepreneurs—they can tell better stories.

I spoke to Stone upon release of his book *The Upstarts: How Uber, Airbnb, and the Killer Companies of the New Silicon Valley Are Changing the World*. Stone argues that Chesky, like many of today's successful startup founders, is not like the "awkward and introverted" entrepreneurs Stone has covered in years past. "They are extroverted storytellers, capable of positioning their companies in the context of dramatic progress for humanity and recruiting not only armies of engineers but drivers, hosts, lobbyists, and lawmakers to their cause."[1]

The market is changing and so are the skills that are in demand. According to Stone, "In the past, tech companies were able—to a large degree—to ignore the world around them, other than their customers, of course. They certainly didn't have to engage in the political process for many years."[2] Stone reminds us that nonstop controversy followed startups like Airbnb and Uber in their early years, and they continue to do battle with cities, regulators, and customers today. "They [upstarts] had to be politicians very early on," says Stone.

In addition to challenging the regulatory market in their host cities, Airbnb had to overcome a major stumbling block—one that continues to place hurdles on its growth in some countries: trust. "They [Uber, Airbnb] were asking us to do something our parents told us never to do . . . get into a stranger's car or stay in a stranger's home," says Stone.[3] "They had to persuade people to be comfortable with something that felt unnatural."

Brian Chesky uses a proven storytelling method to build trust. He follows a structure that almost all successful Hollywood movies share: the three-act structure.

Screenwriting expert Syd Field popularized the structure in his 1979 book, *Screenplay: The Foundations of Screenwriting*. Directors James Cameron, Judd Apatow, and many others have used Field's book, which is considered the bible of screenwriting. A writer for *Saturday Night Live* was struggling with a screenplay and had gone through, in her words, "a million drafts." She picked up Field's book and struck gold by following the formula. Tina Fey's 2004 comedy *Mean Girls* went on to make more than $130 million.

Field didn't make up the model. He analyzed hundreds of successful movies and noted that they all follow a dramatic structure, one that our friend Aristotle first identified. According to Field, "To tell a story, you have to set up your characters, introduce the dramatic premise (what the story is about) and the dramatic situation (the circumstances surrounding the action), create obstacles for your characters to confront and overcome, then resolve the story."[4] Best of all, says Field, building a story is a craft that can be learned and applied to any storytelling platform, including business.

Technology enhances the way movies are made, how they look, and how they're delivered to your home or theater, but technology alone cannot fix a bad script. The art of storytelling remains constant. The same principle applies to communication in the workplace. You can design slides with advanced presentation tools, speak face-to-face with colleagues thousands of miles away, hold a webinar and invite people to watch from anywhere in the world, or give a presentation in San Jose, California, and appear as a hologram in India (I saw it happen at a Cisco Systems presentation). But, as in Hollywood, technology alone cannot fix a bad script.

According to Syd Field, great stories use the following structure, a paradigm that's also consistent with great business presentations[5]:

The Three-Act Storytelling Structure

	Act I	Act II	Act III
	The Set-up	The Confrontation	The Resolution
Hollywood screenplay	The characters are introduced and we learn about the hero's world before the adventure starts.	The hero's world is turned upside down and we learn about obstacles the hero must overcome.	The problem is solved. The hero's world is transformed and everyone lives happily ever after.
Business presentation	The status quo is described, the current state of the company or industry.	Obstacles are outlined and solutions to overcome them are discussed.	The company's product, service, or strategy solves the problem and the company or industry thrives.

Hollywood producers are enamored of the three-act structure and they will turn to specific pages of a script to see how the acts play out. The script for a standard two-hour movie runs about 110 pages. The first 10 pages set up the film. Act two begins around page 25, and act three starts around page 85 and runs through the end. The structure doesn't stifle creativity; it gives you the freedom to be more creative. After all, we've been using it since humans began telling stories and drawing on cave walls. A structure simply makes a narrative easier to follow and more satisfying, and still allows plenty of room to surprise, delight, and inspire.

Screenwriter Blake Snyder took the three-act structure one step further, demonstrating that all winning movies are made up of "beats" within the acts, 15 beats in total. These 15 sequences keep the story moving and give the narrative its emotional resonance. A beat is a unit of storytelling. For our purpose, it's not necessary to dissect every beat. A great business presentation follows the three-act structure and hits at least two critical beats: *the catalyst* and *all is lost*.

In Snyder's beat process, *the catalyst* appears near the end of act one and triggers the hero's adventure. This is the point at which the hero decides that the status quo cannot continue. It's when Luke Skywalker discovers that his family has been killed in *Star Wars* and decides to join the Resistance. It's when Elle Woods's boyfriend breaks up with her at dinner in *Legally Blonde*. It's when Moana decides to sail the seas in search of a solution to the curse that has caused problems on her island. *The catalyst* sets up the break into act two.

Within act two, there's a scene when *all seems lost*. It appears around page 75 of a well-written screenplay. The hero's life is bleak and a satisfying conclusion seems unlikely. In *Star Wars*, the walls are literally closing in on Luke Skywalker and the others as the trash masher is about to end their lives. Thankfully, R2-D2 shuts down the compactor and Luke, Leia, Han Solo, and Chewbacca are free to fight another day.

Most romantic comedies follow the structure to the letter: boy meets girl, boy loses girl, boy and girl are reunited after a madcap chase and live happily ever after. It's no coincidence that Richard Curtis, the screenwriter who brought us *Notting Hill*, also brought us *Four Weddings and a Funeral*, *Bridget Jones's Diary*, and *Love Actually*. He's mastered the structure, as have most successful screenwriters.

Joseph Campbell's 1949 book *The Hero with a Thousand Faces* "is perhaps the closest any theorist has come to a universal formula for storytelling," writes Derek Thompson in *Hit Makers: The Science of Popularity in the Age of Distraction*.[6] "Campbell reached back thousands of years to show that, since before human beings could write, we have been telling the same heroic story over and over," writes Thompson.

In Campbell's theory, the universal myth is nearly identical in every epic heroic story: a hero goes on a journey, survives key trials, and emerges better than before—the hero is transformed. "It is the story of *Harry Potter* and Luke Skywalker, Moses and Muhammed, Neo in *The Matrix* and Frodo in *The Lord of the Rings*," writes Thompson. Ultimately, the Hero's Journey inspires us because we see ourselves in the hero's flaws, courage, and transformation. The hero's setbacks and successes provide the suspense and keep the audience alert. If the hero is relatable, their journey becomes our journey and we're inspired by their conquest.

Let's return to the art of business communication. An "inspiring" leader is, by definition, a storyteller who tells tales of heroes and epic adventures. Brian Chesky is one such storyteller; he consistently tells Airbnb's story using the three-act structure.

Airbnb and the Three-Act Structure

Act I: The set-up

Two friends share an apartment in San Francisco and struggle to pay rent. Brian and Joe put three air mattresses on the floor and rent them out for $80 each. The two entrepreneurs decide to make a business of it. They hire a former roommate (Nathan) to design a simple website called airbedandbreakfast.com. The three friends launch their startup at the popular South by Southwest conference. Far from being a huge success out of the gate, they only get two bookings.

Catalyst: The Democratic National Convention comes to town and it sparks an idea. The co-founders repackage cereal and design novelty boxes: *Obama O's* and *Cap'n McCains*. They charge $40 a box and raise $30,000. It's enough money to keep the adventure going.

Act II: The conflict

The co-founders are running short on cash. All seems lost. When Chesky reaches this scene in his public presentations, he builds up the tension. "I would wake up in a panic. Everyone thought it was crazy. No one supported us. We had no money. It was the best weight-loss program ever. I lost 20 pounds. I didn't have any money for food. I would wake up in the morning with my heart pounding. During the course of the day I would convince myself that everything would work out. I went to bed at night really confident. Like a reset button, I would be jolted out of bed with my heart pounding."[7]

Chesky reminds audiences that many people were skeptical of the service in its early years. And they regret it. According to Chesky, "Twenty investors had been introduced to Airbnb. Any one of them could have owned 20 percent of the company for $100,000. Fifteen of them didn't even reply to my e-mail. I met with one investor at a cafe. In the middle of drinking his smoothie, he got up, left, and I've never seen him again."

Act III: The resolution

Just when all hope seems lost, Airbnb seeks admission to Y Combinator, the highly selective Silicon Valley accelerator that provides seed funding and coaching for startups. It is Chesky's last-ditch effort, but in another all-is-lost moment, Chesky misses the deadline to apply. The tension rises. "If we didn't get in, we would not exist," Chesky's co-founder Joe Gebbia says in his presentations. But at the last minute they manage to apply late and are invited to interview. The tension rises again. Y Combinator founder Paul Graham is initially skeptical. "People actually do this?" he asks the founders. "I wouldn't want to stay on anyone else's sofa." The tension breaks when Graham decides to jump on board. He figures that anyone who could convince people to pay $40 for a $2 box of cereal is worth taking a chance on.

Thanks to Y Combinator's $20,000 investment and its coaching, Airbnb bookings begin growing steadily, soaring 40 to 50 percent a month. Investors like Andreessen Horowitz, Sequoia Capital, and celebrity Ashton Kutcher come knocking. By 2014, Airbnb reaches a value of $10 billion. Within six years of renting air mattresses on the floor, Brian, Joe, and Nathan are each worth $1.5 billion. Today Airbnb is valued at $30 billion and worth more than any hotel chain in the world. Set-up, conflict, resolution, and 30 billion reasons to live happily ever after.

Airbnb did not create the sharing economy, but by building trust between homeowners and renters it provided the fuel for the market to grow. "Both Uber and Airbnb had to create trust where suspicion existed," Brad Stone told me.[8] Without trust, argues Stone, companies like Airbnb and Uber would not exist. Most people did not feel comfortable sleeping in a complete stranger's bed, and many still don't. Airbnb continues to fight restrictive zoning laws, entrenched businesses, and unions. Establishing a trusted brand is Chesky's secret weapon and storytelling is the tool to build that weapon.

"I've covered tech for twenty years. I've interviewed people like Mark Zuckerberg and the Google founders early in their careers. They didn't have to be good storytellers because their businesses spread virally and their products stood for themselves," Stone told me. "Uber and Airbnb are different. These companies required a different kind of CEO—a good storyteller who could charismatically rally customers to their cause."

With each product launch and public presentation, Chesky puts on a master class in storytelling.

In March 2017, Airbnb introduced "Trips," a service that allows its customers to book tours and experiences. Truffle hunting in Tuscany, exploring the best surf spots in Southern California, or checking out Havana's music scene with an award-winning vocalist are all examples of experiences.

Stealing a page from Hollywood, the ads for the new service were designed to look like movie posters. "Great travel is a lot like the characters' experience in great movies," Chesky told an audience gathered at the historic Orpheum Theatre in Los Angeles.[9] He explained that the new service was inspired by mythologist Joseph Campbell's Hero's Journey. According to Chesky, "A character starts in their ordinary world. They cross the threshold—think Wizard of Oz—to this new magical world, where they meet people . . . They have a moment of transformation and they return to the ordinary world." As the Airbnb team explored the Hero's Journey, a lightbulb went off: "Sharing homes and rooms is only one small part of a great travel journey. People remember the magic of an experience."

In his keynote presentation, Chesky took the audience on his own journey, telling personal stories to explain the *why* of the product before revealing *how* the service worked. "I want you to think back to your earliest memories. Think about the first big trip you ever took," Brian Chesky began.[10] "I remember mine. I was raised in Niskayuna, New York, a small town outside of Albany. The first trip we ever took was to Saint Louis. To get there, you've got to fly. It was the first time I was in an airplane. It was totally magical."

Jeff Jordan, the former CEO of Open Table and a partner at Andreessen Horowitz, serves on Airbnb's board of directors. In an interview for *Business Insider*, Jordan said his experience with Airbnb's founders has convinced him that there's one skill every entrepreneur needs. "Every great founder can really tell a great story," he said.[11] "If a founder doesn't have it, it's harder to get funding, attract employees, or get attention."

Chesky is the right CEO for the times and the times reward great story-tellers.

Why does the three-act structure work? Why does it build trust and create deeper relationships between people? Neuroscientists have found a possible answer. And it all starts with the love molecule.

Releasing the Love Molecule

One hundred and forty-five college students walked into a lab in 2009 to watch a short video. "Ben's dying," a father says into the camera. Ben—his two-year-old son—is playing in the background. Ben has a brain tumor and doesn't know it's taking his life. It's a sad story and it's true. Half of the participants in the study saw the two-minute video. The other half watched a different video. Ben's father narrates that video, too, but there's no mention of the boy's illness. Instead of showing the child in a hospital, the video shows father and son at a zoo.

The participants were asked a series of questions to gauge their emotional reaction to the videos they had just seen. Before they left, the students were asked if they'd like to make a small donation to a children's cancer charity. They didn't have to give, but if they chose to donate it would be taken from the small fee they were paid to take part in the study. There was one more detail to this study. Blood samples were taken from each of the participants before and after the videos, first to test for baseline levels of oxytocin, the neuromodulator that increases social bonds and builds trusts, and then to see how it rose in response to the two different stories.

The study, conducted by Paul Zak and Jorge Barraza at Claremont Graduate University, reached three important conclusions that improve our understanding of persuasion.[12] First, the emotional video about the dying boy increased oxytocin levels in participants' blood plasma by 47 percent over the "neutral" video of the parent and child at the zoo. Second, there was a strong correlation between the degree of empathy the participants said they experienced and the change in oxytocin in their bloodstream. Third, those who were more empathetic donated more money to the charity. A lot more. The Zak and Barraza experiment was the first to show direct evidence that emotional videos and stories trigger a release of oxytocin. Zak calls oxytocin the "love molecule" because of its social bonding properties. His research shows just show powerful the bond can get and exactly what triggers it.

Zak has subsequently conducted several major studies on oxytocin and generosity, and he has begun to theorize about the kinds of stories likely to produce the effect. He explains that the story of father and son at the zoo had a flat structure, with no narrative tension. Participants were not sure what they were supposed to learn, if anything. Most lost interest within a minute. The story about Ben's illness has a dramatic arc. It has dramatic tension, conflict, and a resolution by the father that he will choose to be happy and positive in front of his son. According to Zak, the emotional story is better at "sustaining attention and causing empathetic transportation." In further experiments, Zak administered synthetic oxytocin intranasally (through the nose so it would reach the brain faster). The participants in those studies donated 56 percent more money to charities than those in the placebo group.

Zak's conclusion is that some stories are better than others. Stories with an emotional trigger alter our brain chemistry, which makes us more trusting and open to new ideas.

McKinsey's Three-Act Presentation Structure

As we learned in chapter 7, McKinsey is the most selective consulting firm on the planet. It's a launchpad for aspiring leaders. One survey found that more than 70 past and present Fortune 500 CEOs have come from McKinsey's ranks. McKinsey has been nicknamed the "CEO factory" for good reason. When I attended a McKinsey meeting overseas, the regional head told the 700 people assembled in the room that 50 of them would go on to become CEOs.

The coveted consulting powerhouse receives more than 200,000 applications a year and accepts just 1 percent, making McKinsey more selective than Harvard or Stanford business schools. Those who are accepted usually have an MBA or advanced degree from a top university, but those are the minimum qualifications. They must also demonstrate emotional resonance and strong interpersonal communication skills. Clients pay McKinsey millions of dollars in fees to identify and analyze problems and to present solutions to those problems in a way that's easy to understand, digest, and act upon. McKinsey's main asset is trust. If they lose a client's trust, they lose the business. Great storytellers build trust.

McKinsey's leaders understand the power of storytelling to win new business and build deeper relationships with current clients. They teach new consultants a method of storytelling that's nearly identical to the three-act structure followed by Hollywood screenwriters. The McKinsey storytelling structure goes by the acronym SCR. It stands for: situation, complication, and resolution.[13]

In a McKinsey presentation, the situation is, essentially, a set-up. It describes the current state of the client's business. The complication is just that—the challenge the client faces now or will face in the future. The resolution is McKinsey's answer to the problem and a happy ending.

Although McKinsey consultants use PowerPoint to present a proposal, they are taught to start with the three-part structure to refine their thinking and to take the client along on a journey. PowerPoint is the method of transmission, but the story comes first. The hook to a play, a great movie, or a business always starts with the story.

Storytelling Hooks Your Audience

A great story hooks your audience the same way a great pop song hooks its listeners. In the world of pop music, the bliss point, the lines and beats that turn a song into a hit, is called the "hook." A handful of writer-producers have mastered the winning formula and are responsible for most of the ear candy we have stuck in our heads.

If you've ever hummed Backstreet Boys' "I Want It That Way," Britney Spears's "Baby One More Time," or Taylor Swift's "Shake It Off," then you can thank (or blame) Swedish producer Max Martin. Martin has more top 10 singles than Madonna, Elvis, or The Beatles. According to John Seabrook in *The Song Machine*, "Ninety percent of the revenues in the record business come from ten percent of the songs," and most of the 10 percent are written by Martin and a handful of others.[14]

Martin's songs are irresistible because they follow a structure Seabrook calls "track-and-hook." A producer starts the process by laying down some tracks—chords, beats, instruments. The producer then sends the track to "hook writers" who add the earworms, the short melodies that get stuck in your head.

The hooks follow a structure. Seabrook calls it melodic math. Max Martin's collaboration with Katy Perry is a great example of how this formula turns songs into hits. For example, many of the lines in Perry's hit albums have two parts and each half has the same number of syllables. In "Chained to the Rhythm," Perry sings: "Turn it up, it's your fav-rite song/Dance, dance, dance to the dis-tor-tion." The way Perry sings it, each half has eight syllables.

Some readers might be thinking that it's too formulaic. Well, formulas are followed because they work. People like to hear things that sound something like what they've heard before—in music and conversation. The journalist Derek Thompson reveals in his book *Hit Makers* why some pieces of art, music, or design catch on. Hit makers, he argues, marry the new with the old. In the psychology of aesthetics, there is a name for the moment between the anxiety of confronting something new and the satisfying click of understanding it. It is called an "aesthetic aha." Popular music and great speeches both exploit this with rhythm and repetition.

For example, if I ask you to recite one line from John F. Kennedy's inauguration speech—considered one of the best speeches of the twentieth century—what might you remember? I'd be willing to bet your answer is: "Ask not what your country can do for you; ask what you can do for your country."

The line resonates because it's a speech hook. It's an earworm. Each half of the sentence is a mirror image of the other. Kennedy relied on a popular speech method called antithesis—juxtaposing two opposing ideas in the same sentence while keeping the number of syllables roughly in balance. He also used another speech formula, popular in poetry, called alliteration: "Whether it wishes us well or ill." There are 21 instances of alliteration in Kennedy's inauguration speech.

What line do you remember from Martin Luther King Jr.'s famous speech on the steps of the Lincoln Memorial? You would probably answer: "I have a dream . . ." The sequence of sentences that begin with "I have a dream . . ." is an example of anaphora, a popular rhetorical device where successive sentences begin with the same word or phrase. These structures give speech their rhythm.

Writers and speakers often stick to a structure because it works. "The architecture of the human mind is ancient, and the most basic human needs—to belong, to escape, to aspire, to understand, to be understood—are eternal," writes Thompson.[15] Stories are irresistible because the brain is hardwired for narrative. If your audiences are wired for a three-act narrative, give it to them. If you want people to pay attention to you, wrap your idea in a story. The story provides the bliss point, the moment your audience falls in love. Even hardened investors are enamored of story.

Pitch competitions are growing in popularity around the world, but the most famous pitch event of all airs once a week on ABC: *Shark Tank*. In the show, five investors watch entrepreneurs pitch their products or ideas and then the moguls decide to invest or not. The money the investors put up is their own. In 2016, a human behavior expert ran a massive experiment on 495 pitches from the show's first seven seasons. The deals were almost evenly split: 253 entrepreneurs won deals and 242 did not. The difference between the two, according to Vanessa Van Edwards, is that captivating entrepreneurs included "conversational sparks" in their pitches. A spark is often a story. Fifty-eight percent of successful pitches had a story. About 30 percent of successful pitches specifically followed the three-act Hero's Journey.

"Everyone loves a good story," says Van Edwards.[16] "Some kind of captivating narrative—an experience or personal anecdote—told by the entrepreneur provides context and interest and, done well, can humanize your pitch. Try framing your personal story as a Hero's Journey—a time-tested formula in which you were inspired to try something difficult, struggled for a while, and then finally succeeded."

The billionaire investor Vinod Khosla once told me, "Facts alone are not enough. You have to do storytelling." Stories educate, entertain, inspire, build trust, and ultimately fire up our collective imagination. Tell great ones and structure them well.

Five-Star Principles:

- Follow the classic three-act storytelling formula in your next pitch or presentation: set-up, conflict, and resolution. It's a formula as old as storytelling itself, and it works.

- Keep your audience in suspense (and alert) by including some hurdles the hero must overcome before they successfully accomplish the mission.
- Trigger a release of oxytocin in the brains of your listeners by telling stories with a dramatic arc that includes tension, struggle, and a happy ending.

12

DELIVER THE BIG PICTURE

You have five seconds to grab my attention.

—GEOFF RALSTON, investor, Y Combinator

A hit movie or TV show starts with a winning logline. No logline, no deal. The logline is one sentence that sells the idea. In Hollywood pitch meetings, everybody listens for one; everyone comes prepared with one. It's the hook. A good one reels people in, and they'll want to see the rest of the script. Here are some famous loglines that went from pitch meeting to blockbuster:

- The aging patriarch of an organized crime dynasty transfers control of his clandestine empire to his reluctant son.—*The Godfather*
- A male nurse meets his girlfriend's parents before proposing, but her suspicious father is every date's worst nightmare.—*Meet the Parents*
- An undercover police officer has to track down and arrest the fugitives responsible for stealing electronics from a semi-truck, but has a hard time turning them in because he falls in love with one of them.—*The Fast and the Furious*

In as few words as possible, a winning logline conveys the main character, the character's goals, and a conflict. You might be able to guess the title of this next movie from one of the greatest loglines ever written:

- A police chief, with a phobia for open water, battles a gigantic shark with an appetite for swimmers and boat captains, in spite of a greedy town council who demands that the beach stay open.—*Jaws*

It's a well-established fact in Hollywood that most scripts—95 percent—are terrible or, at best, just decent. About 4 percent are good, while 1 percent or less are considered good to truly great. And a great logline is often an indication of something great.

Loglines are effective because they deliver what the brain craves—the big picture. According to University of Washington biologist John Medina, the human brain doesn't record every detail of an event. It's better at seeing patterns and gleaning the general meaning of an experience—the gist of it. Medina likes to use the analogy of our primitive ancestors running into a tiger. In that encounter our ancestors did not ask, *"How many teeth does the tiger have?"* Instead, they asked, *"Will it eat me? Should I run?"* And they had to make a decision in a split second. We remember the emotional components of an experience and the big picture. Great persuaders use this knowledge about our evolutionary heritage to create messages that grab our attention.

Don't Cram All You Know on One Slide

During the week of TED's annual conference in 2017, I had the opportunity to speak directly to some of that year's most prominent speakers. One professor, Adam Alter, is *The New York Times* bestselling author of *Irresistible*, a book that tracks the rise of addictive technologies: smartphones, video games, apps. Alter is a social psychologist and an associate professor of marketing at the Stern School of Business at New York University. Although Alter's book runs 80,000 words, he was asked to deliver a TED talk that ran no longer than nine minutes. To make it more difficult, the book is chock-full of compelling stories and detailed explanations of the neuroscience behind behavioral addiction.

Alter told me that if he really wanted to flesh out the major concepts in the book, he'd have to create a 90-minute presentation. Clearly, that was unacceptable at TED. Fortunately, as a lecturer and psychologist, Alter knew how to handle his dilemma. "The one thing you want to do is avoid cramming everything you know in a presentation," he told me.[1] "And you can't condense your ideas and jam them into a nine-minute presentation."

Alter's strategy was to focus on one idea and one idea only. The rest of the presentation would support the one idea with stories, examples, and data. It's an approach that sounds easy in theory but is hard to apply. "Each idea is like a child," says Alter. "You want to keep all your children in the talk, but ultimately you've got to pick favorites. *Your instinct is to hold on to as many ideas as you can, but it's a mistake*" (italics mine).

Alter settled on one key message that actually makes up a very small section of his book: stopping cues. According to Alter, "One of the major reasons we can't stop using technology today is that tech companies have erased our stopping cue, a signal that you should move on to something new."

TED conference organizers give similar instructions to all their speakers: pick one idea and make it as clear, concrete, and vivid as possible. TED curator Chris Anderson says many talks and presentations are meandering and have no clear direction. Anderson suggests that speakers spend time developing the overall theme, the narrative arc. Instead of a "logline," Anderson calls it the "throughline." "Think of the throughline as a strong cord or rope, onto which you will attach all the elements that are part of the idea you're building," writes Anderson.[2]

Alter wasn't completely thrown off by the exercise. He first realized the power of focusing on the one thing while working at a law firm before his career as a university professor. The common wisdom among lawyers at the time was to bombard a judge with multiple arguments. If an attorney had 12 ways to argue a particular point, they'd walk the judge through all 12, hoping one would stick. People who study persuasion in the legal field found that presenting too many arguments and giving each one equal weight dilutes the force of each idea. It made all of them sound less convincing.

The successful advocates concentrated their fire. In clear and brief language, they presented a judge with their one strongest argument followed by the evidence to support the point. "The greatest mistake a lawyer can make in briefing or oral argument is to keep the court in the dark as to what the case is about until after a lengthy discussion," said Judge Luke M. McAmis.[3] "Always start with a statement of the main issue before fully stating the facts."

A VC's Five-Second Rule

Whether you're selling an idea to Hollywood producers, delivering an argument to a judge, or making a pitch to investors, the logline rules. Geoff Ralston, partner at the iconic investment firm Y Combinator, puts it succinctly: "If a story is too complicated, it doesn't stick. The simpler a story is, the easier it is for us to join that narrative."[4]

Ralston says you have five seconds to grab someone's attention. Every investor in a pitch meeting has a smartphone and will begin checking e-mails as soon as they've checked out of your presentation. "You will lose them really fast. You need a hook," says Ralston. "The best hook for a startup is a very quick way of articulating *why* what you do matters. This is how our brains work. The simpler the concept, the easier it is for us to fit it into your world."

Geoff Ralston gives you five seconds to make an impression. He's not alone. Neuroscientists who study first impressions say we really do form impressions about a speaker very quickly, in as little as 5 to 15 seconds.

Researchers use a common expression—"snap judgments"—to describe this phenomenon, and it makes sense. Some studies have found that students will form an impression of a teacher within two seconds of meeting that teacher—and the snap judgment lasts throughout the semester. Research into business presentations has found that audiences will often give a speaker a little more time, but not much. Several comprehensive studies have shown people will make up their minds about a speaker's message within 7 to 15 seconds of beginning to watch a pitch or presentation.

Snap judgments are the brain's way of evaluating whether a person is a friend or a foe. Like it or not, we're stuck with these quick assessments. In a business setting, the first several seconds of an encounter might not activate our flight-or-fight response, but we will make a snap decision on whether or not we'd like to hear more. Don't give your audience an excuse to tune out. Create an irresistible logline to keep them hooked.

Five-Star Principles:

- Great presentations have one theme. Everything else supports that key message.
- Think of your next pitch or presentation as the logline to a Hollywood movie. If you had one sentence and one sentence only to pitch your idea, what would you say?
- Introduce your one big idea within 15 seconds of starting your presentation.

13

SMART WORDS MAKE THE GRADE

He has never been known to use a word that might send
a reader to the dictionary.

—WILLIAM FAULKNER, Nobel Prize–winning author,
on Ernest Hemingway

Three minutes after takeoff from New York's LaGuardia Airport, U.S. Airways flight 1549 struck a flock of geese. Passengers heard the thud and saw the engines catch fire. The plane lost all engine power. After weighing his options, Captain "Sully" Sullenberger decided to make an unpowered landing into the river. Sully gave the following instruction over the cabin's public address system, the only words the passengers would hear: "This is the captain. Brace for impact."

Brace for impact: three words that triggered the flight attendants into action. They instructed the passengers on how to prepare for the sudden landing. All 155 people on board survived the Miracle on the Hudson.

"Brace for impact" is a perfect sentence. In three words it triggers hundreds of hours of training, which can save lives. The sentence contains no adverbs, no passive voice, and there's no alternative sentence that's easier to read. In fact, it can be understood by the average second-grader.

About 60 seconds before addressing the passengers, Sully told the control tower he had an emergency: "Mayday. Mayday. Mayday." Mayday is the universal distress signal for ships and aircraft. Pilots are taught that a short word repeated three times leaves no room for miscommunication. When ground operators suggested it might be possible for Sully to turn back toward LaGuardia or a nearby airport, Sully responded: "Unable. We're gonna be in the Hudson." Simple. Direct. No room for misunderstanding.

"Simplicity is one of the most deceptive concepts on earth," writes Ken Segall, who led some of Apple's iconic marketing campaigns and put the lower case "i" in the iMac.[1] Simple words and phrases, argues Segall, are "the most potent weapon in business—attracting customers, motivating employees, outthinking competitors, and creating new efficiencies. Yet rarely is it as simple as it looks. Simplicity takes work."

Segall's former boss, Steve Jobs, agreed with him. "Simple can be harder than complex," Jobs once said. "But it's worth it in the end because once you get there, you can move mountains."

Stanford biology professor Robert Sapolsky is one of the world's leading neuroscientists. He studies the biology of humans at their best and at their worst. Oliver Sacks, the famed neuroscientist whom actor Robin Williams played in the movie *Awakenings*, called Sapolsky "one of the best scientist-writers of our time."

At TED 2017, Sapolsky was asked to present one big idea from his new book, *Behave*. In the book, Sapolsky explores the biology of violence and aggression through the lens of several scientific disciplines: neuroscience, anthropology, psychology, genetics, evolutionary biology, political science, and communication theory. It's a hefty book that runs 800 pages.

Within minutes of walking off the iconic red circle that's become synonymous with TED and leaving the stage, Sapolsky spoke to me about how he simplifies complex information. Deciding on just one topic, as we covered in the previous chapter, is the first step to building a simple, engaging presentation. In order to condense 800 pages into a 14-minute presentation, Sapolsky took the same advice he gives to his graduate students. Before presenting their research, Sapolsky asks them for one paragraph that describes the key discovery. He then asks them to distill it again, this time to one sentence. One short sentence speaks volumes. Short words do, too.

Explain Ideas in Grade-School Language

You may recall the health insurance company in chapter 6 that wrote its material using words a third-grader could read. The lesson is worth expanding on here because so few companies, instructors, leaders, and entrepreneurs pay attention to the grade level of the words they use. Big words aren't better; they're confusing.

If you want your ideas to catch people's attention, the Readability Index is a must-have tool. It's a reliable algorithm that textbook publishers in the United States use to evaluate the grade level of content. A book written in twelfth-grade language might be appropriate for high school seniors, but too confusing for students in lower grades. Studies have shown the average American reads and understands content best when it is written at a tenth-grade level, or slightly lower.

Before you throw up your hands in protest, keep in mind that as reading levels climb, clarity can suffer. For example, this chapter is readable by the average eighth-grade student. Eighth-grade readability is considered a good score. Higher scores do not necessarily mean that the writing is better. If I wrote long, convoluted sentences and packed each paragraph with scientific jargon, this chapter would have a much higher score because of its density. It might make me feel smarter, but it wouldn't help the average reader. As it turns out, when famed neurobiologist Robert Sapolsky is speaking to a general audience, he uses seventh-grade words.

I inserted the text from Sapolsky's academic papers into a popular tool for measuring readability. The app is called Hemingway, named after the author whose prose often scored as "low" as the fifth grade, despite his adult audience. Sapolsky's papers generated an average readability of 16—post-graduate level. And his TED talk? It generated a readability level of grade seven. An analysis of the 2,400 words that made up his TED presentation found 18 percent of his sentences were "very hard to read." In Sapolsky's academic papers, 83 percent were very hard to read.

Sapolsky is one of the smartest neurobiologists on the planet today, but when he wants to reach the greatest number of people, he uses simple, short words so the greatest number of people will understand.

A Famous Twentieth-Century Speech That's
Four Minutes Shorter Than a TED Talk

In chapter 1, we talked about John F. Kennedy and how the power of his words inspired a generation to look to the moon. One of the reasons why JFK's words continue to resonate today is because Kennedy was a good editor.

On a visit to the John F. Kennedy library in Boston, I was struck by the large number of edits Kennedy had made to the inaugural speech now on display in the museum. The speech, delivered on January 20, 1961, was the fourth shortest inaugural address in presidential history. And JFK wanted it that way. "I don't want people to think I'm a windbag," Kennedy told his speechwriter, Ted Sorensen. "Make it short." Think about it. Kennedy's speech was 13 minutes and 42 seconds. One of the greatest speeches in American history is four minutes shorter than a TED talk.

Sorensen had worked closely with Kennedy for years and understood how best to articulate his ideas. But despite Sorensen's gorgeous prose, Kennedy made *31* changes in the last few hours, and most were aimed at streamlining the language. You can see the edits in red. Until the last minute Kennedy was crossing out phrases, replacing long words with short ones, and eliminating entire sentences. For example, Kennedy crossed out the following sentence: "The world is very different now, empowered as it is to banish all form of human poverty and all form of human life." Kennedy removed the words "empowered" and "banish" and wrote a simpler, stronger sentence that sounds better to the ear: "For man holds in his mortal hands the power to abolish all form of human poverty and all form of human life."

The most famous line even went through edits. Kennedy crossed out "will" and replaced it with "can." He cut out three words, too. The sentence finally read: "Ask not what your country can do for you—ask what you can do for your country." As noted above, while the concept is profound, the sentence is made up of short words that a fourth-grader could read.

Another famous sentence tests at a third-grade readability level because it's made up of mostly one-syllable words: "We shall pay any price, bear any burden, meet any hardship, support any friend, oppose any foe . . ."

Imagine if Kennedy had been speaking in the language of contemporary politics. He might have said, "We should consider the effort to be worth any cost or encumbrance associated with the initiative . . ." If he had, we would not have remembered the speech. Fewer, shorter words are more memorable.

Kennedy studied two speechmakers to sharpen his writing skills: Abraham Lincoln and Winston Churchill. Lincoln, as we learned earlier, was a master storyteller. It's said that crowds of villagers from far and wide would flock to his events when he was running for president. Great orators stir the soul, and Lincoln was one of the best.

Lincoln, of course, is also known for writing one of the most famous short speeches in history—the Gettysburg Address. Kennedy and Sorensen analyzed the speech and concluded that Lincoln used the fewest words possible to get his idea across. He chose one-syllable words when there were two- and three-syllable alternatives available. In other words, Lincoln made the speech simple to deliver, hear, and understand. And he kept it short. The orator Edward Everett spoke for two hours before Lincoln took the stage to dedicate a military cemetery in Gettysburg, Pennsylvania, during the Civil War. Lincoln only required two minutes to read his 272-word speech. When Lincoln ended and put the notes back into his pocket, no one said a word. They stood transfixed, awestruck at how a speaker could articulate America's values in so short a time. For a few seconds Lincoln thought the audience didn't like it. Then they broke into applause. On YouTube, you'll find hundreds of thousands of videos showing students in America and around the world reciting the speech. Lincoln could never have foreseen the introduction of streaming video, but he did appreciate the magnitude of the event. When it came time to make sure his ideas would be recalled by future generations, he kept his words short and succinct.

Churchill is also known for replacing long words with short ones. "Short words are best," he once said. "The shorter words of a language are usually the most ancient."

After the Royal Air Force staged an impressive victory in the Battle of Britain, Churchill, referring to the actions of British pilots, wrote:

"Never in the field of human conflict has so much been owed by so many to so few." *So much, so many, so few.* In six words, Churchill spoke volumes about heroism and sacrifice.

In his groundbreaking book, *Thinking, Fast and Slow,* Nobel Prize–winning psychologist Daniel Kahneman writes, "If you care about being thought credible and intelligent, do not use complex language where simpler language will do."[2] Effective leaders speak in simple language.

It's good to celebrate inspiring leaders. Their stories bring out the best in us. John F. Kennedy once said, "A person may die. Nations may rise and fall, but an idea lives on." True, but convoluted ideas will never live on because they don't catch on. Great communicators are great editors and JFK, Winston Churchill, and Abraham Lincoln were among the best.

If you're having trouble condensing your words, try scientist Neil deGrasse Tyson's method. The astrophysicist uses an old-fashioned tool to help him write for a general audience: quill and ink. Tyson says he likes to write by candlelight, dipping a quill pen into an inkwell. It's almost like he's channeling the brilliant thinkers who came before him, who wrote their works using the tools of the day. But beyond the metaphysical, there's a practical point to Tyson's method. "If you look at memorable speeches of the past, the rhythms happen to be in five- to seven-word pulses. Then you learn that a single dip of a quill got you five or seven words. It may be that the rhythm was shaped by how much ink could sit in the shaft of a quill pen. As I write, I'm conscious of this. When you give a speech you don't want your sentences to be too long."[3]

Sell Your Idea in 10 Minutes

Selling your idea in 10 minutes is a valuable career skill. While I was writing this book, I visited an elite class of military officers who spend 13 months training on the most sensitive national security issues of our time. My books *Talk Like TED* and *The Storyteller's Secret* are required reading in the class because crafting and delivering a compelling presentation is a key skill they have to learn. To be effective, they must learn to sell their ideas with emotion and in a concise amount of time . . . 10 minutes or less.

"Why only 10 minutes?" I asked one of the instructors.

"The generals, leaders, and lawmakers these officers will be presenting to have a cascade of information coming at them from all directions. They need information fast. They don't have the time to pore through hundreds of pages of documents or endless PowerPoint slides. Our officers will be expected to analyze a potential threat, develop a short presentation, deliver three possible plans of action, and make an argument for the best one, in their opinion. Condensing the argument into 10 minutes makes it tighter, stronger, and easier for the listener to absorb."

In general, people seem to like 10-minute pitches. I met an executive at Intel who told me about one of his first meetings with legendary CEO Andy Grove.

"How long is this presentation?" Grove asked the speaker.

"Twenty minutes."

"Give me the 10-minute version," Grove responded.

The executive must have left a good impression because he grew within the company, but he never forgot the fear he felt when he had to cut down his presentation on the spot.

An unusual pitch competition is held at Richard Branson's home on Necker Island, his private island in the British Virgin Islands. It's called The Extreme Tech Challenge. It begins months earlier as 2,000 entrepreneurs enter the competition. Among the entries, 10 finalists are chosen to pitch their startup ideas on stage at the giant CES conference in Las Vegas. The top three are invited to pitch to Branson and a panel of judges at Necker Island. You might think the tropical breeze would put participants at ease, but it's an intense competition for the finalists, who might get an investment and support from the billionaire entrepreneur.

Each speaker is given 10 minutes to pitch their idea. One finalist—and eventual winner—once told me that a coherent value proposition must be made clearly and quickly. "You must clearly explain why you're making the product, what problem it solves, and why Branson should want to join the journey. If it's not crystal clear in ten minutes, you've lost your audience."

What's so special about 10 minutes? University of Washington biologist John Medina has one of the best answers. In his book *Brain Rules*, Medina observes that in a class of medium interest (not too exciting and not too boring), most students will mentally tune out at exactly 10 minutes.

According to Medina, peer-reviewed studies confirm that people tune out of a presentation before the first quarter hour is over. "The brain seems to be making choices according to some stubborn timing pattern, undoubtedly influenced by both culture and gene. This fact suggests a teaching and business imperative: Find a way to arouse and then hold somebody's attention for a specific period of time."[4]

The Intel manager, the winner of Branson's pitch competition, and the military officers in training all remind us that the art of selling your idea in 10 minutes or less is a real career advantage. If you have 20 or 30 minutes for a presentation, that's fine. But get to the point in the first 10 minutes before your listener's mind begins to wander.

Let's put this in perspective. Abraham Lincoln inspired generations in a speech that lasted two minutes. John F. Kennedy took 15 minutes to shoot for the moon. Martin Luther King Jr. articulated his dream of racial unity in 17 minutes. Steve Jobs gave one of the most famous college commencement speeches of our time at Stanford University in 15 minutes. If you can't sell your idea or your dream in 10 to 15 minutes, keep editing until you can.

Ideas don't sell themselves. Be selective about the words you use. If they don't advance the story, remove them. Condense, simplify, and speak as briefly as possible. Have the courage to speak in grade-school language. Far from weakening your argument, these tips will elevate your ideas, making it more likely you'll be heard.

Five-Star Principles:

- Download text readability software like the Hemingway app. These are mobile or desktop tools that use reliable algorithms that judge the grade level of your text. They'll show you the lowest education level required to read and understand whatever piece of writing you tell the software to analyze. If you have too much jargon, it will result in a higher grade level. Simpler words and phrases—which we're aiming for—will return lower grade levels. Remember, in this case lower means better.

- Edit your work, edit again, and edit some more. JFK had one of the world's great speechwriters by his side and yet still improved his work by editing and then reediting. Great communicators make their work look effortless because they put a lot of effort into making it work.

- Keep in mind that your audience will tune out after approximately 10 minutes. Some neuroscientific studies have found that attention spans last a bit longer, but not much . . . up to 15 minutes. There seems to be a built-in evolutionary reason for people to check out after a particular period of time. Put simply, the brain gets bored. Get to the point and get there quickly.

14

HOW TO GIVE YOUR IDEAS "VERBAL BEAUTY"

The computer is a bicycle for our minds.

—STEVE JOBS

In 1967, a 37-year-old stock market investor and self-made millionaire accompanied his wife to hear a charismatic preacher. Fifty years later, the investor—Warren Buffett, now the richest man in the world—still remembers the exact words that "took me out of my seat." When Dr. Martin Luther King Jr. quoted the poet James Russell Lowell near the end of his speech, it changed Buffett's life. King said, "Truth forever on the scaffold, wrong forever on the throne. Yet that scaffold sways the future."[1]

On that day Buffett heard "one of the most inspiring" speeches of his life, one that sparked his interest in civil rights and, later, philanthropy. Around the time that Buffett saw King speak in person, the civil rights leader had been using the poetic line in speeches that ran upward of 7,500 words in length. But it was the analogy of the scaffold and throne that Buffett remembered and could still recite 50 years later. Why? Once again, Aristotle provided us with the answer more than 2,000 years ago, and, once again, modern science proves that he was right.

In *Rhetoric*, Aristotle observes that the most persuasive individuals pepper their speech with metaphors and analogies. He says these rhetorical devices energize listeners and move them to action. They make language sweet and bring about clarity. They "make learning pleasant," according to Aristotle. Metaphors, he says, have "qualities of the exotic and the fascinating" and provide an idea's "verbal beauty."

A brief lesson on verbal beauty. "Analogy" is the broad umbrella term for a comparison of two different things to show how they're similar. It forces the listener to think differently about an idea. In everyday language, there are several forms of analogies. Metaphor is one of them. A metaphor is a literary device through which we describe one thing in terms of another, replacing the meaning of one word with another. For example, when William Shakespeare wrote, "Juliet is the sun," he was using a metaphor. Juliet isn't really the sun, but in four words we learn a lot about her. Juliet is a bright light in Romeo's world and the center of his universe. Romeo speaks those words at the balcony at night, but Juliet's radiance transforms the darkness. Shakespeare was good at this stuff.

"In many arguments, whoever has the best analogy wins," writes John Pollack, a former speechwriter for American president Bill Clinton.[2] "Evidence suggest that people who tend to overlook or underestimate analogy's influence often find themselves struggling to make their arguments or achieve their goals. The converse is also true. Those who construct the clearest, most resonant and apt analogies are usually the most successful in reaching the outcomes they seek."

As we learned earlier, Warren Buffett is a strong proponent of improving one's public-speaking skills. He says it instantly boosts a person's value by 50 percent. Buffett was captivated by the speaking ability of Martin Luther King Jr. and adopted one of King's most powerful linguistic devices to stir people's emotion—the analogy.

In May 2017, more than 40,000 Berkshire Hathaway shareholders descended on Omaha, Nebraska, to watch Buffett and his longtime partner, Charlie Munger, hold court. According to a *Fortune* magazine reporter who attended the event, "What is most remarkable about the annual meeting is the way Buffett and Munger distill their responses to complex, technical questions into eloquent and pithy nuggets of wisdom that even novice investors can understand."[3]

Buffett uses analogies to make the complex, simple. Analogies are repeatable because they help us understand material we know little about. By comparing the abstract with the familiar, analogies give us a framework to explain and to understand complex topics.

In the HBO documentary *Becoming Warren Buffett*, Buffett's expertise at using analogies is on frequent display. In one instance, Buffett cites a book by baseball legend Ted Williams called *The Science of Hitting*. Williams divided the strike zone into squares. "If he waited for the pitch that was really in his sweet spot, he would bat .400," explained Buffett.[4] "If he had to swing at something on the lower corner, he would probably bat .235. The trick in investing is to watch pitch after pitch go by and wait for the one right in your sweet spot." In other words, only invest in companies in your "circle of competence," the sweet spot where an opportunity meets domain knowledge.

Buffett is especially fond of medieval analogies. He looks for companies that are like "an economic castle" with a strong moat that prevents competitors from taking the castle. Buffett takes the analogy one step further, placing a knight—a strong leader—as the head of the castle. "In capitalism, people are going to try to take that castle from you so you want a moat around it and you want a knight in that castle who is pretty darn good at warding off marauders."[5]

Buffett made yet another analogy in the documentary, comparing his early investment strategy to a cigar butt. He would look for a company that was like "a discarded cigar butt and had one more smoke in it." Buffett said the goal was to buy the company at the right time to take advantage of the last smoke.

According to *The Financial Times*, Buffett can "barely get through a sentence" without using an analogy or metaphor. "Even when Mr. Buffett is talking about something as complex, impersonal and abstract as finance, they allow him to make it sound simple, human and concrete."[6]

Mastering the ancient art of persuasion requires an understanding of the art and science of analogy. Persuasion cannot exist in the absence of analogy. Analogies force people out of conventional thinking. When an idea or a concept is truly different from what's come before, unconventional thinking is required to sell to it. "Analogies work because they make the unfamiliar familiar," writes Pollack.[7] "They help the mind navigate new terrain by making it resemble terrain we already know."

Analogy Is the "Fabric of Our Mental Life"

When Doug Hofstadter's daughter was about two years old she said she wanted to "undress" a banana. She didn't know the verb—peel—so her brain connected the experience to something she did know—undressing a doll. Hofstadter paid attention to the girl's comment because nobody has studied analogy more than he has. "Analogy is the key mechanism for all our thinking," he said.[8] "It is the fabric of our mental life."

Hofstadter is a Pulitzer Prize–winning cognitive scientist. He disputes the common perception that artificial intelligence gives computers human-like intelligence. If a computer crashes and goes to the trash heap in the sky, we don't miss it. When a person dies, we miss her terribly. In a beautiful passage from his award-winning book, Hofstadter writes, "In the wake of a human being's death, what survives is a set of afterglows, some brighter and some dimmer, in the collective brains of those who were dearest to them . . . Though the primary brain has been eclipsed, there is, in those who remain . . . a collective corona that still glows."[9]

The difference between a human and a computer, argues Hofstader, is analogy. Humans are wired to process the world through analogy, which is a very different way of thinking than that of artificially created cognitive systems.

How many times has this happened—you tell someone about an experience and the other person responds, "The same thing happened to me!" They tell you about their incident and it has nothing to do with yours. Although it may seem as though they're trying to tell a better story than you, their brain is simply trying to find an analogous situation to categorize the event that happened to you. The human brain is always on a quest to save energy. Analogies are efficient. They help us make sense of a concept while conserving brain power.

We make analogies all day. Most are small comparisons like the banana peel, while others change the world. "Analogies lie at the very center of human cognition, from the humblest of everyday activities to the most exalted discoveries of science," writes Hofstadter.[10]

In the field of physics, a famous analogy has become known as the Ship and the Tower. In 1624, the astronomer Galileo Galilei conducted experiments to disprove the popular belief that the Sun revolved around the Earth. Galileo's critics said if the Earth was moving, a rock dropped from a tower would not land at the base of the tower, as it always did. The rock would fall away from the tower. Galileo used a simple analogy to prove them wrong. He dropped a rock from the mast of a moving ship. The rock landed at the base of the mast. Tower is to Earth as mast is to ship. The analogy would turn out to be true, of course, but it didn't sit well with others. Galileo was found guilty of heresy and spent the rest of his life under house arrest.

Galileo's analogy worked too well. In the seventeenth century, standing out often meant a death sentence. In the twenty-first century, standing out puts you on the map. Standing out is essential to thriving in a rapidly changing world.

The Analogy That Put LinkedIn on the Map

In 2004, LinkedIn co-founder Reid Hoffman went on a search for a $10 million round of funding. At the time, the social gaming site Friendster boasted 10.5 million users, and MySpace had 2 million users. Hoffman's company—LinkedIn—had only 900,000 users, no market leadership, and not a dime in revenue. Hoffman couldn't tell a data story because the data was weak, but he could pitch a concept story. The concept revolved around a core analogy, as he later related.

"If we had framed LinkedIn as only a 'jobs/classifieds' website, most smart venture capitalists would not have invested," Hoffman said in a blog post deconstructing LinkedIn's original pitch.[11] "Most technology revolutions are founded on one or two simple concepts. Our simple concept was: The network provides the platform for a new kind of people search, which can be a platform to many other businesses."

The idea may have sounded simple, but Hoffman would have to persuade investors that moving from directories to networks would produce real value. He needed an analogy, and that's exactly what Hoffman showed on slide number five of his presentation.

The slide had two company logos. On the left, Hoffman had placed an image of a newspaper that had put its classified ads online. The ads were a failure. On the right, a photo of eBay, a red-hot success. Hoffman told investors, "eBay has a network. It has reputation. It has transactional histories. Adding a network to online classifieds made it valuable."[12]

Hoffman's comparison worked and LinkedIn became the leading professional-networking site in the world. In 2016, it would, at $26 billion, become the biggest acquisition in Microsoft's history.

Now a billionaire, Hoffman is a partner at Greylock Partners, where he urges entrepreneurs to use the very same strategy that put LinkedIn on the map—pitch by analogy. He says that investors don't have a lot of time and entrepreneurs don't often have a lot to show. Connect your idea to a company that investors already understand.

Greylock Partners see 5,000 pitches a year. They decide to take a closer look at no more than 800. They'll invest in two deals a year, or 0.04 percent of the year's pitches. What makes an investor stand out? For starters, if Greylock's investors don't understand the long-term implications of an entrepreneur's idea, there is zero chance that entrepreneur will be among the winners. Analogies increase the likelihood an entrepreneur will make it to the winner's circle.

Pope Francis and Drinking Gin on an Empty Stomach

In his surprise appearance at TED 2017, Pope Francis made an analogy that generated more than 6,000 shares on Twitter and appeared in more than 1,000 headlines: "Power is like drinking gin on an empty stomach," Pope Francis said.[13] "You feel dizzy, you get drunk, you lose your balance, and you will end up hurting yourself and those around you, if you don't connect your power with humility and tenderness."

Pope Francis relies on analogy in nearly every speech. "For Mother Teresa, mercy was the salt which gave flavor to her work," he once said. The church, he often says, is like a "field hospital" that works on the margins of society and goes in search of "the wounded."

In a major paper on marriage and the family, Pope Francis cited the Psalms and wrote: "Your children are as the shoots of an olive tree."[14] He makes comparisons between Earth and family. "Our common home

[Earth] is like a sister with whom we share our life and a beautiful mother who opens her arms to embrace us. This sister now cries out to us because of the harm we have inflicted on her . . . She pleads, cries out . . . our common home is falling into serious disrepair. The Earth, our home, is beginning to look more and more like an immense pile of filth."

Pope Francis credits his writing and speaking style to a Jesuit training in homiletics (the art of preaching). Today he advises young seminarians to build their skills as speakers. Using a series of analogies to describe the importance of speaking, he says evangelism is to be "animated by the fire of the spirit" to "inflame the hearts of the faithful."

Entrepreneurship is replete with the metaphorical language used in the Bible. Entrepreneurs are said to be *evangelists* on a *mission* to create *believers*. Investors look for entrepreneurs who have *passion* and a *fire in the belly*. Great communicators *inspire* audiences (in religious terms, "inspire" means to be infused with the spirit).

It's no coincidence that startups rely on the same analogies as spiritual leaders. Faith is knowing something is real, even if you don't see it. Investors need a lot of faith to put their money behind an entrepreneur who has little to show beyond an idea. How the idea is framed could mean all the difference. And nobody could frame an idea better than the master of metaphor, Steve Jobs.

The Master of Metaphor

Speechwriter John Pollack, whom we met earlier in this chapter, calls Steve Jobs the master analogist. Pollack argues that Jobs's obsession with user-friendly design was "fundamentally analogical." For example, in 1983, few people outside of that Xerox research facility had heard of the term "graphical user interface." Jobs didn't call it that, either, at least when speaking to a non-techie. Instead he described it as a computer's desktop. Documents could be organized in folders, which you could move on the desk or throw away in the trash can. Jobs had to make the unfamiliar approachable. He had to make the complex simple. He had to make the abstract tangible. Analogy was his winning ticket.

Jobs once read a study in *Scientific American* that measured the energy required for different species to move a particular distance. Oxford

University engineering instructor S. S. Wilson wrote the 11-page article in 1973. The condor was the most efficient; humans came in about one-third of the way down the list, far behind the horse but ahead of a salmon or a bee. But put a human on a bicycle and it blew past everything, making humans the most energy-efficient species. Jobs later used the comparison to describe the core of his business: "What a computer is to me is the most remarkable tool that we've ever come up with. It's the equivalent of a bicycle for our minds."[15]

Jobs explained ideas using many figures of speech, but chief among them were analogy and metaphor. "We want to make a product like the first telephone. We want to make mass-market appliances," Jobs said about the first Macintosh in 1984. He explained the analogy further by explaining that, in 1844, most predicted that the telegraph would be in every home in America. It didn't happen because the majority of people couldn't learn to use it. The sequence of Morse code (dots and dashes) was simply too daunting. Alexander Graham Bell's telephone was much simpler. Jobs challenged the Macintosh team to make the first "telephone of the computer industry," a computer easy enough for the average person to learn, use, and enjoy.

Jobs was once asked why he created conflict and tension among his teams. Jobs answered in, what else, a metaphor:

> When I was a kid, there was a widowed man who lived up the street. I got to know him a little bit. One day he invited me into the garage and pulled out a dusty old rock tumbler. It had a motor and a can. We got some old, ugly rocks from the backyard. We put them in the can with a little liquid and powder and turned the motor on. I came back the next day and we took out these amazingly, beautiful polished rocks. The same common stones that had gone in, through rubbing against each other, creating a little friction, a little noise, had come out beautiful, polished rocks. That's my metaphor for a team working hard on something they're passionate about. It's through the team of incredibly talented people bumping up against each, having arguments, having fights sometimes, making some noise. Working together, they polish their ideas and what comes out are these really beautiful stones.

"To be a master of metaphor is the greatest thing by far . . . it is also a sign of genius," Aristotle once wrote. Average communicators deliver straightforward prose. The verbal genius uses analogies to stand apart.

Five-Star Principles:

- Analogies and metaphors give your language its "verbal beauty."
- Start keeping an eye out for analogies and metaphors. You'll find them everywhere.
- To find ideas, read Warren Buffett's annual newsletter and John Pollack's book, *Shortcut: How Analogies Reveal Connections, Spark Innovation, and Sell Our Greatest Ideas.*

15

LEONARDO, PICASSO, AND YOU

It's rare that a fresh idea comes up out of nowhere.
More often we put together disparate ideas that
nobody has put together.

—JAMES PATTERSON

On a visit to an aquarium at Six Flags Marine World in 1992, Andrew, a young writer/director, began thinking about how cool it might be to capture an undersea world in computer animation. It was an intriguing project, he thought, but it didn't come full circle until five years later. Andrew was taking his son to the park and realized he was being an overprotective dad. "Don't touch that, don't go there, put that down," he recalls saying to his son. Suddenly, both experiences came together to create magic.

Andrew called a pitch meeting together. He had an idea for a movie about fish, but not just any fish. This fish tale would strike an emotional chord. For one hour, Andrew mesmerized his colleagues by telling a story about a dad who undertakes an epic journey to find his abducted son. It was the story about a struggle—a child searching for independence and a parent struggling to retain control. Andrew's passionate pitch was contagious because it was based on an intensely personal experience. He used the ocean as a metaphor for life—an exciting, intriguing place with risks and uncertainties. Andrew outlined the entire narrative and voiced the characters.

Andrew ended the pitch and the room went silent. Andrew's boss— John Lasseter—brought the house down when he simply said, "You had me at the word 'fish.'" Andrew Stanton got the green light to write and direct *Finding Nemo*. The Pixar movie went on to become the highest-grossing animated film (at that time).

Pixar president Ed Catmull recalled Stanton's pitch in his book, *Creativity, Inc.* Catmull called the pitch "a tour de force . . . nothing short of magnificent."

Four Simple Mind Hacks to Spark Original Ideas

Ideas that are communicated in unique and unusual ways grab people's attention and inspire them to look at the world differently. But before you can pitch an original idea, you need to have a novel idea. Thanks to neuroscience, we know more than ever about history's most prolific idea creators. Their lessons can help each of us unleash our best ideas.

1. Connect ideas from everywhere

The billionaire founder of Oracle, Larry Ellison, was best friends with Steve Jobs for 25 years. "He was brilliant," Ellison recalled after Jobs died. "He was our Edison. He was our Picasso."

Ellison's comparison makes sense—Edison, Picasso, and Jobs were inventors and innovators. "Picasso is an appropriate metaphor for Steve Jobs because he was innovative in many ways, one of which was his ability to look at reality in a different way. He looked at the language of art in a different way," says Dr. Enrique Mallen, director of the online Picasso Project at Sam Houston State University.[1] "Picasso could have taken the conventional approach of his time and he could have done it well for the rest of his life, but, like Jobs, he tried to change things."

I contacted Dr. Mallen because he is one of the leading authorities on Pablo Picasso. His online project represents the most detailed catalog of Picasso's life and work. Specifically, I wanted to know why Ellison chose to compare Jobs to Picasso and why Steve Jobs himself was fond of one of Picasso's most famous quotes: "Good artists copy; great artists steal."

According to Mallen, "to copy" is to do something exactly like somebody else. A good painter can copy another work or style, but it doesn't qualify as an innovation. Picasso and Jobs were innovators because they didn't copy; they searched for the best ideas from outside their fields or experiences to create innovations the world had never seen.

For example, Picasso's famous 1907 painting *Les Demoiselles d'Avignon (The Young Ladies of Avignon)* and Steve Jobs's Macintosh are both examples of "stealing" ideas to create something entirely new. They represented radical departures from the status quo.

Picasso's oil painting created a scandal in the art world because it violated the "rules" of art on several levels. First, Picasso's depiction of prostitutes as characters was not an "appropriate" subject at the time. Second, Picasso blended two influences on the same canvas, which represented a radical departure from the status quo. Search for a photo of the painting on the Internet and you'll see two types of faces on the subjects. The three women on the left are painted using ancient Iberian style (outlined eyes, large ears, noses in profile) and the two women on the right are influenced by an African style characterized by colorful mask-like features. By applying two techniques and two styles to the same canvas, Picasso challenged the status quo and, in doing so, set the stage for an entirely new form of art—cubism.

Fast-forward to 1984, and we find Steve Jobs applying the very same creative process to revolutionize another field—computing. Interestingly, Jobs, too, was influenced by art. He took a calligraphy course at Reed College for no reason other than the fact that he enjoyed it. In 1971 calligraphy had no practical application to his life, but years later he would blend the two influences—computers and art—into one product, one canvas.

"Reed College at that time offered perhaps the best calligraphy instruction in the country," Jobs told Stanford graduates in 2005.[2] "I learned about serif and sans serif typefaces, about varying the amount of space between different letter combinations, about what makes great typography great. It was beautiful, historical, artistically subtle in a way that science can't capture, and I found it fascinating . . . Ten years later, when we were designing the first Macintosh computer, it all came back to me. And we designed it all into the Mac. It was the first computer with beautiful typography."

Jobs was creative precisely because he opened himself up to new experiences—studying calligraphy and Zen Buddhism, visiting an ashram in India, strolling the kitchen appliance section at Macy's (the Apple II was modeled after a Cuisinart), or copying the Ritz-Carlton's steps of service in the Apple Store (though the Genius Bar dispenses advice, not alcohol). Jobs experienced the world and built on those experiences to improve upon what has been done. Creativity, said Jobs, "comes down to exposing yourself to the best things that humans have done and then try to bring those things in to what you're doing."[3]

When Jobs said he was "shameless about stealing great ideas," he meant it in the Picasso context. Anyone can copy a competitor. True innovation occurs when you build on the ideas that came before you.

"Steve Jobs taught me about 'zooming,' looking beyond the boundaries of the industry you're in," says former Apple CEO John Sculley.[4] "Steve was a designer at heart. He loved calligraphy. It made a huge impression on him. Then he went to Xerox to see what they were working on. He saw experimental work-stations that used the first graphical user interface and connected the dots."

Sculley calls it "zooming" or "connecting the dots." You might know it as an "epiphany" or a "shower moment." Your best ideas don't always show up when you want them to. They don't always arrive on your schedule or while you're staring at a computer screen. Fortunately, we know how original ideas are formed, where they come from, and when they're delivered in our mental mailbox.

One of the most talked-about slides in corporate history first appeared in 2011 during Steve Jobs's launch of the iPad 2. The slide showed the intersection of two street signs. One sign read "Technology." The other sign read "Liberal Arts." Jobs said that technology alone was not enough to build great products. It's the intersection—the marriage—of technology and liberal arts that made his "heart sing." Jobs's biographer, Walter Isaacson, brought up the slide in his book about another creative genius, Leonard da Vinci.

"Today we live in a world that encourages specialization, whether we are students, scholars, workers or professionals. We also tend to exalt training in technology and engineering, believing that the jobs of the future will go to those who can code and build rather than those who can be creative,"[5] Isaacson writes. The innovators of the future, argues Isaacson, are those who, like Leonardo and Jobs, study the art of science and the science of art.

More than 7,000 pages of Leonardo's extensive notes still exist. They teach us that Leonardo was relentlessly curious about the world. He let his mind wander across arts, sciences, engineering, and the humanities. He didn't distinguish between science and art. History's most creative genius become a genius because he saw that everything connects. And so Leonardo saw himself as a scientist, engineer, artist, inventor, anatomist, philosopher, painter, and storyteller. Leonardo studied math and developed a system to measure size, space, and perspective. He studied the scientific properties of light. In Florence, he studied the art of painting under the masters of his day. He connected these ideas to create the *Mona Lisa* and *The Last Supper*.

Leonardo is considered history's greatest genius because he connected different fields to arrive at novel ideas. When Andrew Stanton connected several ideas from his personal experiences to create *Finding Nemo*, he was simply following in the footsteps of the ancient artists. And you can, too.

In 2015, a group of researchers in Austria and Denmark performed a remarkable experiment. They discovered that when people were too familiar with a specific domain, it blocked their creativity, because they stopped looking outside of their area of expertise for ideas. The researchers interviewed hundreds of roofers, carpenters, and in-line skaters. The three categories were chosen because—while they are completely different fields—they share an analogous problem: encouraging the use of safety gear to prevent injuries. Roofers use safety belts, carpenters use safety masks, and in-line skaters use knee and elbow protectors.

The researchers conducted 306 interviews. The participants were asked for their best ideas on the following topic: improving safety gear for the market they are experts in and for the other two categories. A panel of safety gear experts evaluated the responses. The findings were extraordinary: the more distant the field, the more novel the solution the participants came up with. In other words, members of each group were better at coming up with an innovative solution for a field other than their own.

The experiment gives us insight into the minds of creative geniuses. They're not geniuses because they are smarter; they are geniuses because they're open to connecting ideas from different fields. When asked what made the Macintosh a revolutionary computer, Steve Jobs answered: "Part of what made the Macintosh great was that the people working on it were musicians, poets, and artists, and zoologists and historians." They also happened to know computer science, Jobs added. Jobs's goal wasn't to be average. His goal was to be great. And greatness, he said, comes from connecting ideas.

2. Find your theme song

While I was writing my first book on Steve Jobs and his presentation skills, I used a background track. Since Jobs was a fan of Bob Dylan, I played Dylan music to inspire me. It put me in a creative state of mind. But if you had to choose just one music style to do your best writing, thinking, and creating, what would it be? Speechwriters and scientists have weighed in on the topic. The answer: film scores. It makes sense. Bono, the singer for U2, once said that a great melody is like a great idea; both are instantly memorable. All great presentations should begin with the written word, words that ebb and flow like a satisfying melody. Great communicators don't open a PowerPoint and randomly insert photos or type out bullet points. They think about what they want to say and how they want to say it. A memorable presentation builds like a great movie—it has tension, conflict, and a rousing ending.

Since a presentation tells a story with heroes and villains, why not listen to a style of music that complements heroic stories on the big screen? Ronald Reagan's speechwriter Peggy Noonan is a fan of listening to film scores as background music. In an article titled "Music in the Key of America," Noonan talks about the scores that remind her of America and its values. Noonan says Leonard Bernstein's score for *On the Waterfront* is "dramatic, crashing, tender . . . it reminds me of the importance of everyday human endeavor—that even if you think you're just a beat-up nobody, a former contender with a one-way ticket to Palookaville, you can find within yourself a nobility you never guessed was there."[6] That's a lot of insight from a piece of music.

In a documentary about film scores, aptly titled *Score*, psychology professor Dr. Siu-Lan Tan says movie soundtracks trigger many structures of the brain simultaneously. Melody and pitch are processed by one system in the brain, tempo and rhythm are processed in other parts of the brain. She says certain kinds of music trigger neurochemicals in the reward centers of the brain—the ventral striatum and nucleus accumbens. In non-scientific language, the music makes you feel good.

Movie music can evoke a range of emotions. It can make you cry (*Schindler's List*), run into battle (*Braveheart*), or just run (*Rocky*). Film scores and public speaking sometimes combine to make magic. In *Score*, composer Trevor Rabin recalls the night Barack Obama accepted the Democratic Party's nomination in Chicago. Rabin's music from *Remember the Titans* was growing louder and louder as Obama finished his speech and waved to the crowd. The audience was delirious with joy, many were crying and cheering. Words, music, and emotion were connected that evening. "If it gives me goose bumps, it's pretty likely it will give other people goose bumps," Rabin said.[7] It sure did.

Film scores drive narrative. Movies wouldn't be the same without them. Perhaps listening to scores will infuse your next presentation with a little movie magic. It's worth a try. The worst that can happen is you'll feel like taking on the world.

3. Read more books to become a better speaker

Retired U.S. Navy admiral James Stavridis has 4,000 books in his home library. On one side of his business card his title reads: Dean, Fletcher School of Law and Diplomacy, Tufts University. On the other side is his favorite quote by Thomas Jefferson: "I cannot live without books."

Stavridis spent more than 37 years in active service in the U.S. Navy, commanding destroyers and a carrier strike group in combat. He spent four years as the allied supreme commander at NATO and has written books that are required reading at the U.S. Naval Academy. His love of books runs deep. I caught up with Stavridis to talk about his book *The Leader's Bookshelf*. "A personal bookshelf is critical to developing the ability to inspire others in the pursuit of worthy goals," he told me.[8] In our conversation, Stavridis offered three reasons why books help leaders become more effective, clear, and inspiring communicators.

THERE ARE VERY FEW PROBLEMS THAT ARE NEW CHALLENGES

"Almost always you can reach back in history (fiction, memoirs, biographies) and find a problem that is similar to the problem you face today," he says. As Stavridis prepared to take command of a navy destroyer 20 years ago, he read the 20 classic sea novels of Patrick O'Brian. As he followed Captain Jack Aubrey's experiences in *Master and Commander,* Stavridis challenged himself and asked, *What would I do in that situation?*

READING ENHANCES A LEADER'S ABILITY TO CREATE POWERFUL, EMOTIONAL RHETORIC TO GALVANIZE A TEAM

Communication, says Stavridis, is at the heart of any leader's suite of tools. The one book that's always on his desk is an anthology of great speeches. "When I'm locked up on a communication idea, I'll read an oration by Socrates, Churchill, FDR, or John F. Kennedy. Reading those speeches will unlock your own rhetoric," Stavridis says. "Leadership is creating an idea and convincing others that it matters and that it will solve a challenge. To do that you have to communicate the challenge, why it matters and a coherent way to address it."

READING GOOD, CRISP, WELL-WRITTEN PROSE MAKES YOU A BETTER WRITER

"Over time, I became a reasonably good writer because I was an inveterate reader as a child," says Stavridis. "It's very hard to teach someone to write, but by reading you become a better writer. Good leaders must be good communicators, and the hard work of writing is best sharpened on the whetstone of reading."

Admiral Stavridis isn't the only great leader who's a voracious reader, of course. While the average American spends 19 minutes a day reading, billionaire Warren Buffett spends 80 percent of his office time—about six hours—reading newspapers, magazines, and books. Elon Musk is a prodigious reader, at times going through two books in one day. Bill Gates reads about 50 books a year. Billionaire Mark Cuban reads three hours a day, while Mark Zuckerberg reads a book every two weeks. Yes, success leaves clues.

In 2009, researchers at Carnegie Mellon were the first scientists to discover that reading actually rewires the brain, especially in children, whose brain tissue is in the process of forming.[9] Writing in the journal *Neuron*, the scientists found that reading increased the quality of white matter, the brain tissue that carries signals between areas of gray matter, where information is processed. By improving the "integrity" of the white matter, children are able to communicate better and express their ideas with more eloquence. Although the research was conducted on 8- to 10-year-olds, recent research into brain plasticity has shown that our brains can form new connections even through adulthood. It seems as though reading books will keep your mind young and your communication skills sharp.

4. Take a trip to the unfamiliar

Just as Steve Jobs came up with his best ideas while studying products outside of his field, Lin-Manuel Miranda came up with his best idea 3,800 miles away from Broadway. "It's no accident that the best idea I've ever had in my life—perhaps maybe the best one I'll ever have in my life— came to me on vacation," Miranda told Arianna Huffington.[10] "The moment my brain got a moment's rest, *Hamilton* walked into it."

Miranda and his wife had taken a vacation to Playa del Carmen, Mexico. Miranda, another voracious reader, dropped into a bookstore and found an 800-page biography of Alexander Hamilton. As he relaxed next to the hotel's pool, he opened the book and started reading. By the second chapter, he was thinking about who might play George Washington in the musical.

These lightbulb moments don't surprise Emory University neuroscientist Gregory Berns. "To see things differently than other people, the most effective solution is to bombard the brain with things it has never encountered before. Novelty releases the perceptual process from the shackles of past experiences and forces the brain to make new judgments," Berns writes in his book *Iconoclast*.[11]

According to Berns, epiphanies rarely occur in familiar places. A simple change in environment is usually effective, he says. Traveling to another country entirely is even more effective, particularly when its physical makeup and culture are radically different from your own. "When confronted with places never seen before, the brain must create new categories. It is in this process that the brain jumbles around old ideas with new images to create new syntheses . . . The key to seeing like an iconoclast is to look at things that you have never seen before. Breakthroughs in perception do not come from simply staring at an object and thinking harder about it. Breakthroughs come from a perceptual system that is confronted with something that it doesn't know how to interpret. Unfamiliarity forces the brain to discard its usual categories of perception and create new ones. Sometimes the brain needs a kick start."[12]

"In order to have a eureka breakthrough, you have to be deeply immersed in a problem. But then you have to let go of it," writes Olivia Fox Cabane in *The Net and the Butterfly*.[13] According to Cabane, neuroscience has recently discovered the secret to triggering original ideas. Breakthroughs happen when the ancient brain switches between two modes: the executive network and the default network.

Using a clever analogy, Cabane describes the default network as a council of geniuses inside your brain, talking and exchanging ideas. It's the source of creativity. The executive network is focused on accomplishing specific tasks. Consider it the front office. When the front office takes a break, it goes to the genius lounge, where it can brainstorm with geniuses in a relaxed setting. It's where you'll see "Leonardo da Vinci sitting in a corner doodling on his sketch pad. Napoleon playing with toy soldiers . . . and Steve Jobs telling Einstein he's not thinking big enough."[14] To put it simply, the brain's executive network walks into the genius lounge and defines the goal—we need a hit! Then it takes a break and takes a walk while the geniuses go to work.

A common theme throughout this book is that ideas don't sell themselves. But sometimes we need a little help to trigger those novel ideas in the first place. When it comes to creativity, Leonardo, Picasso, and Jobs are good friends to have. Call on them when you need a spark.

Five-Star Principles:

- A person cannot *will* an original idea into existence. It must be *allowed* to appear by creating the ideal conditions for epiphanies.

- Kick-start your brain by connecting ideas from different fields, listening to film scores, reading books, or taking a walk. Better yet, do it while on a trip to a totally new location.
- When planning a presentation to deliver your original ideas, don't start with the slides. Put yourself in a creative space and think through the elements of the narrative before creating slides or documents. Remember, people aren't moved by slides; they're moved by the emotional components of your story.

16

CONQUER THE FEAR THAT HOLDS YOU BACK

*It is not possible to foster iconoclastic thinking
when fear is pervasive.*

—GREGORY BERNS, neuroscientist

A world-famous pastor who captivates audiences at sold-out stadiums once admitted that in his first year as a minister, his hands would shake as he approached the lectern. His palms would sweat and his heart would race. He had severe stage fright. The minister told me that when he overheard a critical comment about his speaking, he would focus on it and replay it over and over in his head.

How did you get over it? I asked him.

"I started speaking to myself in a more positive way. Instead of tearing myself down, I built myself up," he said.

The minister also began to practice. He rehearsed for hours and hours ahead of every sermon. The latest neuroscience research concludes that the preacher intuitively did two things right—reappraisal and rehearsal.

Reappraisal: Changing the Channel

The minister told me he overcame the fear of public speaking by "changing the internal channel." Instead of focusing on what had gone wrong—or the negative comments he overheard—he focused on what he did right and how people were moved by his message.

The minister was engaging in what psychologists and neuroscientists call "cognitive reappraisal." According to neuroscientist Gregory Berns, "cognitive reappraisal is the act of reinterpreting emotional information in such a way that the emotional component is diminished."[1]

Berns and others have found that "reappraisal" inhibits the amygdala, the source of the fight-or-flight response in our brains (which elevates our heart rate when speaking in public). Reframe your internal thoughts and you'll tame the amygdala.

Berns's observation has been validated by many scholarly research experiments in the last few years. In a paper titled "Rethinking Feelings: An fMRI Study of the Cognitive Regulation of Emotions," researchers at Columbia University conclude: "We can change the way we feel by changing the way we think, thereby lessening the emotional consequences of an otherwise distressing experience."[2]

Reframing the way we think about external events is nothing new, of course.

This observation has been made throughout history. From Marcus Aurelius to William Shakespeare, great leaders and great writers have always known that while we can't control events that happen to us, we can choose how to interpret those events and experiences. As Shakespeare wrote in *Hamlet*, "There is nothing either good or bad, but thinking makes it so."

Dr. Sian Beilock is a psychology professor at the Human Performance Lab at the University of Chicago. She wrote the book *Choke* to explain why some people stumble when the pressure is on while others thrive. She tested people in high-pressure situations, including sports, test taking, and public speaking.

Part of the reason why many people choke when the stakes are high is because we put added stress on ourselves, stress we can remove *if we choose*. For example, Beilock says people are more likely to bomb a presentation "when worries and self-doubt flood the brain."[3] It's very hard to function at peak performance when you're worried about what people will think. "Anticipation of an event, and specifically anticipation of others judging you, is enough to put pressure on before you have even arrived at the performance stage."

Reappraisal stops the cycle cold.

According to Beilock, "The prefrontal cortex is also the seat of our ability to reappraise a situation or event. Reappraisal is one of the main cognitive tools we use to reflect on what others do and change our own emotional responses accordingly."[4]

Rehearsal: Training Under Pressure

In addition to reappraisal, Beilock recommends "pressure training" to overcome nerves and stress. This works for athletes as well as business professionals preparing for a public-speaking opportunity. "Even practicing under mild levels of stress can prevent you from choking when high levels of stress come around," Beilock writes.[5]

An example of mild stress would be gathering a few friends or peers to watch you practice your upcoming presentation. Have them watch a "dress rehearsal," in a conference room, office, or at your house. According to Beilock, "Simulating low levels of stress helps prevent cracking under increased pressure, because people who practice this way learn to stay calm, cool, and collected in the face of whatever comes their way."[6]

In his book, *Social*, UCLA psychology professor Matthew Lieberman explains the difference between suppressing our nerves and reappraising the way we look at a situation. In public speaking, suppressing your emotions means walking on stage, putting on a broad smile, and saying to yourself, "I'm not nervous. I'm not nervous. I'm not nervous." The problem is—you *are* nervous. You might *look* less distressed to your audience, and that's fine, but it won't make you feel in peak condition for next time.

Rehearsal and reappraisal will help you reach a high-performance state of mind. If you change your perspective about public speaking and rehearse under stress, you might find yourself looking forward to your next presentation instead of dreading it.

Overcoming the fear of speaking up takes on greater importance for those who are not satisfied with being average. Above-average performers— five-star persuaders—must have the courage and confidence to take the stage and make their voices heard.

If you have a fear of public speaking, don't be too hard on yourself. You're in good company. Many of the world's most successful people have recently talked openly about stage fright. These men and women include: *Grey's Anatomy* creator and mega-producer Shonda Rhimes, billionaires Richard Branson and Warren Buffett, musicians such as Barbra Streisand and Adele. *Shark Tank* investor and real estate mogul Barbara Corcoran acknowledges a terrifying fear of public speaking early in her career. She volunteered to teach real estate classes to help get over the nerves. Corcoran once said, "If you're going to be in business, the single most important thing is the ability to communicate your idea to every single person you meet." Corcoran knew she'd fail at the single most important thing if she didn't have the courage to stand up and be heard.

Having an original idea isn't enough to guarantee success. Originals must, by definition, advocate for those ideas. But they will fail in their advocacy if they cannot overcome fear and doubt. The good news is fear and doubt are often self-imposed. If we place these limits on ourselves, we also have the power to lift them off and lift ourselves up.

Remember, you have stage fright because you're supposed to. We are hardwired to crave acceptance among our social groups. If our primitive ancestors were banished from the tribe, they wouldn't have survived on their own. Today, the worst that can happen is that your pitch will fall flat, but our physiology still reacts as it did hundreds of thousands of years ago.

Stage fright is as engrained in our psyche as an aversion to spiders. In 1991, psychologist Graham Davey at City University London found that about 75 percent of undergraduates were mildly or severely afraid of spiders, even if they had no negative experience or "spider trauma" to draw on. According to Davey, we are born with the fear. It's an adaptive response that's been hardwired in us since our species appeared.

In both cases—fear of spiders and fear of public speaking—people rarely eliminate their fight-or-flight response entirely, but they learn to *manage* it. And how do psychotherapists recommend people manage their fear of spiders or fear of public speaking? By repeated exposure, beginning in small steps and adding a "little stress" each time. For spiders it might mean putting pictures of spiders around the house before coming face to face with a real tarantula. For public speaking, as we've discussed, it means rehearsing in front of others.

We can't manage fear if we don't face our fears. It's how the pop singer Adele manages her stage fright. Several years ago, Adele said she preferred to play smaller or low-key venues to cope with her nerves. She gradually worked up the courage to play London's 20,000-seat O2 arena in 2016. Adele gradually exposed herself to bigger and bigger venues—from tiny spiders to the tarantula in the room. As she received more positive feedback, her self-doubt diminished and her confidence built. Today, Adele says her stage fright is being replaced by "performance energy." It's a great phrase and a great example of reappraisal. Stage fright provokes more fear; performance energy means a person cares about her audience.

Face the fear. It's the only way to manage it and, eventually, to conquer it. Conquer the fear and you'll replace it with the joy that comes with connecting with an audience. You should be thrilled to share your ideas. After all, they might change the world, and that's exceptionally exciting.

Five-Star Principles:

- Great communicators are made, not born. Many of the world's most inspiring speakers—from historical figures to today's business leaders—have overcome anxiety, nerves, and stage fright. You can, too.
- Neuroscientists have identified two techniques that will help you shine when the pressure is on: reappraisal and repetition.
- Reappraisal simply means reframing the way you think about yourself and the events in your life. Turning thoughts from negative to positive is the key to winning. Once you've transformed your thoughts, you have to put in practice time. Repeating a presentation over and over will boost your confidence for the big day.

CONCLUSION

Find the Tune That Makes Your Heart Sing

Words from the heart enter the heart.

–Jewish Proverb

In his 36-year career as an instructor in economics and entrepreneurship at the University of Waterloo, Dr. Larry Smith has had more than 23,000 career conversations with his students. Those conversations have convinced him that two qualities are required to achieve success in any field: passion and communication.

Passion comes first. "The link between excellence and passion is the ability to innovate," Smith told me in our conversations about the topic.[1] "I defy anyone to be innovative in a field or a subject they really don't care about." According to Smith, people can get a salary, status, and promotions, but if they don't care—really care—about the domain, then they won't tweak, learn, and find better ways of solving problems. The mind cannot stop thinking about that which it loves.

"Passion lies at the heart of career success today," Smith explained. "Fifty years ago we could have said that passion is a desirable quality, but not absolutely necessary. A strong work ethic and good sales skills were often sufficient. Today, the economy has become less gentle and more competitive: More and more professional work will be automated. Now, if you want a great career, you must be an innovator, and you cannot innovate without passion. That's the difference between us and the robots. Give me a passionate problem-solver against a machine and I'll bet on the passionate problem-solver any time."

Passion was the ticket to success for one British entrepreneur who built a global brand from her kitchen table.

When Jo was 15 years old, a teacher told her that she wouldn't make anything out of her life (Jo had dyslexia, a largely misunderstood condition at the time). She dropped out of school, but was determined to prove the teacher wrong. Today, Jo Malone is the name behind a fragrance empire. The British perfumer and entrepreneur launched Jo Malone London from her kitchen table and sold it to Estee Lauder for millions.

I met Jo Malone at a book festival in Dubai, where we both were invited to speak. As we sat on cushions in the desert enjoying a traditional feast, Malone expanded on the story that she wrote in her autobiography, *Jo Malone: My Story*.

Passion, she said, is more than having a passing interest in a field. It's something that's core to your identity—you might leave it, but it doesn't leave you. Malone discovered that she had an acute sense of smell while helping her mother, who worked for a skin-care clinic. Malone couldn't read the jars, but she memorized every ingredient by smell. Malone recalls childhood memories in scent: "the damp wood of the garden shed" and "the linseed oil and turpentine scent from dad's paintings."

Malone launched her own brand in 1988. She began mixing ingredients at her kitchen table with four plastic jugs and two saucepans. She started with 12 clients. But the scents she created began to catch on. "Fragrance not only flooded me with ideas but it made me feel complete, fueling an almost obsessive drive of creativity," Malone said.[2]

Malone uses the word "obsession" to describe her enthusiasm. She's on to something. I once asked Google investor Michael Moritz, whom we met earlier, about what he looks for in an entrepreneur. "Passion," he answered. But when I asked Moritz to define passion, he said, "The people who do remarkable things are completely captivated by an obsession that they simply cannot imagine conducting their life without . . . they have a calling that tugs at their emotions."[3]

The tug of emotion. When it comes calling, don't resist it. According to Smith, passion is a necessary ingredient for success in today's winner-take-all, rapidly changing economy—but it's not sufficient. The second piece of the puzzle is the ability to sell ideas persuasively. "In my experience, many great ideas get lost because no one can advocate for them. Ideas do not unfortunately sell themselves," says Smith.[4] "The world needs to know why you are different, and why this difference makes you highly valuable." Passion and enthusiasm, creativity and communication, will help you make an impact on the world. Smith, along with many others, believes that developing great communication skills is so critical to success in life and work that the skills should be taught as early as grade school.

As a former schoolteacher, billionaire Jack Ma, whom we met in chapter 10, believes that we shouldn't teach kids to be like machines. Instead of teaching rote memorization, we should teach students to be innovative, creative, and empathetic. According to Ma, "A machine does not have a heart. A machine does not have a soul. A machine does not have a belief. Human beings have souls, beliefs, and values."[5] Speaking at a Bloomberg conference in New York, Ma argued that those who will survive and thrive in the age of automation and artificial intelligence will not be those with high IQs, necessarily, but those who have both EQ (emotional intelligence) and a new term he coined—LQ. "To be respected, you must have LQ: the love quotient. It's something machines will never have."

Persuasion Is an Art That Should Be Taught Early

"In the twenty-first century, presentation literacy should be taught in every school," argues TED talks curator Chris Anderson.[6] "Done right, a talk can electrify a room and transform an audience's worldview . . . when we peer into a speaker's eyes; listen to the tone of her voice; sense her vulnerability, her intelligence, her passion, we are tapping into unconscious skills that have been fine-tuned over hundreds of thousands of years. Skills that can galvanize, empower, and inspire."

I, too, along with Anderson, Smith, Warren Buffett, Richard Branson, and others you've heard from in this book, believe that communication is a skill that can be learned. Inspiring speakers are not born; they're made. The education can and should start early.

Alexa Cousin is a 12-year-old girl who attends The Benjamin School in North Palm Beach, Florida. The middle school's mission is to transform students into independent, collaborative, and fearless learners. And fearlessness requires overcoming the fear of public speaking.

In 2017, The Benjamin School earned the right to put on a TEDx event, an independent, locally organized event associated with the global TED conference. Alexa was the first speaker. In a four-minute presentation, Alexa explained how she used Aristotle's rhetorical principles of Logos, Pathos, and Ethos to persuade her parents to do what children across America want their parents do—buy a puppy.

"My parents wanted nothing to do with a puppy," Alexa began.[7] "So, how did I get one? Rhetoric, the art of persuading an audience," she said confidently.

> For Logos, I appealed to science. I used compelling evidence such as: "Mom, a puppy will lower your blood pressure in stressful situations" and "Puppies help children develop greater empathy, higher self esteem and participation in social activities."
>
> Ethos is ethics. I told them how a puppy would make us good and noble people. Two-point-seven million animals are put to death every year. We can rescue a dog.
>
> Finally, I used pathos. For this, I needed my little sister. She came in with a stuffed animal that resembled a Golden Doodle. She gave my mom a face she couldn't resist, looked Mom in the eye, curled her upper lip and said, "Mommy, would you get me a Golden Doodle?"
>
> And that was how I got my Golden Doodle . . . Tucker.

Tucker the puppy then joined Alexa on stage. Alexa ended her presentation with words that showed maturity beyond her 12 years. Alexa said, "Persuasion is an art that everyone should try and master. It'll be worth it."

It will be worth it. It'll be worth it when you live the life you imagined.

It'll be worth it when you make a mark in your career and leave a mark on this world. It'll be worth it when you start a company, build a product, sell a service, or manage a nonprofit that makes people's lives better and more meaningful. Above all, it'll be worth it when you inspire other people to dream bigger and seek out their own marvelous adventures.

ACKNOWLEDGMENTS

I'd like to thank the winning team that made this book possible. My wife, Vanessa, provided invaluable support, feedback, and editing skills as I worked on the manuscript. I once heard a quote in a movie that reminds me of what we share: "A love like ours comes but once in a lifetime." I couldn't agree more.

St. Martin's Press executive editor Tim Bartlett added his remarkable insights to clarify and strengthen my ideas. Editorial assistant Alice Pfeifer and managing editor Alan Bradshaw also made sure the process ran smoothly. I'm also extremely grateful to Laura Clark, George Witte, and Sally Richardson for their support and enthusiasm.

To the people in my life who encourage me to dream big: Roger Williams, my extraordinary literary agent and friend, and Tom Neilssen and Les Tuerk, my enthusiastic speaking agents at the BrightSight Group. Thank you, gentlemen, for your wisdom and guidance.

I'm also grateful for idea generators in my close circle of friends and family. To Carolyn Kilmer for her dedication and professionalism in the Gallo Communications Group. My nephews, Francesco and Nick, keep me apprised of communication challenges facing their generation. My brother and sister-in-law, Tino and Donna Gallo, provide great wisdom. Thanks to Ken and Patty for raising the wonderful woman who became my wife, and our two daughters, Josephine and Lela, who are great communicators in the making. Finally, to my mother, Giuseppina, and my late father, Francesco: It took uncommon courage to leave their beloved home to give their sons an opportunity to rise.

NOTES

Introduction: Rise Up!

1. Lin-Manuel Miranda and Jeremy McCarter, *Hamilton: The Revolution* (New York: Grand Central Publishing, 2016), 16.
2. Thomas L. Friedman, "Average Is Over," *The New York Times*, January 24, 2012, http://www.nytimes.com/2012/01/25/opinion/friedman-average-is-over.html?mcubz=0 (accessed July 17, 2017).
3. Tyler Cowen, *Average Is Over: Powering America Past the Age of the Great Stagnation* (New York: Dutton, 2013), 5.
4. Anthony Goldbloom, founder and CEO of Kaggle, in discussion with the author, August 18, 2016.
5. Ibid.
6. Ibid.
7. Noriko Arai, "Can a Robot Pass a University Entrance Exam?" TED.com, April 2017, https://www.ted.com/talks/noriko_arai_can_a_robot_pass_a_university_entrance_exam (accessed October 2, 2017).
8. Carl Benedikt Frey and Michael A. Osborne, "The Future of Employment: How Susceptible Are Jobs to Computerisation?" Oxford Martin, University of Oxford, September 17, 2013, http://www.oxfordmartin.ox.ac.uk/downloads/academic/The_Future_of_Employment.pdf (accessed July 11, 2017).
9. "How AI Will Change Everything," *The Wall Street Journal*, March 6, 2017, https://www.wsj.com/articles/how-artificial-intelligence-will-change-everything-1488856320 (accessed July 18, 2017).
10. Neil Jacobstein, chair of artificial intelligence and robotics at Singularity University, in discussion with the author, March 17, 2017.

11. Kate Davidson, "Employers Find 'Soft Skills' Like Critical Thinking in Short Supply," *The Wall Street Journal*, August 30, 2016, http://www.wsj.com/articles/employers-find-soft-skills-like-critical-thinking-in-short-supply-1472549400 (accessed July 11, 2017).

12. Ibid.

13. Burning Glass Technologies, "The Human Factor: The Hard Time Employers Have Finding Soft Skills," Burning-glass.com, November 2015, http://burning-glass.com/wp-content/uploads/Human_Factor_Baseline_Skills_FINAL.pdf (accessed July 11, 2017).

14. Hay Group, "Today's Graduates: Worth Their Weight in Gold?" Haygroup.com, http://www.haygroup.com/~/media/files/resources/documents/worth_their_weight_in_gold_final.ashx (accessed July 11, 2017).

15. Anthony Goldbloom, founder and CEO of Kaggle, in discussion with the author, August 18, 2016.

16. Investors Archive, "Bill Gates and Warren Buffett: Student Q&A 2017," Youtube.com, March 23, 2017, https://www.youtube.com/watch?v=1CCcheNC1sw (accessed July 18, 2017).

17. Alex Crippen, "Warren Buffett's $100,000 Offer and $500,000 Advice for Columbia Business School Students," CNBC, November 12, 2009, http://www.cnbc.com/id/33891448 (accessed July 18, 2017).

18. Adam Grant, *Originals: How Non-Conformists Move the World* (New York: Penguin Books, 2016), 69.

Chapter 1: Poetry, Power, and Moonshots

1. Ron Chernow, *Alexander Hamilton* (New York: Penguin Group, 2004), 56.

2. Ibid., 4.

3. Andrew M. Carton, "I'm Not Mopping the Floor—I'm Putting a Man on the Moon: How NASA Leaders Enhanced the Meaningfulness of Work by Changing the Meaning of Work," The Wharton School, University of Pennsylvania, paper to be published in *Administrative Science Quarterly*, provided to author in April 2017.

4. Ibid.

5. Bill Gates, "Accelerating Innovation With Leadership," Gatesnotes, October 6, 2016, https://www.gatesnotes.com/About-Bill-Gates/Accelerating-Innovation?WT.mc_id=10_06_2016_06_AcceleratingInnovation_BG-LI_&WT.tsrc=BGLI (accessed April 4, 2017).

6. Eli Harari, co-founder of SanDisk, in discussion with the author during author's time working with SanDisk in 2008.

Chapter 2: Winning the War of Ideas

1. Cade Metz, "Inside Liberatus, the Poker AI That Out-Bluffed the Best Humans," Wired.com, February 1, 2017, https://www.wired.com/2017/02/libratus/ (accessed July 10, 2017).

2. Haseeb Qureshi, software engineer at Airbnb, in discussion with the author, September 22, 2016.

3. Phys.org, "New Research Finds CEOs Who Appear on CNBC Can See Their Pay Rise Over $200,000 Per Year," Home, Other Sciences, Economics and Business, June 12, 2017, https://phys.org/news/2017-06-ceos-cnbc-year.html (accessed July 18, 2017).

4. Andrew Grove, *Only the Paranoid Survive: How to Exploit the Crisis Points That Challenge Every Company* (New York: Doubleday, 1999), 4.

5. Matt Ridley, *The Rational Optimist* (New York: HarperCollins, 2010).

6. Deirdre McCloskey, *Bourgeois Equality: How Ideas, Not Capital or Institutions, Enriched the World* (Chicago: University of Chicago Press, 2016), 21.

7. Ian Goldin and Chris Kutarna, *Age of Discovery: Navigating the Risks and Rewards of Our New Renaissance* (New York: St. Martin's Press, 2016), 139.

8. Johan Norberg, Swedish historian and author, in discussion with the author, January 10, 2017.

9. Goldin and Kutarna, *Age of Discovery*, 88.

10. Norberg, discussion with the author.

11. Peter H. Diamandis and Steven Kotler, *Abundance: The Future Is Better Than You Think* (New York: Free Press, 2014), x.

12. McCloskey, *Bourgeois Equality*, 106–110.

13. Ibid., 492.

14. Gerry Antioch, "Persuasion Is Now 30 Per Cent of US GDP," Australian government, *Economic Roundup*, Issue 1, 2013, https://treasury.gov.au/publication/economic-roundup-issue-1-2013/economic-roundup-issue-1-2013/persuasion-is-now-30-per-cent-of-us-gdp/ (accessed November 20, 2017).

15. McCloskey, *Bourgeois Equality*, 490.

Chapter 3: Aristotle Was Right and Neuroscience Proves It

1. Avinash Kaushik, digital marketing evangelist at Google, in discussion with the author, September 9, 2016.

2. Chris Dixon, "How Aristotle Created the Computer: The Philosophers He Influenced Set the Stage for the Technological Revolution That Remade Our World," *The Atlantic*, March 20, 2017, https://www.theatlantic.com/technology/archive/2017/03/aristotle-computer/518697/ (accessed July 11, 2017).

3. Scott F. Crider, *Aristotle's Rhetoric for Everybody* (Kindle edition only: The Arts of Liberty Project, 2014), pagination changes depending on font size set by individual Kindle users.

4. Ibid.

5. John J. Medina, "Why Emotional Memories Are Unforgettable," *Psychiatric Times*, Molecules of the Mind, May 2008, http://www.brainrules.net/pdf/JohnMedina_PsychTimes_May08.pdf (accessed July 11, 2017).

6. Ibid.

7. Rohan Ayyar, "Why a Good Story Is the Most Important Thing You'll Ever Sell," *Fast Company*, October 24, 2014, https://www.fastcompany.com/3037539/why-a-good-story-is-the-most-important-thing-youll-ever-sell (accessed July 18, 2017).

8. Megan Beck and Barry Libert, "The Rise of AI Makes Emotional Intelligence More Important," *Harvard Business Review*, February 15, 2017, https://hbr.org/2017/02/the-rise-of-ai-makes-emotional-intelligence-more-important (accessed July 12, 2017).

Chapter 4: The Human Capacity to Dream Big

1. Big Jocko Willink and Leif Babin, *Extreme Ownership: How U.S. Navy SEALs Lead and Win* (New York: St. Martin's Press, 2015), 12.

2. Ibid., 34.

3. Ibid., 45.

4. Ibid., 49.

5. Geoff Ralston, founder and partner of Imagine K12, in discussion with the author, March 23, 2017.

6. Sam Altman, "2017 YC Annual Letter," Sam Altman blog, http://blog.samaltman .com/2017-yc-annual-letter (accessed July 11, 2017).

7. Ibid.

8. Carmine Gallo, "The Apple Store's New Redesign Celebrates Steve Jobs' Legacy," *Forbes,* April 26, 2017, https://www.forbes.com/sites/carminegallo/2017/04/26 /the-apple-stores-new-redesign-celebrates-steve-jobs-legacy/#7849c10f67f9.

9. CBS News, "Angela Ahrendts Talks Apple Store Makeover, Why Tim Cook Hired Her," *CBS This Morning,* April 25, 2017, http://www.cbsnews.com/news/angela -ahrendts-apple-svp-of-retail-redesign-today-at-apple/ (accessed July 11, 2017).

10. Ibid.

11. Ibid.

12. Ibid.

13. HCAHPS online, "HCAHPS Survey," http://www.hcahpsonline.org/Files/V4%20 0%20Appendix%20A%20-%20HCAHPS%20Mail%20Survey%20Materials%20 %28English%29.pdf (accessed July 18, 2017).

14. Halee Fischer-Wright, *Back to Balance: The Art, Science, and Business of Medicine* (New York: Disruption Books, 2017), 12.

15. Adrienne Boissy and Timothy Gilligan, *Communication the Cleveland Clinic Way: How to Drive a Relationship-Centered Strategy for Exceptional Patient Experience* (New York: McGraw-Hill Education, 2016), xiii.

16. Cleveland Clinic, "Empathy: The Human Connection to Patient Care," Youtube.com, February 21, 2013, https://www.youtube.com/watch?v=cDDWvj_q-o8 (accessed July 18, 2017).

17. Teresa Keller, director of training and development, Kiawah Island Golf Resort, in discussion with the author, September 7, 2016.

18. Garry Kasparov, "Don't Fear Intelligent Machines. Work With Them," TED.com, April 2017, http://www.bostonmagazine.com/news/blog/2016/05/12/lola-travel -app/ (accessed July 11, 2017).

Chapter 5: The Scientists

1. Neil deGrasse Tyson, American astrophysicist, in e-mail exchange with the author, March 20, 2017.

2. Neil deGrasse Tyson, *Astrophysics for People in a Hurry* (New York: W. W. Norton & Company, Inc., 2017), 1.

3. Ibid, 121.

4. Ibid., 122.

5. Ibid., 190.

6. deGrasse Tyson, e-mail exchange with the author.

7. Ibid.

8. deGrasse Tyson, *Astrophysics for People in a Hurry*, 192.

9. CBS, *The Late Show with Stephen Colbert,* March 15, 2017, viewed by author live.

10. deGrasse Tyson, e-mail exchange with the author.

11. Ann Roemer, manager for astronaut selection program, NASA, in discussion with the author, August 26, 2016.

12. Ibid.

13. NASA, "NASA Astronaut Talks With Cancer Patients About Cancer Research on the International Space Station," Youtube.com, September 16, 2016, https://www.youtube.com/watch?v=gEUrPrDUMK0 (accessed July 11, 2017).

14. NASA, "Astronauts Talk About Research in the ISS," Youtube.com, July 13, 2016, https://www.youtube.com/watch?v=nNsaQPy4bBY (accessed July 11, 2017).

15. Angry Birds, "Angry Birds Space: NASA Announcement," Youtube.com, March 8, 2012, https://www.youtube.com/watch?v=lxI1L1RiSJQ (accessed July 11, 2017); Roemer, discussion with the author.

16. NASA Jet Propulsion Laboratory, "NASA TRAPPIST-1 News," Youtube.com, February 22, 2017), https://www.youtube.com/watch?v=cURfn6FH1Hs (accessed July 18, 2017).

17. Ibid.

18. Anders Sahlman, founder of Researchers' Grand Prix, in discussion with the author, January 18, 2017.

19. Ibid.

20. Steven Sloman and Philip Fernbach, *The Knowledge Illusion: Why We Never Think Alone* (New York: Riverhead Books, 2017), 108.

21. Neil Jacobstein, chair of artificial intelligence and robotics at Singularity University, in discussion with the author, March 17, 2017.

22. Ibid.

23. Ibid.

24. Ibid.

25. Ibid.

Chapter 6: The Entrepreneurs

1. Scott Hartley, *The Fuzzy and the Techie: Why the Liberal Arts Will Rule the Digital World* (New York: Houghton Mifflin Harcourt, 2017), 1.

2. Scott Hartley, author of *The Fuzzy and the Techie*, in discussion with the author, June 29, 2017.

3. Rajaie Batniji, co-founder and chief health officer of Collective Health, in discussion with the author, July 6, 2017.

4. Sarah Kliff, "Do You Understand Health Insurance? Most People Don't," *The Washington Post*, Wonkblog, August 8, 2013, https://www.washingtonpost.com/news/wonk/wp/2013/08/08/do-you-understand-health-insurance-most-people-dont/?utm_term=.88b38c920d94 (accessed July 10, 2017).

5. Collective Health, "Your 2017 Health Benefits" pamphlet, given to author in July 2017.

6. Batniji, discussion with the author.

7. David Pakman, partner in Venrock, in discussion with the author, June 22, 2017.

8. John Patrick Pullen, "How a Dollar Shave Club's Ad Went Viral," Entrepreneur.com, October 13, 2012, https://www.entrepreneur.com/article/224282 (accessed July 10, 2017).

9. Pakman, discussion with the author.

10. Ibid.

11. Ibid.

12. "The Top 20 Venture Capitalists Worldwide," *The New York Times*, March 27, 2017.

13. "In Defense of the Deck," Above the Crowd.com, July 7, 2015, http://abovethecrowd.com/2015/07/07/in-defense-of-the-deck/ (accessed July 18, 2017).

14. Carmine Gallo, "7 Top VCs Say These Communication Skills Will Set You Apart," Forbes.com, March 28, 2017, https://www.forbes.com/sites/carminegallo/2017/03 /28/7-top-vcs-say-these-communication-skills-will-set-you-apart/#6847266a65df (accessed November 20, 2017).

15. Ibid.

16. Ibid.

17. Ibid.

18. Sir Michael Jonathan Moritz, KBE, venture capitalist with Sequoia Capital, in discussion with the author, October 23, 2015.

19. Carmine Gallo, "7 Top VCs Say These Communication Skills Will Set You Apart."

20. Ibid.

21. Molly Rubin, "Full Transcript: Tim Cook Delivers MIT's 2017 Commencement Speech," Quartz.com, https://qz.com/1002570/watch-live-apple-ceo-tim-cook -delivers-mits-2017-commencement-speech/ (accessed July 12, 2017).

22. Richard Branson, "Storytelling: What Does It Take to Master the Art?" Virgin.com, March 1, 2017, https://www.virgin.com/richard-branson/dream-0 (accessed July 12, 2017).

23. Richard Branson, "5 Skills and Abilities That Successful Entrepreneurs Share," Virgin.com, January 30, 2017, https://www.virgin.com/richard-branson/5-skills-and -abilities-successful-entrepreneurs-share (accessed July 12, 2017).

24. Caline Malek, "UAE Needs Generations of Engineers and Scientists," *The National*, March 8, 2017, https://www.thenational.ae/uae/education/uae-needs-generations-of -engineers-and-scientists-to-secure-post-oil-future-sheikh-mohammed-bin-zayed -tells-students-1.70436 (acccessed November 20, 2017).

25. Bill J. Bonnstetter, "New Research: The Skills That Make an Entrepreneur," *Harvard Business Review*, December 7, 2012, https://hbr.org/2012/12/new-research -the-skills-that-m (accessed July 12, 2017).

26. Thomas L. Friedman, *Thank You for Being Late: An Optimist's Guide to Thriving in the Age of Accelerations* (New York: Farrar Straus and Giroux, 2016), 87.

Chapter 7: The Professionals

1. Sharon is an assigned name to maintain confidentiality, executive at Fortune 100 company, in discussion with the author.

2. Adam Grant, *Originals: How Non-Conformists Move the World* (New York: Penguin Books, 2016), 3.

3. Gregory Berns, *Iconoclast: A Neuroscientist Reveals How to Think Different* (Boston: Harvard Business School Publishing Corporation, 2008), cover.

4. Matthew is an assigned name to maintain confidentiality, civil engineer, in discussion with the author.

5. E-mail exchange with author, September 21, 2017.

6. Thomas L. Friedman, *Thank You for Being Late: An Optimist's Guide to Thriving in the Age of Accelerations* (New York: Farrar Straus and Giroux, 2016), 87.

7. Ibid., 211.

8. The Association of American Colleges and Universities by Hart Research Associates, "It Takes More Than a Major: Employer Priorities for College Learning & Student Success," April 10, 2013, https://www.aacu.org/sites/default/files/files/LEAP /2013_EmployerSurvey.pdf (accessed July 13, 2017).

9. Susan Vitale, chief marketing officer for iCIMS, in discussion with the author, April 28, 2017.

10. Craig is an assigned name to maintain confidentiality, in discussion with the author.

11. Anna Hensel, "The 1 Incredibly Detailed Job Interview Question Elon Musk Always Asks," Inc.com, February 14, 2017, https://www.inc.com/anna-hensel/the-1 -incredibly-detailed-job-interview-question-elon-musk-always-asks.html (accessed July 13, 2017).

12. James F. Peltz, "Headhunter James Citrin Tells Millennials How to Land Jobs and Keep Them," *Los Angeles Times*, June 11, 2015, http://www.latimes.com/business /la-fi-qa-citrin-20150611-story.html (accessed July 13, 2017).

13. Slide Heroes, "The Advanced Guide to McKinsey-Style Business Presentations," Slide-heroes.com, https://www.slideheroes.com/advanced-guide-to-writing-mckinsey-style -presentations/ (accessed July 13, 2017).

14. Shu Hattori, *The McKinsey Edge: Success Principles From the World's Most Powerful Consulting Firm* (New York: McGraw-Hill Education, 2015), 66.

15. Claire is an assigned name to maintain confidentiality, a financial services professional, in discussion with the author.

16. Mike is an assigned name to maintain confidentiality, a corporate sales professional, in discussion with the author.

17. David J. Deming, "The Growing Importance of Social Skills in the Labor Market," May 24, 2017, file:///C:/Users/Vanessa%20Gallo/AppData/Local/Microsoft/Windows /INetCache/Content.Outlook/03CQ1ZRH/David%20Deming_SkillsLaborMarket .pdf (accessed July 18, 2017).

18. David Deming, professor in the Harvard Graduate School of Education and a faculty research fellow at the National Bureau of Economic Research, in discussion with the author, June 14, 2016.

19. Harvard Extension School, "10 Soft Skills Every IT Professional Should Develop," https://www.extension.harvard.edu/inside-extension/10-soft-skills-every-it -professional-should-develop (accessed November 20, 2017).

20. Ibid.

21. Burning Glass Technologies, "The Human Factor: The Hard Time Employers Have Finding Soft Skills," Burning-glass.com, 2015, http://burning-glass.com/wp -content/uploads/Human_Factor_Baseline_Skills_FINAL.pdf (accessed July 13, 2017).

22. "Andy Bryant Says CIOs Need Better Communication Skills: The Intel Chairman Offers Advice on How to Deal With Boards and Fellow Executives," *The Wall Street Journal*, February 10, 2016, https://www.wsj.com/articles/andy-bryant-says-cios -need-better-communications-skills-1455083007 (accessed July 13, 2017).

23. Sir Michael Jonathan Moritz, KBE, venture capitalist with Sequoia Capital, in discussion with the author, October 23, 2015.

Chapter 8: The Leaders

1. Sundar Pichai, "'AI First' Google I/O 2017, All About Artificial Intelligence Keynotes Full Presentation," Youtube.com, May 2, 2017, https://www.youtube.com /watch?v=Y2VF8tmLFHw (accessed July 18, 2017).

2. Brain Rules, "The Brain Cannot Multitask," Brain Rules blog, March 16, 2008, http://brainrules.blogspot.com/2008/03/brain-cannot-multitask_16.html (accessed July 18, 2017).

3. Nancy Duarte, "Do Your Slides Pass the Glance Test?" *Harvard Business Review*, October 22, 2012, https://hbr.org/2012/10/do-your-slides-pass-the-glance-test (accessed July 18, 2017).

4. Chris Anderson, *TED Talks: The Official TED Guide to Public Speaking* (New York: Houghton Mifflin Harcourt, 2017), 117.
5. "The Science of Storytelling: Prasad Setty, Google People Analytics," Youtube.com, May 24, 2016, https://www.youtube.com/watch?v=ncTXE7iLUnw (accessed July 18, 2017).
6. Ibid.
7. Julia Rozovsky, "The Five Keys to a Successful Google Team," re:work.com, The Water Cooler blog, November 17, 2015, https://rework.withgoogle.com/blog/five-keys-to-a-successful-google-team/ (accessed July 18, 2017).
8. Charles Duhigg, "What Google Learned From Its Quest to Build the Perfect Team," *The New York Times Magazine*, February 25, 2016, https://www.nytimes.com/2016/02/28/magazine/what-google-learned-from-its-quest-to-build-the-perfect-team.html?mcubz=0 (accessed July 18, 2017).
9. David Feinberg, president and CEO for Geisinger Health, in discussion with the author, September 16, 2016 .
10. David Feinberg, "One Patient at a Time," YouTube.com, August 2, 2011, https://www.youtube.com/watch?v=cZ5u7p-ZNuE (accessed on November 20, 2017).
11. Scott Simmons and Christie Fraser, "Why Hospitals Don't Deliver Great Service," Gallup.com, Business Journal, August 21, 2012, http://www.gallup.com/businessjournal/156701/why-hospitals-don-deliver-great-service.aspx (accessed July 18, 2017).
12. David Rock, "Managing With the Brain in Mind," Strategy+Business.com, Organizations & People, August 27, 2009, https://www.strategy-business.com/article/09306?gko=5df7f (accessed July 18, 2017).
13. CME Group survey answers provided to author during a visit in May 2016.
14. Rock, "Managing With the Brain in Mind."
15. Gino Blefari, CEO for HSF Affiliates, in discussion with the author, March 3, 2017.
16. Matthew D. Lieberman, *Social: Why Our Brains Are Wired to Connect* (Oxford, United Kingdom: Oxford University Press, 2014), 259.
17. PepsiCo, " 'Following Your Dreams' With Indra Nooyi," Youtube.com, August 31, 2011, https://www.youtube.com/watch?v=WG9IUKhSMf0 (accessed July 18, 2017).
18. Narrative: The Business of Stories, "Change Storytelling by Indra Nooyi," Youtube.com, March 3, 2017, https://www.youtube.com/watch?v=DsABAnILwj0 (accessed July 18, 2017).
19. Ibid.
20. Maria Popova, "David Foster Wallace on Leadership," Brain Pickings.org, February 17, 2014, https://www.brainpickings.org/2014/02/17/dfw-leadership-debbie-millman/ (accessed July 18, 2017).

Chapter 9: The TED Stars

1. Richard Turere, "My Invention That Made Peace With Lions," TED.com, February 2013, https://www.ted.com/talks/richard_turere_a_peace_treaty_with_the_lions (accessed October 2, 2017).
2. Chris Anderson, *TED Talks: The Official TED Guide to Public Speaking* (New York: Houghton Mifflin Harcourt, 2017), xiv.
3. Turere, "My Invention That Made Peace With Lions."
4. Shah Rukh Kahn, "Thoughts on Humanity, Fame and Love," TED.com, April 2017,

https://www.ted.com/talks/shah_rukh_khan_thoughts_on_humanity_fame_and
_love/transcript?language=en (accessed July 14, 2017).

5. Sir Ken Robinson, "Ken Robinson Says Schools Kill Creativity," TED.com, June 2006,
http://www.ted.com/talks/ken_robinson_says_schools_kill_creativity.html?qsha
=1&utm_expid=166907-20&utm_referrer=http%3A%2F%2Fwww.ted
.com%2Fsearch%3Fcat%3Dss_all%26q%3Dken%2Brobinson (accessed July 14, 2017).

6. Anderson, *TED Talks*, 60.

7. Shonda Rhimes, "My Year of Saying Yes to Everything," TED.com, February 2016,
https://www.ted.com/talks/shonda_rhimes_my_year_of_saying_yes_to
_everything (accessed July 14, 2017).

8. Anderson, *TED Talks*, 30.

9. Pope Francis, "Why the Only Future Worth Building Includes Everyone," TED
.com, April 2017, https://www.ted.com/talks/pope_francis_why_the_only_future
_worth_building_includes_everyone (accessed July 14, 2017).

10. Robert Ballard, *Titanic* explorer, in discussion with the author, February 18, 2013.

Chapter 10: The Pathos Principle

1. Phil Knight, *Shoe Dog: A Memoir by the Creator of Nike* (New York: Scribner,
2016), pagination changes depending on font size set by individual Kindle users.

2. Eric Ransdell, "The Nike Story?: Just Tell it!" Fastcompany.com, December 31, 1999,
https://www.fastcompany.com/38979/nike-story-just-tell-it (accessed July 14, 2017).

3. Ibid.

4. Knight, *Shoe Dog*.

5. Alan Alda, *If I Understood You, Would I Have This Look on My Face?: My Adventures in the Art and Science of Relating and Communicating* (New York: Random
House, 2017), xvii.

6. Ibid., introduction.

7. Ibid., 158.

8. Uri Hasson, "This Is Your Brain on Communication," TED.com, February 2016,
https://www.ted.com/talks/uri_hasson_this_is_your_brain_on_communication
?language=en (accessed July 19, 2017).

9. Duncan Clark, "How Self-Made Billionaire Jack Ma Used Charisma and Masterful
Speaking Skills to Build the Alibaba Empire," *Business Insider*, April 14, 2016,
http://www.businessinsider.com/the-billionaire-founder-of-alibaba-has-been
-giving-a-similar-speech-for-17-years-heres-how-he-always-engages-his-audience
-2016-4 (accessed October 2, 2017).

10. Ibid.

11. Ibid.

12. La Logiciel, "Today Is Hard, Tomorrow Will Be Worse," Youtube.com, April 17, 2016,
https://www.youtube.com/watch?v=kL41UMHBZpQ (accessed October 2, 2017).

13. Phil Wall, founder of WeSeeHope, in discussion with the author, May 18, 2016.

14. Ethan is an assigned name to maintain confidentiality, in discussion with the author.

15. Bruce N. Pfau, "How an Accounting Firm Convinced Its Employees They Could
Change the World," *Harvard Business Review*, October 6, 2015, https://hbr.org
/2015/10/how-an-accounting-firm-convinced-its-employees-they-could-change-the
-world (accessed on November 20, 2017).

16. Ibid.

17. Dwight Clark, San Francisco 49ers football legend, in discussion with the author,
November 21, 2016.

18. David Aaker and Jennifer Aaker, "What Are Your Signature Stories?" *California Management Review*, Spring 2016, vol. 58, no. 3, http://cmr.berkeley.edu/browse /articles/58_3/5818/ (accessed November 20, 2017).
19. Ibid.

Chapter 11: The Three-Act Storytelling Structure

1. Brad Stone, *The Upstarts: How Uber, Airbnb, and the Killer Companies of the New Silicon Valley Are Changing the World* (New York: Hachette Book Group, 2017), 11.
2. Brad Stone, senior executive editor for technology at Bloomberg News, in discussion with the author, February 23, 2017.
3. Ibid.
4. Syd Field, *Screenplay. The Foundations of Screenwriting: A Step-by-Step Guide From Concept to Finished Script*, revised edition (New York: Delta Trade Paperback, 2005), 3.
5. Ibid., 21.
6. Derek Thompson, *Hit Makers: The Science of Popularity in an Age of Distraction* (New York: Penguin Press, 2017), 109.
7. Bruce N. Pfau, "How an Accounting Firm Convinced Its Employees They Could Change the World," *Harvard Business Review*, October 6, 2015, https://hbr.org /2015/10/how-an-accounting-firm-convinced-its-employees-they-could-change-the -world (accessed July 19, 2017).
8. Stone, discussion with the author.
9. Airbnb, "Welcome to a World of Trips: Airbnb Open Los Angeles," Youtube.com, November 17, 2016, https://www.youtube.com/watch?v=efNyRmTLbjQ (accessed July 15, 2017).
10. Ibid.
11. Avery Hartmans, "This Is the One Quality Every Startup Founder Needs," *Business Insider*, September 25, 2016, http://www.businessinsider.com/jeff-jordan -andreessen-horowitz-startup-founders-2016-9 (accessed July 15, 2017).
12. Jorge A. Burraza and Paul J. Zak, "Empathy Toward Strangers Triggers Oxytocin Release and Subsequent Generosity," Values, Empathy and Fairness Across Social Barriers, New York Academy of Sciences, vol. 1167 (2009): 182–189, http://www .neuroeconomicstudies.org/images/stories/documents/empathy-towards-strangers .pdf (accessed July 15, 2017).
13. Ian Davis, David Keeling, Paul Schreier, and Ashley Williams, "The McKinsey Approach to Problem Solving," McKinsey Staff Paper, no. 66, July 2017, published on slideshare.net, October 6, 2016, https://www.slideshare.net/interviewcoach/the -mckinsey-approach-to-problem-solving-pdf (accessed July 19, 2017).
14. John Seabrook, *The Song Machine: Inside the Hit Factory* (New York: W. W. Norton and Company, Inc., 2015), 12.
15. Thompson, *Hit Makers*, 6.
16. Science of People, "The 10 Secrets to the Perfect Shark Tank Pitch," Scienceofpeople .com, 2016, http://www.scienceofpeople.com/2016/09/the-10-secrets-to-the-perfect -shark-tank-pitch/ (accessed July 15, 2017).

Chapter 12: Deliver the Big Picture

1. Adam Alter, associate professor of marketing at New York University's Stern School of Business, in discussion with the author, May 10, 2017.

2. Ibid.

3. Bryan Garner, *Winning Oral Argument: Enduring Principles With Supporting Comments From the Literature*, course book, 2d ed. (St. Paul, MN: Thomson/West, 2009), 40.

4. Geoff Ralston, founder and partner of Imagine K12, in discussion with the author, March 23, 2017.

Chapter 13: Smart Words Make the Grade

1. Ken Segal, *Think Simple: How Smart Leaders Defeat Complexity* (New York: Penguin Random House LLC, 2016), 1.

2. Daniel Kahneman, *Thinking, Fast and Slow* (New York: Farrar Straus and Giroux, 2011), 63.

3. Chris Kornelis, "Neil deGrasse Tyson on What Every Child Should Know About Science," *The Wall Street Journal*, May 18, 2017, https://www.wsj.com/articles/neil-degrasse-tyson-1495122652 (accessed July 15, 2017).

4. John Medina, *Brain Rules* (Seattle, WA: Pear Press, 2008), 106.

Chapter 14: How to Give Your Ideas "Verbal Beauty"

1. HBO, *Becoming Warren Buffett*, Hbo.com, documentaries, 2017, https://www.wsj.com/articles/neil-degrasse-tyson-1495122652 (accessed July 15, 2017).

2. John Pollack, *Shortcut: How Analogies Reveal Connections, Spark Innovations, and Sell Our Greatest Ideas* (New York: Avery, 2014), xv.

3. Jen Wieczner, "9 Best Warren Buffett Quotes From the Berkshire Hathaway Annual Meeting," *Fortune*, May 18, 2017, http://fortune.com/2017/05/08/warren-buffett-berkshire-hathaway-annual-meeting-quotes/ (accessed July 19, 2017).

4. Ibid.

5. Ibid.

6. Sam Leith, "How to Do Folksy Like Warren Buffett," *Financial Times*, April 28, 2014, https://www.ft.com/content/68afbbb8-ca14-11e3-ac0500144feabdc0?mhq5j=el (accessed July 19, 2017).

7. David Zax, "How Steve Jobs's Mastery of Analogies Sent Apple Skyrocketing," Fast Company.com, October 14, 2014, https://www.fastcompany.com/3037014/my-creative-life/how-steve-jobss-mastery-of-analogies-sent-apple-sky-rocketing (accessed July 19, 2017).

8. "Douglas Hofstadter: Analogies Are the Core of Thinking," Youtube.com, January 4, 2017, https://www.youtube.com/watch?v=vORB92BU7zk (accessed July 19, 2017).

9. Ibid.

10. Ibid.

11. Reid Hoffman, "LinkedIn's Series B Pitch to Greylock: Pitch Advice for Entrepreneurs," reidhoffman.org, February 9, 2017, http://www.reidhoffman.org/485-business-and-entrepeneurship/2135-linkedin-s-series-b-pitch-to-greylock (accessed July 15, 2017).

12. Ibid.

13. Pope Francis, "Why the Only Future Worth Building Includes Everyone," TED.com, April 2017, https://www.ted.com/talks/pope_francis_why_the_only_future_worth_building_includes_everyone (accessed July 14, 2017).

14. Pope Francis, "Post-Synodal Apostolic Exhortation Amoris Laetitia of the Holy Father Francis to Bishops, Priests and Deacons, Consecrated Persons, Christian Mar-

ried Couples and All the Lay Faithful on Love in the Family," downloadable pdf, https://www.youtube.com/watch?v=vORB92BU7zk (accessed July 19, 2017).

15. Carlton Reid, "How the Bicycle Beats Evolution and Why Steve Jobs Was So Taken With the Fact," bikebook.info, March 14, 2015, http://www.bikeboom.info /efficiency/ (accessed July 17, 2017).

Chapter 15: Leonardo, Picasso, and You

1. Enrique Mallen, director of the online Picasso Project at Sam Houston State University, in discussion with the author, September 13, 2013.
2. Stanford University, "'You've Got to Find What You Love,' Jobs Says," Stanford Report, June 14, 2005, Steve Jobs commencement address, delivered on June 12, 2005, http://news-service.stanford.edu/news/2005/june15/jobs-061505.html (accessed April 11, 2013).
3. PBS, Triumph of the Nerds: Starring Robert X. Cringely, PBS.org, KQED, http://www.pbs.org/nerds/part3.html (accessed July 19, 2017).
4. Natalie Walters, "Former Apple CEO John Sculley Shares the Most Important Thing He Learned From Steve Jobs," Business Insider, January 12, 2016, http://www .businessinsider.com/john-sculley-shares-lesson-from-steve-jobs-2016-1 (accessed July 19, 2017).
5. Walter Isaacson, "The Lessons of Leonardo: How to Be a Creative Genius," The Wall Street Journal, September 29, 2017, https://www.wsj.com/articles/the-lessons-of -leonardo-how-to-be-a-creative-genius-1506690180 (accessed October 2, 2017).
6. Peggy Noonan, "Music in the Key of America," The Wall Street Journal, November 26, 2015, https://www.wsj.com/articles/music-in-the-key-of-america-1448575880.
7. Score: A Film Music Documentary, https://www.score-movie.com (accessed November 20, 2017).
8. James Stavridis, dean of Fletcher School of Law and Diplomacy, in discussion with the author, March 31, 2017.
9. Mario D. Garrett, "Brain Plasticity in Older Adults: Learning New Tricks in Older Age," Psychology Today, April 27, 2013, https://www.psychologytoday.com/blog /iage/201304/brain-plasticity-in-older-adults (accessed October 2, 2017).
10. Ana Almendrala, "Lin-Manuel Miranda: It's 'No Accident' Hamilton Came to Me on Vacation," Huffington Post, June 23, 2016, http://www.huffingtonpost.com/entry /lin-manuel-miranda-says-its-no-accident-hamilton-inspiration-struck-on-vacation _us_576c136ee4b0b489bb0ca7c2 (accessed July 17, 2017).
11. Gregory Berns, Iconoclast: A Neuroscientist Reveals How to Think Different (Boston: Harvard Business School Publishing Corporation, 2008), 8.
12. Ibid, 33.
13. Olivia Fox Cabane and Judah Pollack, The Net and the Butterfly: The Art and Practice of Breakthrough Thinking (New York: Penguin Random House LLC, 2017), 13.
14. Ibid., 28.

Chapter 16: Conquer the Fear That Holds You Back

1. Gregory Berns, Iconoclast: A Neuroscientist Reveals How to Think Differently (Boston: Harvard Business School Publishing Corporation, 2008), 78.
2. Kevin N. Ochsner, Silvia A. Bunge, James J. Gross, and John D. E. Gabrieli, "Rethinking Feelings: An fMRI Study of the Cognitive Regulation of Emotion," Massachusetts Institute of Technology, Journal of Cognitive Neuroscience 14, no. 8 (2002): 1215–1229,

https://pdfs.semanticscholar.org/51a0/83a0702159cddc803ce7126d52297e94821b
.pdf (accessed July 18, 2017).

3. Sian Beilock, *Choke: What the Secrets of the Brain Reveal About Getting It Right When You Have To* (New York: Free Press, 2010), 123.

4. Ibid., 249.

5. Ibid., 34.

6. Ibid.

Conclusion: Find the Tune That Makes Your Heart Sing

1. Larry Smith, professor of economics, University of Waterloo, in discussion with the author, April 12, 2016.

2. Jo Malone, *Jo Malone: My Story* (New York: Simon and Schuster, 2016), 169.

3. Sir Michael Jonathan Moritz, KBE, venture capitalist with Sequoia Capital, in discussion with the author, October 23, 2015.

4. Smith, discussion with the author.

5. Lila MacLellan, "Alibaba Founder Jack Ma Says to Be a Successful Leader You Need EQ, IQ, and LQ," Quartz Media, September 20, 2017, https://qz.com/1082709/alibabas-jack-ma-says-successful-leaders-need-eq-iq-and-lq-baba/ (accessed October 6, 2017).

6. Chris Anderson, *TED Talks: The Official TED Guide to Public Speaking* (New York: Houghton Mifflin Harcourt, 2017), xii.

7. TEDx Talks, "Aristotelian Rhetoric and Golden Doodles: Alexa Cousin," Youtube.com, April 19, 2017, https://www.youtube.com/watch?v=MphqZ-phoGY (accessed July 18, 2017).

INDEX